Photoshop® Studio Secrets™, 3rd Edition

DEKE McCLELLAND, KATRIN EISMANN, AND JENNIFER ALSPACH

PHOTOSHOP®
STUDIO SECRETS™

3RD EDITION

Hungry Minds™

New York, NY ▲ Cleveland, OH ◆ Indianapolis, IN

Photoshop® Studio Secrets™, 3rd Edition

Published by
Hungry Minds, Inc.
909 Third Avenue
New York, NY 10022
www.hungryminds.com

Library of Congress Cataloging-in-Publication Data
2001089294

ISBN: 0-7645-3576-5

Printed in the United States of America

10 9 8 7 6 5 4 3 2 1

3K/RU/QV/QR/IN

Distributed in the United States by Hungry Minds, Inc.

Distributed by CDG Books Canada Inc. for Canada; by Transworld Publishers Limited in the United Kingdom; by IDG Norge Books for Norway; by IDG Sweden Books for Sweden; by IDG Books Australia Publishing Corporation Pty. Ltd. for Australia and New Zealand; by TransQuest Publishers Pte Ltd. for Singapore, Malaysia, Thailand, Indonesia, and Hong Kong; by Gotop Information Inc. for Taiwan; by ICG Muse, Inc. for Japan; by Intersoft for South Africa; by Eyrolles for France; by International Thomson Publishing for Germany, Austria, and Switzerland; by Distribuidora Cuspide for Argentina; by LR International for Brazil; by Galileo Libros for Chile; by Ediciones ZETA S.C.R. Ltda. for Peru; by WS Computer Publishing Corporation, Inc., for the Philippines; by Contemporanea de Ediciones for Venezuela; by Express Computer Distributors for the Caribbean and West Indies; by Micronesia Media Distributor, Inc. for Micronesia; by Chips Computadoras S.A. de C.V. for Mexico; by Editorial Norma de Panama S.A. for Panama; by American Bookshops for Finland.

For general information on Hungry Minds' products and services please contact our Customer Care department within the U.S. at 800-762-2974, outside the U.S. at 317-572-3993 or fax 317-572-4002.

For sales inquiries and reseller information, including discounts, premium and bulk quantity sales, and foreign-language translations, please contact our Customer Care department at 800-434-3422, fax 317-572-4002 or write to Hungry Minds, Inc., Attn: Customer Care Department, 10475 Crosspoint Boulevard, Indianapolis, IN 46256.

For information on licensing foreign or domestic rights, please contact our Sub-Rights Customer Care department at 212-884-5000.

For information on using Hungry Minds' products and services in the classroom or for ordering examination copies, please contact our Educational Sales department at 317-572-3168 or fax 317-572-4168.

For press review copies, author interviews, or other publicity information, please contact our Public Relations department at 317-572-3168 or fax 317-572-4168.

For authorization to photocopy items for corporate, personal, or educational use, please contact Copyright Clearance Center, 222 Rosewood Drive, Danvers, MA 01923, or fax 978-750-4470.

Hungry Minds™ is a trademark of Hungry Minds, Inc.

To all my teachers and mentors: From Mrs. Maybe and Mrs. Armstrong
to Willie Osterman, Judy Levy, Douglas Ford Rea, and Jeff Weiss.
The lessons you taught me I still learn from today.
— with deepest appreciation, Katrin

To my Arizona support system of Diane Taylor, Becky Dutcher, Melanie Rejebian, and Sue Ingram.
(Without Sue's support, this book never would have been finished.) You are always here to push, nudge,
and encourage me to do my best. I'll cherish your friendships forever.
— Jen

FOREWORD

As the editorial lead for the largest gathering of Photoshop users in the country, I have spent many years consuming books, articles, and lectures on how to best use what is arguably the most powerful and deepest imaging application in the world.

As with many Photoshop users, I have examined the dozens of technical reference books that have been written by Photoshop experts over the years. These books tend to serve as deeper, more insightful replacements for the documentation that is included with the software. These books talk about the *right* way to use the program and dissect what menu commands and filters do to your images.

Photoshop Studio Secrets, 3rd Edition, is definitely a breath of fresh air. It takes an approach that not only reveals crucial features of the software but also opens up completely new ways to using those capabilities.

I had the pleasure of working with artist Glenn Mitsui a few years back when we put together the first Technique Conference, where artists (not techie Photoshop users) came together to show off their art and discuss how they used Photoshop to create it. It opened my eyes to some amazing Photoshop realities.

I saw artists who broke several cardinal rules (they used Contrast and Brightness instead of Levels or Curves). They created stunning compositions without touching the Layers palette. They used the data-destroying Dodge and Burn tool to create very cool 3D effects. In a nutshell, their use of Photoshop was *wrong*, but after seeing their creations, I learned that there is no *right* way to use Photoshop. These artists were too busy creating award-winning art to bother with convention.

Several of these artists and their innovative approaches have been profiled in this book. The combination of their unconventional techniques with Deke McClelland's, Katrin Eismann's, and Jennifer Alspach's supreme product knowledge and ability to translate these techniques onto paper have created a book that clearly demystifies while it inspires.

I have learned a lot from this book. I hope you enjoy it as much as I have.

Steve Broback
President and CFO
Thunder Lizard Productions

PREFACE

When I was in grade school, I read an account of Pablo Picasso eating a fish and admiring the way its exposed skeleton lay on his plate. Perhaps on a whim, perhaps merely to impress his interviewer, he gathered the skeleton and worked it into a slab of clay. Then, he molded the clay into a new plate from which he might later suck the bones of another fish.

This simple — if not entirely spontaneous — examination of the artistic cycle has stuck with me ever since. What we see inspires us; what we create becomes a thing from which we can derive use, pleasure, and future inspiration. The beauty of the cycle is that the more you make, the better you become. In other words, as you make art, it makes you.

The purpose of this book is to observe what modern Picassos do with their fish. The only difference is that instead of using skeletons and clay, these artists use digital photographs and a computer program called Photoshop.

YOU ALREADY KNOW HOW TO USE PHOTOSHOP

We won't take up your time explaining the fundamental principles of using Photoshop. This topic is well covered in my *Macworld Photoshop 6 Bible* and *Photoshop 6 for Windows Bible* (from Hungry Minds, Inc., formerly known as IDG Books Worldwide), in addition to scads of other perfectly excellent books.

Nor is this a cookbook of graphic formulas with a blow-by-blow account of every brushstroke the artists apply. Again, that's been done — and done quite well — by several authors before us.

YOU WANT TO KNOW HOW TO MAKE ART

I like to think that this book is something that hasn't been done before. In the pages that follow, we examine proven secrets from top artistic and photographic studios. This is a book of techniques, ideas, philosophies, and inspiration directly from the artists' mouths.

The best way to decide whether this book works for you is to understand our method in creating the book. If you happen not to care for the method, chances are that the book's content won't suit your needs. But if the method appeals to you, I'm guessing that you'll find plenty to like.

- **I would be the student, not the teacher.** The very first decision I made was that if I was going to write yet another Photoshop book, I had better learn something from it. There was no point in sitting down and rehashing yesterday's tips and tricks. I resolved to seek out fresh insights that I had never heard, or perhaps even considered. As it turns out, I succeeded. Speaking purely personally, every chapter is an eye-opener.

■ **Get the best artists.** I decided to concentrate exclusively on the best and the brightest artists in the business. I never sent out a mass e-mail encouraging artists to send me their tips. Undoubtedly, this would have unearthed lots of golden nuggets, but it would have required that I spend too much time sifting through the gravel. Instead, with the help of the able folks at Thunder Lizard Productions, we found the artists whose techniques we most trust and whose work we most admire. Happily, nearly everyone agreed to participate, including several artists who have never consented to show their work in a Photoshop book before.

■ **Focus on clearly defined topics and explore them in depth.** This book covers 20 topics from 20 artists in 20 chapters. This means that you get to spend a leisurely amount of time looking over the artists' shoulders as they concentrate on the tasks that are most near and dear to their hearts.

■ **Cover challenging topics that affect working professionals.** Rather than focus exclusively on Photoshop's features — such as masking or color corrections — this book tackles broad artistic topics. These chapters go beyond the narrow confines of the program and examine the larger Photoshop process. Glenn Mitsui explains how to meet the demands of art directors; Bud Peen mixes watercolor and quill pen with digital media; Katrin Eismann explores the world of digital cameras; Eric Chauvin tells how he creates animated matte paintings for feature films. Even the Photoshop-centered topics — such as Eric Reinfeld's examination of text effects or Greg Vander Houwen's meditations on layers — resonate with each artist's unique perspective.

■ **Respect the artist.** One of the unfortunate trends in publishing is that most computer graphics books treat their artists as commodities. An image and its artist may rate no more than a single caption or paragraph. Whether it's because the author didn't have the expertise to dig deeper or the artist was too busy to share, this practice shortchanges the artist and reader alike. You may learn a little about how the piece was created, but you rarely find out why. I decided to give the artists a chance to show who they are, how they got there, and why they do what they do. By conducting exhaustive, free-form, and sometimes fatiguing interviews, we were able to generate a picture of who each person is, largely in the artist's own voice.

Of course, the qualities that permeate my other books are here, too. I try to keep the topic lively and interesting throughout. (If the text isn't fun to read, there's no way it's going to compete with all this gorgeous artwork!) And although the information comes from some very experienced sources, there's nothing here that a reasonably proficient Photoshop user can't understand.

ABOUT THE WHOLE PLATFORM THING

This is a cross-platform book, which is to say that it's written for both Macintosh and Windows users. If I write ⌘/Ctrl+K, for example, it means to press ⌘+K if you're working on the Mac or Ctrl+K on the PC. A few differences exist between Photoshop for the Mac and Photoshop for Windows, but nothing that affects the content of this particular book.

However, if you take a quick look at the computers that the artists in this book use, you'll notice a strange phenomenon. Virtually every one of them uses a Mac. Ben Benjamin and Michael Ninness also use PCs on the job, and Robert Bowen uses a Unix-based SGI machine. But the computers with which they spend most of their time are Macs.

Does this mean that Macs are the best computers for artists? Or is it simply an indication that these folks have been working on Macs for so long that they don't know any better? I don't know what the reason is, and more important, I don't care. The machines they use are their business.

In fact, the only reason I bring it up is that some folks may wonder why I didn't work a little harder to find artists who prefer Windows. My frank answer is that doing so would have been pointless and counterproductive. I didn't observe any racial, sexual, religious, geographic, or age-based quotas in selecting these artists. Why in the world would I have given even a passing thought to the computer they use? All that matters is that the information in this book is as equally applicable to Photoshop for Windows as it is to Photoshop for the Mac.

SOME MORE PERSONAL TESTIMONY

In short, of all the Photoshop books on the market, this is the one I would be the most likely to buy. It's the one book I've written that reveals mysteries that were previously outside my range of knowledge on virtually every page. That's because this is less a cohesive book than a compilation of 20 unique seminars presented by 20 eminent artists. My biggest contribution is a sense of enthusiasm and wonder as the information unfolds.

As is so often the case, I started thinking that I knew everything, only to learn that I knew nothing. Read these pages and delight in the discovery of how little you once knew.

— *Deke McClelland*

CONTENTS AT A GLANCE

CONTENTS

CHAPTER 3
SPOT-COLOR SEPARATIONS   31

FEATURING JIM POPP

CHAPTER 4
CREATING BUDGET 3D CHARACTERS   47

FEATURING MIKE STRASSBURGER

CHAPTER 7

FROM ILLUSTRATION TO PHOTOREALISTIC IMAGE   79

FEATURING JON-PAUL FAY

CHAPTER 8

MERGING PAST AND PRESENT WITH SUMI BRUSHSTROKES   93

FEATURING HIROSHI GOTO

CHAPTER 9
GLASS, SMOKE, AND REFLECTIONS   109

FEATURING ELIOT BERGMAN

CHAPTER 10
THE TAO OF LAYERING   129

FEATURING GREG VANDER HOUWEN

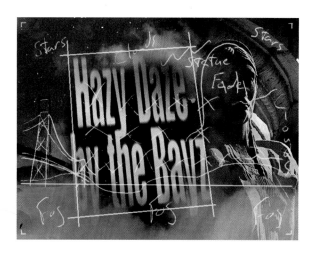

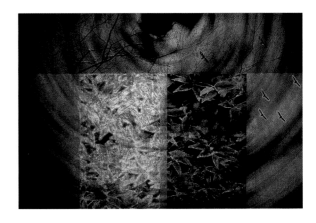

CHAPTER 13
DIGITAL CAMERAS COME OF AGE   177
FEATURING KATRIN EISMANN

CHAPTER 14
PHOTOGRAPHING FOR PHOTOSHOP   193
FEATURING JEFF SCHEWE

CHAPTER 15
CREATIVE QUICKTIME
VIRTUAL REALITY   209

FEATURING JANIE FITZGERALD

CHAPTER 16
HIGH-END TEXTURE MAPPING
FOR 3D IMAGES   233

FEATURING JOE JONES

CHAPTER 17
INVENTING PHOTOREALISTIC
WORLDS 255

FEATURING ERIC CHAUVIN

CHAPTER 18
CREATING IMAGES FOR THE
WORLD WIDE WEB 271

FEATURING BEN BENJAMIN

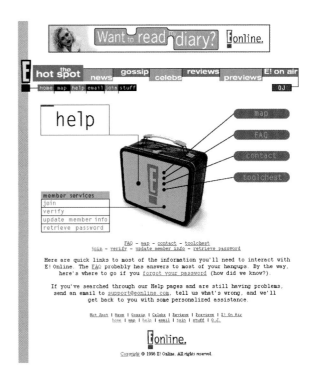

NAATA PRESENTS THE

1994

N FRANCISCO **ASIAN AMERICAN**

INTERNATIONAL

FILM FESTIVAL

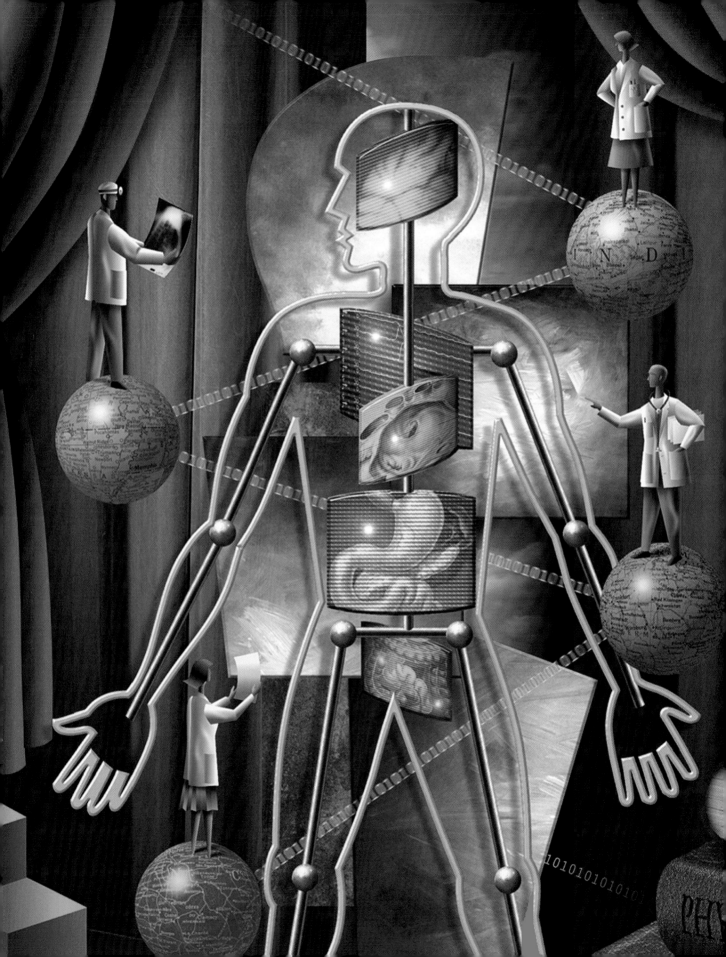

CHAPTER 1
SKETCH TO EXECUTION: THE COMMERCIAL ART PROCESS

Photoshop is, by most accounts, a powerful and well-constructed program, arguably the staple application of the professional graphics industry. But it's the program's price that really forces you to treat it with reverence. Unless you're a highly paid professional type who gets a kick out of image editing in your spare time, Photoshop is too expensive to purchase as a lark. After sinking $500 into the software, and who knows how much into learning it, the best way to recoup your costs is to make money with the program.

We're not proposing to share with you some magic formula for breaking into the computer graphics market. Nor do we have a secret list of art directors who are looking for fresh talent. (If we did, we would be filming infomercials and setting up 900 numbers instead of writing this book.) Having only a vague recollection of the random turn of events that got us where we are today, we're hardly in a position to coach.

But with the help of veteran computer artist Glenn Mitsui, we can paint a picture of what it's like to create a commercial project from start to finish. If you've never sold a piece of artwork to a high-end client, then this little tour is the next best thing to serving six months as a studio apprentice. And if you already make a tidy living with Photoshop, we think you'll find Mitsui's approach uniquely insightful. This chapter shows Mitsui at work, from initial client contact to final product.

With different styles, you can handle a wide variety of jobs, and you're never in a position of having to hammer a round peg in a square hole.

GLENN MITSUI

WHO IS GLENN TO TALK?

Before we launch into what Mitsui does, it might help to know a little bit about who he is and what makes him an expert on this particular topic. Art directors and colleagues recognize him as a rare chameleon of an artist who can shift styles to accommodate the interests and personalities of his clients. Although just about every artist feels compelled to periodically modify his or her style to remain commercially viable, Mitsui seems capable of balancing multiple styles simultaneously.

"If you maintain a single particular style, it's not always possible to force that style into different subject matters. For example, my brightly colored architectural style probably wouldn't work as editorial art for a story about psychology. With different styles, you can handle a wide variety of jobs and you're never in a position of having to hammer a round peg in a square hole. I'm not saying it never works against you — you may find that your identity isn't as strong in one style as in another. And I always have to ask my clients which piece of mine led them to me so I can figure out which style they're looking for. But the mental advantages are well worth it. I don't get bored."

For A'cino, an emerging cosmetics company, Mitsui employed his sleek photo collage style (1.1). "A'cino wanted to create a series of postcards and placards for retail stores. They wanted chic, but they didn't want to look too high tech. So, I tried to create something that was crisp and elegant. And of course, I've always been intrigued by fish swimming beside birds with long legs."

Mitsui used a softer, more traditional style for a poster he did for the Seattle Repertory Theater (1.2). "I'm a big fan of playwright Philip Gotanda, so when they asked me to do a poster for one of his plays, I was very excited. The play's about a 17-year-old girl who grew up on the island of Kauai in the early 1900s. Part of the story is about how she becomes an apprentice for a bitter but very talented pottery artist, and later becomes romantically involved with him. So, I wanted to integrate the elements of natural art, with natural brushstrokes, pottery shards, and the fire from the kiln."

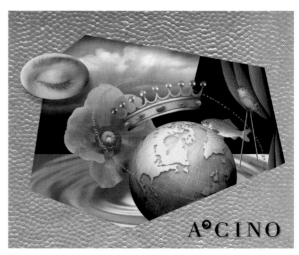

1.1

ARTIST:
Glenn Mitsui

ORGANIZATION:
Studio M D
Seattle, WA

SYSTEM:
Power Mac 7100/66
1GB storage

RAM:
106MB total
70MB assigned to Photoshop

MONITOR:
Radius 17-inch

EXTRAS:
Hewlett-Packard ScanJet IIcx

VERSION USED:
Photoshop 5.0

OTHER APPLICATIONS:
Macromedia FreeHand, Corel Painter, Adobe After Effects

1.2

Folks in the computer industry are likely to see a starkly different side of Mitsui. "Resolution Technology asked me to create an ad for a 3D program of theirs that enables artists to create realistic flythroughs and landscapes. My approach to it was to build a volumetric person made up of various interactive elements (1.3). It resembles a 3D rendering, but I created everything using layers and gradients in Photoshop."

1.3

WORK HISTORY:

<u>1982</u> — Worked as technical illustrator on graveyard shift at Boeing; discovered that women's bathroom had a nap couch.

<u>1987</u> — Created corporate presentation slides on Genigraphics system for Magicmation.

<u>1990–present</u> — Started Studio M D with Jesse Doquilo and Randy Lim; purchased first Macintosh system.

<u>1992</u> — Started creating full-page feature artwork for *Macworld* magazine.

<u>1995</u> — Became board member and speaker for American Institute of Graphics Arts; served as panel judge for Sig-Graph fine arts competition.

FAVORITE '70s TV Shows:

"Green Hornet" (because Bruce Lee played Kato) and "Long Street" (because Bruce Lee played Kung Fu instructor).

Mitsui used the theme of paper kites to symbolize the different nationalities represented at San Francisco's Asian American International Film Festival (1.4). "The Festival includes Chinese films, Japanese films, Korean, Thai, Indonesian, and all kinds of other contributions. I wanted to show that although we're all different in a lot of ways, we're blown by the same

1.4

1.5

wind. Here I tried to emphasize the printed quality of the paper by exaggerating the creases and wrinkles and keeping the halftone dots in the eyes."

One of Mitsui's most recent stylistic developments is what he calls his "big hurkin' icons with Spirograph" approach. "The image of the two hands (1.5) was one of the illustrations I proposed to demonstrate compatibility issues for a new chip from Fujitsu. I feel like this style really emphasizes the power of the line. It lets me elicit humor, anger, and other raw emotions using quick icons. It's like a logo — it either succeeds or fails on first glance."

THE CLIENT AND YOU

Initial contact with a client usually starts with a phone call or e-mail from an art director. "By the time you hear from an art director, the client has probably already seen your work." Does the art director already have a sketch or visual idea in mind? "Sometimes, but mostly not. If I'm doing magazine art, I probably get a copy of the article. If it's an ad, I might get the ad copy or they might send me the product. But the client usually relies on me to come up with a visual concept that relates to what they do."

DEVELOPING QUALITY CONCEPTS

The art director is the client's one and only representative. To satisfy the client, you have to include the art director fully in the decision-making process. "Most problems occur when you don't involve the client enough. The last thing you want to do is surprise your client, as so many digital artists do. That usually happens when you take a concept and run with it on the computer before anybody but you has seen it.

"You can't just tie together a bunch of special effects and expect your artwork to sell. A good illustration is 90 percent concept and 10 percent execution. The concept has got to be strong. If you go to the computer right away, without completely developing the idea, you get 90 percent technique and 10 percent concept. That's simply not going to fly with high-end clients.

"It's really easy to take an idea too far, too fast, when you're working in a program such as Photoshop. That's why I develop the concept with traditional pencil sketches. If I'm on a deadline, I sit down and force the sketches to work. If I have a week to come up with a concept, I sketch when I'm feeling creative. But as a rule, I avoid the computer altogether until the art director has signed off on the concept."

THE IMPORTANCE OF COMMUNICATION

Much as we might like to hope that talent always wins, commercial art is a business like any other. The most successful artists are generally the ones who take the most care in securing and maturing personal relationships. Your ability to get work hinges on effective communication. "If you exclude art directors from the creative process, it can be a big strike against you, particularly if you've never worked with them before. You can almost guarantee that they're going to find things wrong. Whereas, if you get their input at the very beginning and you maintain good relationships, then you avoid surprises and get more jobs in the future. Talk about the project up front. If you don't understand something at the beginning, feel free to ask dumb questions until you know who your client is and what he wants. Don't be nervous, don't feel like you have to apologize. Just patiently feel him out. Now you're working with the art director to get something that he can be comfortable with bringing to his client, and will fight for."

But accommodating your client doesn't mean you have to behave like a wimp. Mitsui advocates that you agree to a reasonable fee up front and stick to it. "The client signs a job estimate before I put pencil to paper for the first sketch. It's a standard contract that I and the others at Studio M D put together a few years back. The estimate is pretty much the exact fee, unless some special circumstances come along. I usually allow for a couple of rounds of revisions before I start charging hourly for anything beyond that. If you do good stuff, and you're predictable and reliable, then you'll always be in demand."

ART ON THE MARCH

Mitsui's work for Advanced Medical Ventures probably illustrates the trials and rewards of creating computer art as well as any piece he's created. "It was an interesting job, all right." The assignment was to create a cover for a medical conference brochure. "The conference was about disorders of the upper stomach. The panelists at this conference were all leading experts in the field of digestive disorders. A bunch of other doctors who treat this illness were invited to come and participate in the audience. Everybody had a keyboard. They posed all questions and received consensus answers from the panelists. There was even going to be a satellite link to show operations beforehand. I can honestly say, it was unlike anything I had done before."

MEDICAL OBJECTIVES AND INTESTINAL DIAGRAMS

"I didn't know anything about stomach disorders—you know, my stomach seems to be working okay—but I agreed to do the job because it sounded as if it would be different. Then, the art director faxed me these two objectives that he wanted me to cover in the artwork (1.6). I don't usually get a list of objectives from a client—not like this, anyway. I looked them over, but for all I could tell, they were written in Greek."

Did the objectives imply that Mitsui should show GERD in action? Was he supposed to highlight the importance of understanding GERD? Or was his

Objective #1: Define dyspepsia, appreciate its epidemiology and clinical significance, and understand the importance of dysomitility in its pathogenesis.

Objective #2: Understand the natural history of gastro-esphageal reflux disease (GERD), the importance of erosive compared to non-erosive esophagitis, and the complications of GERD.

1.6

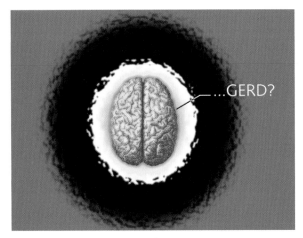

1.7

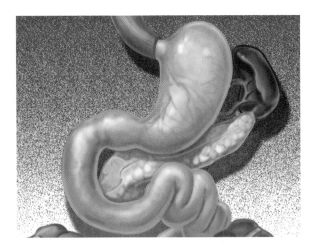

1.8 Reprinted with permission from Advanced Medical Ventures. Artwork by Linda Nye.

mission to produce the artwork while suffering the complications of GERD? Mitsui responds, "I see you have a sense of some of the questions that were going through my head (1.7). Part of the excitement and challenge of being an artist is that you learn so much. Even when you don't want to learn, you get to. It's quite thrilling."

So, how does Mitsui gain a clear understanding of a job when he embarks into such incredibly alien territory? Does he go to the library and search through a few medical encyclopedias? "No way. That might help me understand GERD, but it doesn't get me any closer to knowing the client. The only option is to talk and talk and talk to the art director. I ask every dumb question I can think of until I come across something I can work with. It's better to look like a dope up front than create an illustration that doesn't suit the client's needs."

To make the task more interesting, the art director asked Mitsui to integrate some existing diagrams into his artwork. "He said, 'I'm going to totally leave the creative aspects up to you. But I have a couple of images that I want you to include in your illustration.' And then these intestinal tracts come through (1.8). I thought, whoa, these are pretty. I mean, what is that yellow thing back there? Did this guy swallow a whole cob of corn or something? What in the world am I going to do with this stuff?"

But the client is always right. Who knows, a couple of intestinal diagrams might provide the creative spark that Mitsui is looking for. "Whenever I have something weird like this, I always leave it until the last. That way, I can sit around and worry about it the whole time I'm working on the illustration. It provides motivation."

SKETCH AND CONCEPT

"My personal objective in this project is to come up with a piece of artwork that looks cool and doesn't gross people out. In my first sketch (1.9), I had a little trouble focusing. I think it's Abe Lincoln in a lab coat surrounded by some fire. Even though I didn't use any of this, it was an important part of the process. When you're under a deadline, you don't have any choice. You have to work it out until you hit something that really works for you. For me, sketching is the best way to develop a concept.

"Then, I started brainstorming a little. I looked around the room, paged through books. At some point, I saw some clothes on a hanger, and it reminded me of this petroglyph (1.10). I read the petroglyph as a wire structure with these deelee-boppers hanging down from it, kind of like pots and pans. That's when the basic concept clicked. The body would be the frame, and the organs would hang inside it, like a primitive Visible Man."

With this concept in mind, Mitsui began to sketch in earnest. He quickly settled on a frontal view of the body with the head turned in profile. Then, he arranged a series of globes around the body (1.11). "The conference includes speakers and doctors from all over the world. So the globes demonstrate the international feel of the event.

"As I sketch, I write myself little notes in the margins. These include little comments and ideas I want to remember, bits and pieces I need clarification on, and questions that I have to ask the client. You have to make a real effort to stay on top of the client's needs. By keeping notes, I make sure I don't forget something that could gum up the works."

Mitsui's final sketch adds structure to the illustration (1.12). "The wireframe could look a little flimsy if I just stuck it against a neutral background. By adding some simple, block-like objects—the steps, the curtains, the books—I could convey depth without distracting attention from the primary element. It makes the sketch feel like a more substantial piece of artwork."

At this point, Glenn faxed his sketch to the art director for approval. "He signed off on it right away." Did the quick approval surprise Mitsui? "No, it was a solid concept. After working this long, I think I have a pretty good sense of whether I've nailed it or not. If I don't think I have it, I don't send it."

TRACING THE SKETCH IN FREEHAND

After getting the sketch approved, Mitsui scanned it into Photoshop and scaled it to get the proper width and height dimensions. Then, he saved the sketch as a TIFF image and imported it into FreeHand. Inside FreeHand, Mitsui used the pen tool to trace the main

1.9

1.10

outlines. As we'll see, these paths later served as template elements and selection outlines in Photoshop.

Mitsui likes FreeHand for its simplicity. "It's the 7-Eleven of graphics programs. If you need a Twinkie, you go to 7-Eleven, get in and get out. No one gets hurt. FreeHand is the same way. You get in, trace your paths, get out. No thinking necessary. I don't expect much from it, and it gives me very little in return."

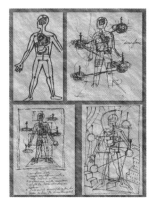 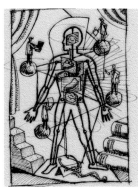

1.11   1.12

We should mention that Mitsui is still using FreeHand 3.1, a program that was last seen in stores about four years ago. "Sure, it's old, but it's easy to use and it does everything I need it to. I can fly around and trace all the paths I need in 15 minutes or so. I don't think I even have the colors loaded anymore; I just use it in black and white."

RASTERIZING AND TRACING IN PHOTOSHOP

"I saved the illustration in the Illustrator 8 format, to use in FreeHand. Then, in Photoshop, I rasterized it at 300 pixels per inch. Because all the paths were black, I opened it as a grayscale image so it came up as fast as possible." FreeHand 10 lets you move between Illustrator and Photoshop without limitations.

Mitsui had no intention of integrating the FreeHand drawing directly into his final artwork; it was merely an architectural template, cleaner and more precise than the original pencil sketch. And in Photoshop, the best place to put a template is in a separate channel. "I went to the Channels palette. Because it was a grayscale image, there was only one channel there. I duplicated it to a second channel and inverted it so it appeared white against black (1.13)."

Mitsui converted the file to the RGB mode and filled the RGB image with black to clear out the rasterized drawing. (The inverted template remained safe in the alpha channel.) He then returned to the alpha channel, now the fourth channel, and traced most of the template outlines with Photoshop's pen tool. "One of the things about using FreeHand 3.1 is

> ### GLENN SAYS, ONE SKETCH, ONE CONCEPT
>
> "Once I get it right, I send just the one sketch. A lot of artists get indecisive and send off two or three sketches just to be safe. That's a bad idea because it confuses the client and asks him to think about issues that are really your responsibility. You have to say, 'Here's my vision. Do you like it, yes or no?' If no, then we talk. If yes, I move on. It's a very clean process this way."

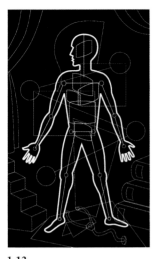

1.13

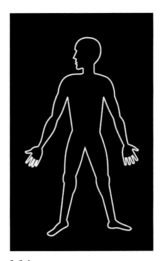

1.14

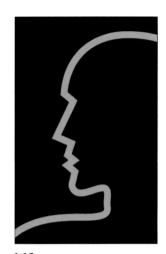

1.15

that you can't bring the paths over directly. But that's okay. Tracing them again gives me the opportunity to further refine the drawing."

MAKING THE BEVELED BODY OUTLINE

So Mitsui redraws every single path? "Not all of them. The outline of the body is something I used as is. I went back to the FreeHand file and copied the body path and pasted it into a file all by itself. Then, I brought that over as a fifth channel in my Photoshop image (1.14). This outline was thick enough to use as a mask all by itself."

The body outline was the first image element that Mitsui added to his illustration. He started by ⌘/Ctrl-clicking the fifth channel in the Channels palette to convert it into a selection outline. Then, he filled the selection with yellow (1.15). To add a beveled edge to the body outline (1.16), Mitsui relied on the third-party Inner Bevel filter, which is part of the Eye Candy plug-in collection from Alien Skin Software. But he could have just as easily applied an Inner Bevel Layer effect in Photoshop 6.0.

1.16

1.17

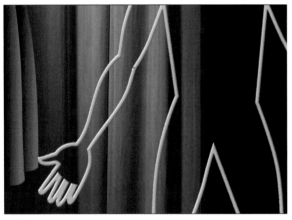

1.18

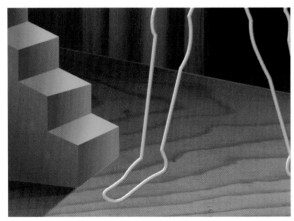

1.19

ADDING THE BACKGROUND STUFF

Mitsui blocked in his background objects on separate layers using gradient fills and stock images. He started by creating red drapes in the upper-left corner of the illustration (1.17). Each fold of the drapery is the result of converting one of his paths to a selection and then filling it with a red-to-black gradation. To make the soft blue drapes at the rear of his virtual auditorium (1.18), he imported a stock photo from the PhotoDisc image library. The floor of the stage (1.19) is a wood pattern that Mitsui shot himself. As with the red drapes, Mitsui created the green steps by converting paths to selection outlines and filling the selections with gradations.

No one can accuse Mitsui of being stingy with his gradient shadows. "My motto is simple. No shadow bad; plenty shadow good." But the astute viewer will notice that Mitsui plays fast and loose with his imaginary light source. "When my students tell me, 'Mr. Mitsui, your light source is inconsistent,' I just say, 'So?' Then they say, 'Your perspective is all screwy,' and I say, 'Yup.' I had my fill of paying attention to that kind of thing when I worked as a draftsman at Boeing. This is my world, darn it. Everybody else is just a nut trying to get a squirrel."

Was it possible that Mitsui was inspired by French post-impressionist Paul Cézanne, who purposely violated perspective in order to focus on abstracted details in his artwork? "Oh, yeah, I'm big on violating stuff. But seriously, people don't come to me to create technically accurate illustrations. They're looking to me to create a mood and a feel and a dynamic."

BINDING THE BOOKS

To highlight the scholarly nature of the conference, Mitsui's sketch called for books in the lower-right corner of the artwork. He created the basic book shapes by reshaping and cloning elements from real books (1.20). But the bindings were generic hard-cover fabric with no markings to identify them as medical volumes (1.21). The challenge was to take words such as Anatomy and Physiology and wrap them onto the curved spines of the books.

"Filter➤Distort➤Shear is great for faking 3D effects. Here, I used the Shear filter to distort the text and medical emblem horizontally (1.22) so they appeared to bend around the sides of the books. Then, I just rotated the elements to match the angle of the spines (1.23). I used to do this kind of stuff in Ray Dream Designer, but now I totally avoid 3D programs. I never did enjoy working in Ray Dream or any of them."

1.20

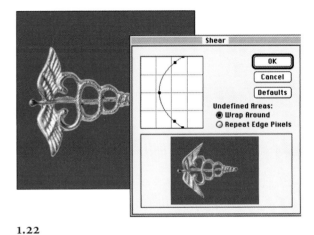

1.22

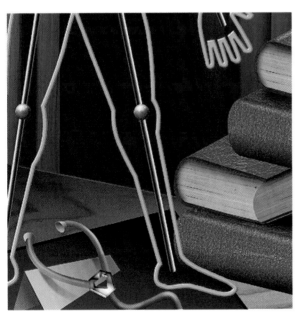

1.21

1.23

CREATING THE GLOBES

For each of his four globes, Mitsui started with a small, square scrap from a scanned map (1.24). Then he applied the Glass Lens Bright filter from Kai's Power Tools 2 to wrap a circular area of the map around a 3D sphere (1.25). "I bet I could've come up with something similar using the Spherize filter that's included with Photoshop, and layering on a couple of radial gradations. But some of those simple KPT filters are really useful."

1.24

1.25

Mitsui wanted to colorize each globe with a different hue, so he converted the globe to a grayscale image. Then, he indexed the color palette using Image➤Mode➤Indexed Color. This permitted him to modify the palette using Image ➤ Mode➤ Color Table. "When you choose the Color Table command, Photoshop lets you edit all 256 colors in the indexed palette (1.26). I just dragged across all the colors in the palette. Then, Photoshop asked me to specify the darkest color in the table and the lightest color. I set them both to shades of blue. Then, Photoshop automatically blended between them (1.27)."

Why not use the Hue/Saturation command? "I don't feel like I have enough control over the process with that command. The ramping between light and dark colors is uneven. As a result, the colors tend to get too hot, and an image like this might start to

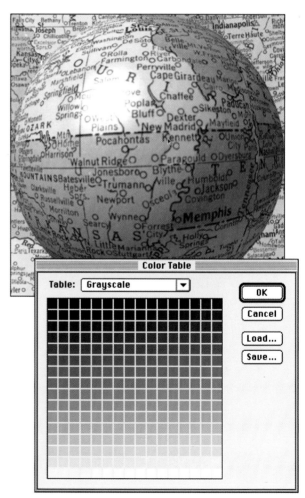

1.26

band. With the Color Table command, I can precisely control the tonal range of colors in one fell swoop." After colorizing each globe, Mitsui selected it with the elliptical marquee tool and dragged it over into his composition (1.28).

HANGING THE INTERNAL ORGANS

"So here I am, almost done with the job. One of the last tasks I have to do is insert the organs into the artwork. I've put it off as long as I can (1.29).

"By now, I've already decided that I'm going to frame the organs inside slanted viewing screens that will hang from the frame that I've set up inside the body. But I'm still a little nervous about integrating the client's images. These doctors are used to seeing internal organs. But it's up to me to make the artwork

palatable to a general audience. I don't want some older couple to walk by the conference room and run away screaming when they see the artwork."

To get a feel for how the organs were going to work, Mitsui started with one of the more enlightened representatives, the brain (1.30). "The brain is another PhotoDisc image. This is one of those cases where I really have to rely on a stock image. I can't walk outside and say, 'Excuse me, could I, uh, saw your head open?

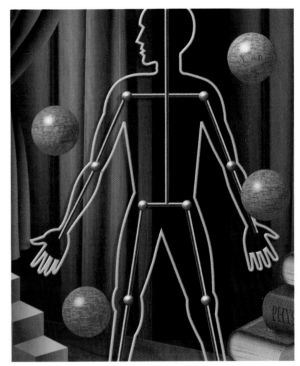

1.28

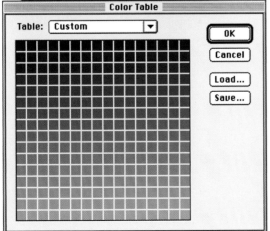

1.27

1.29 Reprinted with permission from Advanced Medical Ventures. Artwork by Linda Nye.

It'll only be for a minute. I have some twine here to tie things back up when we're through.' That's just not going to cut it."

Mitsui converted the brain to grayscale and colored it green using the Color Table trick described earlier (1.31). "I wanted to simulate the look of those old-style green-and-black monitors." To create the effect of interlaced screen lines, Mitsui opened the green brain inside Corel Painter, which offers better texturing capabilities than Photoshop. He selected a horizontal line pattern included in Painter's Art Materials palette (1.32). Then, he applied it to the brain as a paper texture (1.33). (This effect is not impossible to perform in Photoshop, it's just harder. You would have to load the pattern into a separate alpha channel and apply it as a texture map using the Lighting Effects filter.)

After saving the brain out of Painter, Mitsui opened it up again in Photoshop and copied it to the clipboard. Then, he returned to his medical composition and selected the path that traced around the outline of the monitor inside the head. He converted the path to a selection and chose Edit➢Paste Into to paste the green brain inside. Then, he slanted the brain to match the angle of the monitor using Edit➢Transform➢Skew (1.34).

"To give the monitors some depth, I beveled the edges with the Alien Skin filter. That didn't always produce the effect I was looking for, so I hand-brushed in a couple of highlights and shadows along the edges of

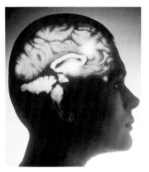

1.30

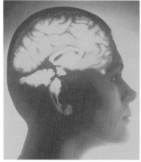

1.31

1.32

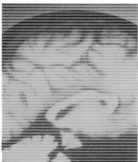

1.33

the paths. Then, I hit each monitor with the Lens Flare filter to create a little reflection on the screen (1.35)."

Mitsui performed the same steps on the other organs with one exception. "I colored the main stomach image orange to set it off from the others (1.36)." Did the client have any problem with Mitsui de-emphasizing the organs by framing them inside monitors? "No, they loved it. I think they understood that it was a modern treatment of the subject that tied in well to the conference angle. You have these little doctor figures analyzing the big body and commenting on the screens. It's like he's their virtual patient."

We imagine the conference organizers were proud indeed to display this piece on the cover of their handouts. It establishes a bold and authoritative mood for the event from the outset, before a word is spoken on stage. The illustration tastefully introduces the topic at hand, explains the relationship between the experts and international attendees, highlights the role of technology at the event, and delivers the scene inside a lush and palpable diorama. Every need satisfied according to plan. This is one conference where the artist will get invited back.

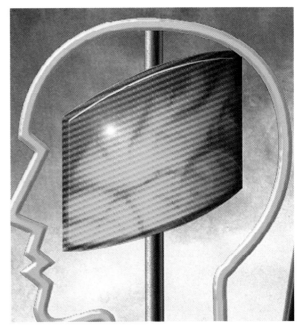

1.35

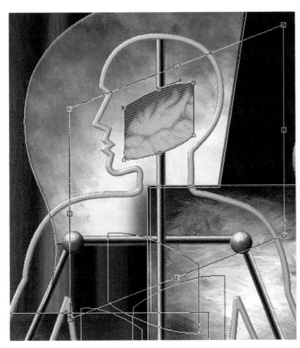

1.34

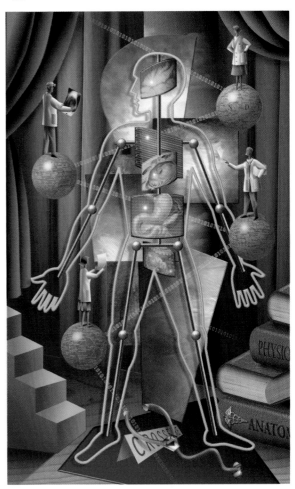

1.36

CHAPTER 2
WORKING STOCK PHOTOGRAPHY INTO GRAPHIC ART

There's a certain tiresome machismo associated with owning big, expensive computer gadgetry. When guys brag about their big disk arrays and their monster memory upgrades, we have to excuse ourselves and visit the little boy's and girl's room. As with everybody else out there, we fully admit that we personally have far too much capital sunk into our machinery, but it's because we can't manage to get by on less, not because we derive any pleasure from owning excessive equipment. Deke, in particular, is one of those crusty old codgers who still remembers fondly how he wrote, designed, and laid out his first book on a Mac 512Ke with two 400K floppy drives and no hard disk. Sure, he lived in a state of perpetual digital torment, but he was too young and stupid to know any better. The fact is, computers are like a sick addiction; we can't seem to live without them, but it's unbecoming to take pride in our depraved predicaments.

Refreshingly, professional illustrator Gordon Studer represents the other extreme. He proves that you can make a living with Photoshop without making the slightest attempt to keep up with the Joneses. Until recently, Studer got by with a Quadra—roughly equivalent to a 486 PC—equipped with 16MB of RAM and a 200MB hard drive. When we wrote the 2nd edition several months after the release of Photoshop 5, Studer was making do with Version 2.5, which, as veteran devotees may recall, lacks layers. He even used a Zip cartridge as a scratch disk. Studer admitted this might not be the wisest solution in the world. "An Adobe representative came up to

The idea is to strip the forms down to their bare minimum and play with unrelated abstractions inside the forms. If the photograph wasn't there to identify the image, it would break down into a bunch of concentric squares.

GORDON STUDER

me once and said, 'You can't tell people that. They're going to destroy their computers!' But I've been doing it for about two years and I haven't had any problems." Now, thankfully, Studer is at least using Photoshop 5.0.

What was Studer doing with his wee system? Creating illustrations that blend his primitive, whimsical style with volumes of royalty-free stock photography and occasional 35mm snapshots. Therefore, Studer's economical system matched his economical approach. "The funny thing is, I get nearly all my images from maybe a dozen PhotoDisc and Adobe CDs. I get my faces from 'Retro Americana' and 'Beyond Retro' (2.1) and my hands from a collection called 'Just Hands.' The 'Retro' collections are wildly popular, but the way I use the photos, no one even recognizes where they come from. I combine a man's head with a woman's eye and another guy's mouth. Then I carve them into simple geometric shapes (2.2). I use the

same photos over and over again, but no one tells me, 'Man, I'm getting tired of that image.' All they see is the artwork."

You can test Studer's hypothesis by trying to spot a separate illustration printed later in this chapter that repeats one of the stock photographs shown here.

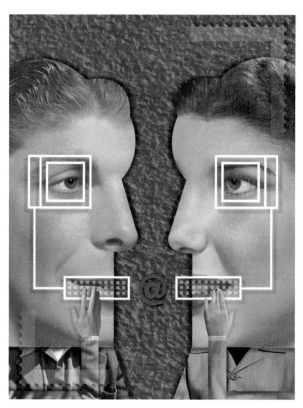

2.2

2.1

ARTIST:
Gordon Studer

STUDIO:
1576 62nd Street
Emeryville, CA 94608
510/655-4256
gstuder363@aol.com

SYSTEM:
When this chapter was first written:
Quadra 840AV
200MB storage
Now:
Power Mac G3/266
6GB storage

RAM:
When this chapter was first written:
16MB total
8MB assigned to Photoshop
Now:
96MB total
60MB assigned to Photoshop

MONITOR:
Apple 17–inch

EXTRAS:
Microtek 300–dpi scanner, PhotoDisc and Adobe Image Library royalty–free images

As you'll discover, the simple act of modifying the shape of the face lends the revised subject its own distinct appearance.

IS IT ETHICAL?

Some might take exception to an artist who makes a living off repurposing a small collection of photographs. Setting aside the fact that the illustrations in this chapter are stylistically unique — being both compositionally and creatively independent of the photographs that populate them — Studer makes ethical use of what is generally accepted to be an ethical system of distribution. A reputable multiuse image dealer such as PhotoDisc or Digital Stock pays its photographers royalties based on how many copies of a CD it sells. Digital Stock estimates that its photographers earn on average $50,000 in the first year for a collection of 100 images — a figure that exceeds the average per-person royalties paid out by traditional stock agencies.

As artists who likewise rely on royalties for a chunk of our income, we would argue that Studer's repeated use of an image is no less scrupulous than you making repeated use of a technique that you learn in this book. It is exceedingly important to observe codes of professional behavior, but it is equally important to evaluate new practices with an open mind. Otherwise, digital manipulation makes pirates and scalawags of us all.

THE TREND TOWARD STOCK PHOTOGRAPHY

Studer's reliance on stock photography is a fairly recent phenomenon. "I made a whole style change about three years ago. Prior to that, I was doing really graphic stuff with sharp lines and abstract forms (2.3). But I grew tired of the fact that everything was so flat. So I started to experiment with textured patterns and designs. To avoid the computer look, I scanned in photographic textures and dropped them inside my basic shapes. It was as if I had wrapped my

2.3

VERSION USED:

When this chapter was first written:
Photoshop 2.5.1
Now:
Photoshop 5.0

OTHER APPLICATIONS:
Adobe Illustrator, Adobe After Effects

WORK HISTORY:

1978 — After deciding football wasn't going to pan out, took up fine arts at Penn State.

1983 — Studied at Corchrain School of Arts; got job as paste-up artist and spot illustrator for Red Tree Associates.

1988 — *Left Oakland Tribune* for *San Francisco Examiner;* was introduced to Illustrator and computer design.

1990 — Created first piece for *MacWeek* "MacInTouch" column, which continued every week for seven years.

1994 — Shifted artistic style from high-contrast graphics to stock photo collage.

1998 — Took up After Effects, illustrated children's book about cats.

FAVORITE WORKING WARDROBE:

Bathrobe ("I got a new one and I just love it.")

artwork in a series of fabric coatings, giving the shapes a richness they didn't have before (2.4).

"About this same time, I was playing around with deconstructing my artwork, reducing it to stark 'circle-head' characters (2.5). It was successful with my editorial clients, but the corporate and ad people were turned off. It was just too weird for them. Then I hit on something that really surprised me. If that same weird shape was filled with a photograph (2.6),

no one seemed to have a problem with it. The client was able to make the jump. It was as if the photograph identified the face as a person instead of a space alien. Then I was free to do whatever I wanted with the outline.

"To keep life interesting, I believe in making a stylistic shift every three or four years. Right now, I'm working on another shift. I'm trying to push the geometry of the shapes even further. For example, I have this one image that's cut out into completely abstract forms that don't even vaguely resemble a head outline (2.7). The idea is to strip the forms down to their bare minimum and play with unrelated abstractions inside the forms. If the photograph wasn't there to identify the image, it would break down into a bunch of concentric squares." From Studer's work of simple abstraction, the photo extends a fragile thread that touches the real world.

GORDONIAN GEOMETRY

"I have two ways I work. One is really geometric — all right angles and circles. Another is more free-form with random cutouts. The illustration I made for Coca-Cola (2.8) is an example of the geometric look. Normally, when you think geometry, you think precision and order. But here, it's a complete abstraction. Nothing in real life is this exact, so the geometry takes you farther away from the real world."

MIXING STATIC BACKDROPS

"Because I'm working without layers, I have to start at the back of the image and work my way forward. So I

2.4

2.5   2.6

2.7   2.8

always lay in the background first." For the Coca–Cola illustration, Studer rendered a circuit board pattern he created in Illustrator and applied the Emboss filter inside Photoshop (2.9). Then he opened a cork texture (2.10), copied the circuit board, and pasted it on top. To merge the two images, he applied the Luminosity blend mode and set the Opacity to 50 percent (2.11).

Studer frequently wallpapers his artwork with static, textured backgrounds. "The cork and chip patterns are good examples. I use these backgrounds, or slight variations on them, in a lot of my work. Like I might colorize the cork brown in one image (2.12) and blue in another (2.13). The idea is to set up similar worlds, so each illustration feels like a room inside the same home."

THE CENTRAL STOCK SUBJECT

"After the background, I lay in the big forms. Usually that's the face, because I like to work everything off the main head in the image (2.14). I always start with a grayscale image. Even if it's in color, I make it grayscale. Then I convert the image to RGB and

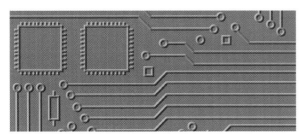

2.9

2.10

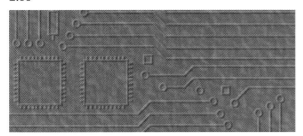

2.11

> **UNDERSTANDING**
>
> **A**ligning an object–oriented pattern such as Studer's circuit board with a face (2.13) or other image can be a tricky matter. Except for scaling, rotating, and the like, you can't edit the pattern in Photoshop, so it's important to nail the alignment in Illustrator or FreeHand. "Before I create the pattern, I save a 72–ppi version of the Photoshop image as an EPS file. Then in Illustrator, I choose Place Art, which gives me a template for how the photographic part is laying out. I can draw the circle exactly around the eyeball or the chip around the mouth. I even have a little circle around the nostril. Then I delete the template, save the illustration, and import it into Photoshop."

colorize it, as opposed to trying to make it look realistic (2.15). The colorizing reminds me of the way I used to work — with pure flat-color fills. Sometimes I add stylized highlights such as rosy cheeks, but only

2.12

2.13

2.14

2.15

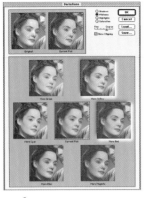

2.16

2.17

2.18

2.19

2.20

2.21

to reaffirm the retro look. The images don't seem like photographs to me; they're more like scraps of color. I like to think of a face as just a big piece of yellow."

Studer's colorizing isn't the vanilla Hue/Saturation type. It's really more of a duotone effect, with hues ranging from yellow to red. "I use the Variations command to saturate the image with yellows and reds. In this case, I selected the Midtones radio button and nudged the slider bar toward Coarse. Then I clicked twice on the Yellow thumbnail and twice on Red (2.16). It's way easier than creating a real duotone, and it gets me the hyper-saturated colors I'm looking for. A while back, Glenn Mitsui showed me a trick where he gets a similar effect by indexing the image and modifying the color table (see Chapter 1). But I don't know — that seems like more work."

To define the shape of the head, Studer superimposed a globe illustration he created in Illustrator. He filled the artwork with white (Ctrl+Shift+Delete in Photoshop 5) and dropped it on the woman's face (2.17). Then he lowered the Opacity to 50 percent to merge globe and face into one element (2.18).

ADDING THE COMPUTER

"I have a small collection of computer pictures that I use over and over (2.19). All of them come from photos I shot myself. For a really brief period of time, I had a $20,000 Kodak digital camera on loan. I just went hog wild with it — I tried to photograph as many things as I could. Then I cut and pasted pieces of the monitors and computers to get a more stylized look. There's a geometric monitor, an orthogonal one, and another that's really irregular. I also colorized the images, airbrushed in shadows, and did whatever it took to convert the computers from photographs to graphics."

COMPOSITION AND DROP SHADOWS

After selecting the least dimensional of his monitors, Studer copied the head and monitor and pasted each one at a time against his background (2.20). "You can see even in the early composition how I'm using simple geometry. The head's a circle, the monitor comes in at 90 degrees. The head is vertically centered on the background, and the green screen of the monitor is exactly centered with respect to the head.

"As each element goes in, I give it a drop shadow. Everyone has a method for making shadows, and whatever yours is, I'm sure it's as good as mine. I'm just going for the basics — feathered edges, black fill. When I add a shadow, it's not intended to convey perspective. I want it to look like I cut out a bunch of photographs and laid them on top of the background (2.21)."

2.22

2.23

THE ANATOMICALLY PRECISE HAND

Second only to faces in Studer's stock photo library are hands. For the Coca-Cola illustration, Studer wanted to add a single hand operating the keyboard. After finding a stock hand that fit his needs (2.22), he colorized it with the Variations command. "I can basically replay the last colorization I applied by pressing the Option/Alt key when I choose the Variations command. If the lighting isn't quite the same, I might have to tweak the settings a little, but usually it only takes a couple of seconds to get it dead on."

Instead of cutting the hand into an abstract shape, Studer carefully selects each and every finger (2.23). "You can't abstract hands the way you can faces. Fingers make hands what they are. Besides, I like the way the detailed treatment of the hands plays off the simple geometry of the head." Studer retouched away the ring by cloning from the third finger. Then he flipped and rotated the hand so it rested on top of the keyboard, detached from the body without even a hint of arm. "Again, the hand sits at a right angle (2.24). Despite the detailing, I have to make it conform to the geometry of the overall illustration."

2.24

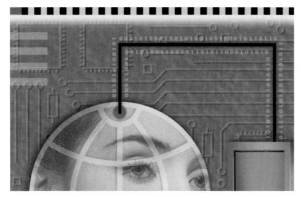

2.25

2.26

2.27

THE FINAL ADJUSTMENTS

"To make that alternating yellow/black accent across the top of the art (2.25), I just create a black square, a yellow square, and clone them over and over again. Of course, I never hit it right on, so I leave a big gap at one end and fill it with red." What is the purpose of this accent? "I've used that pattern since day one, and I have no idea why. No sense questioning it — it just is."

At this point, the image was ready to send off to the client. But as any working artist knows, the job doesn't necessarily end when you turn in the artwork. "The first image (2.8) is the one I submitted. But the art director had me make a bunch of last-minute changes. He had me change the body — it was too pointy — and he had me flip-flop the entire image. He also wanted me to add a little Coke bottle cap at the top of the forehead (2.26)."

Whenever a client dictates modifications to an illustration, there's a chance for damage. The smallest changes can upset a hearty aesthetic balance and send it teetering headlong into a pile of digital goop. "My biggest concern was the flip. I've had so many images where you flip them and they don't look right at all; everything seems off. But because this one was so geometric, it survived pretty well." We guess if your face can tolerate the occasional mirror image as you comb your hair in the morning, a face in a circle can hold up to reflection as well.

FREE-FORM IMAGE CHOPPING

Not all of Studer's images adhere to strict geometric guidelines. Many of his illustrations deliberately shun order in favor of chaos, with carefully clipped cutouts jockeying for attention inside crowded compositions. In an image he did for *CIO* magazine, the assignment was to show a cat working at a computer while his previous lives look on (2.27). "I had to take this one cat and create a bunch of different variations on him. It gave me the opportunity to focus on one element at a time, completely out of context with the others." Studer carved his subjects into human forms, some resembling cartoon skulls, others suggestive of Jimmy Durante in profile.

"The cats are mine. I just shot them with my camera, went down to a one-hour delivery place, and scanned them (2.28). In Photoshop, I cut and pasted the cats into basic arrangements of faces and fur. Then I used the pen tool to shave the cats into the cartoon shapes (2.29)."

ROUGH PIXELS INSIDE SMOOTH OUTLINES

"The resolution of my original photographs was more or less awful. I had to sample them up and sharpen them to get them the way they look in the finished artwork." Is increasing the resolution a wise idea? "If I was working with a flat photograph, probably not. But I've got all kinds of elements coming in at different resolutions. Maybe I'm more cavalier than I ought to be, but I just scale things as I need them. I know I can always deal with any softness or graininess later.

"Besides, I don't think people read a piece of artwork one element at a time; they see the whole piece together, even when it's an obvious composition. The fact that the pen tool edges are nice and sharp makes the entire image look in focus. I've never had a client complain about the resolution or softness of my art."

CACOPHONY OF KITTIES

As before, Studer built his composition off a single image. This time, it was the computer-capable cat in the lower-right corner (2.30). But with no layers at his disposal, Studer was cautious not to go too far too quickly. "I put the bodies in first, because the placement was so tricky. After I got the bodies arranged the way I wanted them, I put in the arms and tails (2.31).

"It was a challenge to get all those cats arranged properly. As I positioned each cat body, I just had to hope that I was making the right decisions. Squeezing that last cat in there was the toughest. I specified in my rough that I was going to do nine cats—for each of the nine lives—but it didn't quite fit. I had to call the art director and say, 'Is it okay if he still has a life left? He's still alive; there he is working. I'd hate to think he could get, like, electrocuted and then drop off for good.' I don't think anyone quite bought my argument, but they gave me a break. So eight cats it is."

2.28

2.29

2.30

2.31

HAVE PHOTOSHOP UPGRADES RUINED GORDON?

Since this chapter was first published, Studer's world has transformed dramatically. He now uses a G3 Power Mac equipped with a 6GB hard drive and 96MB of RAM. He's taken up digital video editing with After Effects. Studer hasn't yet upgraded to Photoshop 6, but he did upgrade from his beloved version of Photoshop 2.5 to Photoshop 5.

That's because of Russell Brown, one of Adobe's creative directors and a member of the Photoshop development team. "Russell invited me to an Adobe training event in Santa Fe and talked me into buying a new computer and getting Photoshop 5. I still own my old machine, and I still use Photoshop 2.5 occasionally. But I spend most of my time now in Version 5."

2.32

2.33

Is that a good thing? "You know, I think it is. It's made a huge difference in the way I work. I used to have to be so organized. I had to dissect the image from back to front and figure out exactly how it was going to lay out. Now, I just start dumping in images — 40 or 50 layers — and then clean it up from there. I used to work with 8MB images, now they grow to 150MB. You'd think that would slow me down, but it doesn't. I'm working faster than ever."

Layers have also permitted Studer to experiment with new techniques. "Instead of cutting just one face into a shape, now I can merge multiple faces into one (2.32). I might take the eyes from one image and the nose from another. I also have more flexibility when experimenting with color and positioning. I feel like I'm much more versatile. I can throw stuff together that before would have been a nightmare."

What about multiple undos? Do they come in handy? "The undos really help. I talk to artists who have been upgrading Photoshop all along, and they act like they've come up with ways to avoid any need for multiple undos by using layers. But because I came across layers and multiple undos at the same time, I use them both. Constantly."

Such a huge leap forward must be downright life-changing. "You wouldn't believe it. I have so much less stress, I feel like I sleep better. When my clients want changes, it's no problem. I don't have to save a million versions of my artwork to Zip files. I can keep it all together in one file."

What will he do now that Photoshop has released Version 6.0? With its many amazing upgrades and shortcuts, Studer soon will go crazy with all the new options Photoshop 6 has to offer. From the upgraded type and crop tools to the improved layering capabilities as well as the addition of Liquify and the constantly improving Web functions, he will have much to go crazy with.

After so much modernization, does Studer have any plans to abandon the retro images in favor of newer material? "Oh, no. If anything, I'm getting more retro than ever. Right now, I'm using After Effects to create movies featuring these '40s and '50s characters (2.33). I still use the abstracted forms, but now they're moving. It carries the abstraction one step farther. It adds another layer of realism and depth, where all I really have are these simple shapes."

TAKE ME TO YOUR RODEO

CHAPTER 3
SPOT-COLOR SEPARATIONS

I n this chapter Jim Popp discusses his technique for making selections from grayscale, CMYK, or RGB channels to create new spot-color channels. He explains how you can still build colors as you do in process printing (he uses spot color in the textile industry). Other topics he covers are maintaining gradients, dealing with dot gain, using spot color with four-color process to replace out-of-gamut colors, addressing fluorescent and metallic colors in preparation work for separations, screen angles, and moiré pattern conflicts, and the weave of the screen mesh for printing versus the weave of the garment.

Popp says, "You're wanting to achieve photorealistic imaging, but you're printing on dark and black T-shirts. Your first answer to this problem might be process color. Although after review of some variables, you'll end up changing your mind and simulated process color will be one of your solutions. Process color, also referred to as CMYK (cyan, magenta, yellow, and black) is composed of different-sized small dots and can make up a rainbow of colors (3.1). This is all great if you are printing on white and light substrates, but process inks are transparent and don't stand up with any brightness on dark backgrounds. Simply printing white under the CMYK will not solve this problem."

Impossible is only an opinion.

JIM POPP

SIMULATED PROCESS COLOR

"Simulated process color can have photorealistic looks without printing CMYK. You're still printing with a halftone image to retain details. So if your image has orange, green, purple, and black, then why

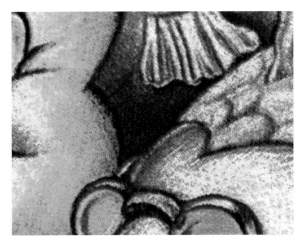

3.1

not print with those colors instead of trying to build them in CMYK? Simulated process color is printed with solid ink, which enables you to achieve a brighter print on dark substrates. Half of the success of separating is understanding the variables of printing on T-shirts and other materials alike."

DOT GAIN

Popp explains, "I'll start with dot gain, because it is what I think is the most pressing issue to address. Dot gain varies depending on your needs, and your computer's stock setting of 20 percent is not enough. Do you need heavy or light penetration and coverage? Let's say that I need heavy coverage because I am printing on sweatshirts. You could be printing with a 50 percent dot gain, and dealing with that you'd better have some tricks up your sleeve or have a very forgiving customer. Printing a color or even white in the opposite field will help reduce the amount of gain. This traps the dot, and when it gains, and it still will gain, it will mix together, reducing the color dots value (3.2).

"Gradients need to be exaggerated, and a reverse dot will help maintain its smoothness between colors in printing. This helps hold the three-quarter tones and quarter tones from gaining too much. Any gain is too much (3.3). Moiré patterns are another battle you need to conquer in printing. Moiré patterns are the interference between two patterns creating sweeping

and checkerboard patterns. This makes your choice of screen angles crucial. Moiré patterns result not only from your art and screen mesh, but also the T-shirt weave. In the graduated print area, you can see banding and moiré patterns caused by the fabric

Dot Gain Simulation

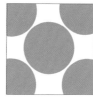

Unaffected dot   Dot with gain   Dot with gain
no gain   out of control   under control

3.2

Black gradient with white   Black gradient printing with dot gain
printing in reverse direction   no control screen

3.3

ARTIST:
Jim Popp

ORGANIZATION:
Popp Art
1700 Iola Street
Aurora, CO 80010
303/366-4876
www.popp-art.com
jim@popp-art.com

SYSTEM:
G3 PowerPC
6GB storage
Mac OS 8

RAM:
128MB total
90MB assigned to Photoshop

MONITOR:
21-inch Super Scan Mc801 RasterOps

EXTRAS:
UMAX Astra 1200S Scanner
La Cie CD Burner
Epson STylus Color 850N printer
Xante Accel-a-Writer 8200 laser printer

VERSION USED:
Photoshop 5.0

weave tweaking the screen-printed image (3.4). Some of the larger separators have published a 75-degree angle. Simulated process is printed dot on dot, all screens at the same angle. The 75-degree angle would be your output angle. This is an ongoing researched factor. One alternative that might help is an elliptical dot configuration. This shape will help you avoid moiré patterns in your 10 and 5 percent dot range (3.5). Don't trust the display of your monitor. The image you view is opaque in color. The last channel in the list of channels will block out channels on the image above with its own channel. Unlike when this image is printed on a T-shirt, the inks will crush into the garment losing some opacity. Where the ink overprints, you will achieve builds of color. One step you can take to adjust what you see in your channel color builds is to reduce the opacity of the color channels. I don't recommend reducing it more than 10 to 20 percent. The reason is because the colors will look pastel in the brighter areas of the image."

3.4

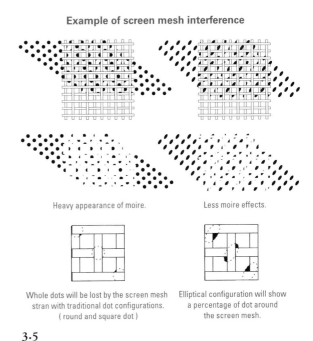

Example of screen mesh interference

Heavy appearance of moire.   Less moire effects.

Whole dots will be lost by the screen mesh stran with traditional dot configurations. (round and square dot)

Elliptical configuration will show a percentage of dot around the screen mesh.

3.5

OTHER APPLICATIONS:
Adobe Illustrator 8.0,
Adobe Streamline 3.0

WORK HISTORY:

1986 — Received associate degree in advertising design from the Colorado Institute of Art.

1986–89 — Started and ran screen print and art department for Competition Design (Denver).

1989–present — Art director, production director for GS Sportswear/Golden Squeegee (Denver).

FAVORITE STATE:
Colorado. From the mountains to the plains, sunrise to sunset, this state is beautiful to all your senses and is a voyeur's paradise. Colorado has it all!

CALLING ALL ALIENS

"The alien image was originally drawn in pencil, and then scanned in as a grayscale document (3.6). Some adjustments were made to smooth out the pencil effects. I like using Gaussian Blur, Despeckle, and Dust and Scratches to smooth out a pencil drawing. Paths were then created of the head, hat, fingers, fence, and the background graphics (3.7). These paths enable you to make consistent selections and deselections so you can modify isolated areas of the image. With a

grayscale image, I now have the job of colorizing. First I'll have to change the mode from grayscale to CMYK. RGB will give you a greater color gamut, but the CMYK mode gives you more color channels with easier information to make the selections from."

THE FUN BEGINS

"Now we can really have some fun. Using the paths made, I make a selection of an area (3.8). Using the Hue/Saturation function, I colorize the selected area of the image (3.9). I like to use a limited palette of colors, knowing that I'll be limited when I go to press. When printing on darks, you could print with six to

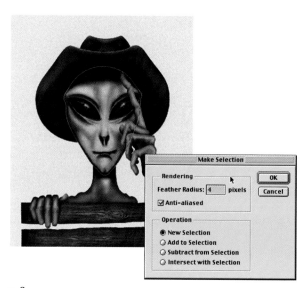

3.6

3.7

3.8

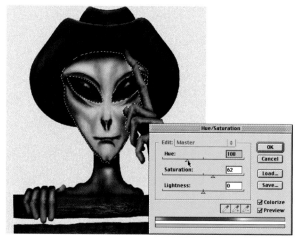

3.9

twelve colors depending on the printer's limitations. One or two of those color screens will be white. With a six-color image, you will only have four color screens. The more colors used, the more you'll be able to break the image down and retain more integrates.

"Before delving into adjusting an image, talk to your printer first to find out its capabilities. If you have finished a full-color image, you'll have the task of breaking it down from millions of colors to just a few. So picture what it will take to rebuild the image in fewer colors. Make a list of the colors in the image, and figure out which colors you can build from and which colors limit your screens. You'll want to use the purest hues of the color ranges used when selecting your color."

COLOR CHANNELS

"When creating new color channels, I'll take the list of colors and create all color channels needed to rebuild the image. Select the new channel option from the Channels palette. Check on Selected Areas, select the color, give it a name, and then click OK (3.10). Choosing Selected Areas enables you to make positive selections of your channel's image information to add, subtract, or modify another channel's image. Hold down the ⌘[Ctrl] key and click the channel (I'll use this later working with the Red channel). Use the paths that were created to make selections (3.11). From the selected area, I'll make copies from the original CMYK channels and paste this image's information into a new color channel. Depending on the copied image, you are more likely to have to adjust it in some way or another."

WORKING WITH CURVES

"Curves are the one tool I use quite often. With the Curve function (⌘+M [Ctrl+M]), you can make local adjustments on isolated areas of the image. Placing the white channel information, I'll make a selection of the whole canvas area of the CMYK channels together. Then I'll copy and paste the information into the new spot white channel (3.12). Next, I'll invert the newly placed image to a negative view (3.13). To see this channel's image because it is white on a white background, I need to make a background channel. I'll make the background channel the color of the T-shirt that I am printing on. I'll label this

3.10

3.11

3.12

channel **SHIRT** so it doesn't get mistaken for a color channel in output (3.14). I'll place the SHIRT channel first in the list of new colors.

"Back on the white channel, I want to curve this information. My objective is to use as little white as possible and use the shirt color through the image. This results in a higher contrast for a more striking image and a softer hand on your print. In the Curves dialog box I moved the 50 percent to 0 percent and the 75 percent to 100 percent (3.15). Then I click the Smooth button in the Curves dialog box until the curved line turns into an S shape with no information under 25 percent (3.16). You need to understand that each image is different and so is the separation. The key point here is to practice, practice, practice. I want the white to really only print under the midtones to highlights, enabling the color screens to be influenced by the shirt. Build

shades and shadows by printing little to no white under the color printing directly on the shirt."

ADDING IMAGE TO THE OTHER COLOR CHANNELS

"I follow some of the same simple steps when adding images to the rest of the color channels. First I make selections of similarly colored image areas. Then I copy and paste the selection into a new color channel. I adjust the new image by using Curves, Dodge, and Burn and any other tool I feel might enhance the

3.13

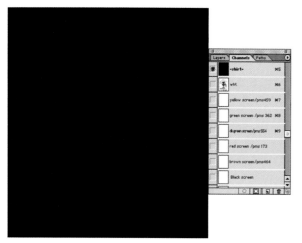

3.14

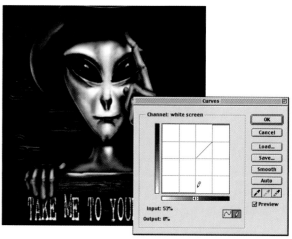

3.15

3.16

image. In the yellow channel, the areas copied are of the skin, fence, hat, and type from the CMYK composite channel. The selected areas are pasted into a new yellow channel, inverted while still selected, and then deselected. I change the Curve back to where I am left with image only in the highlight area (3.17).

The next figure shows the yellow image after the curve adjustments (3.18)."

THE GREEN CHANNEL

"I copied areas from the process yellow channel to make a green channel. Here is a selection of the skin area only (3.19). I pasted the selection into a new green channel, and then deselected (3.20). If you don't

3.17

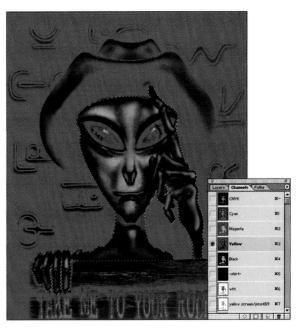

3.19

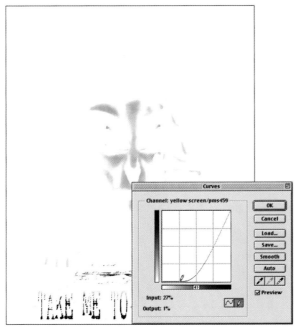

3.18

3.20

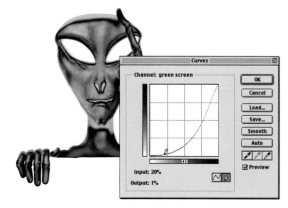

3.21

3.22

3.23

3.24

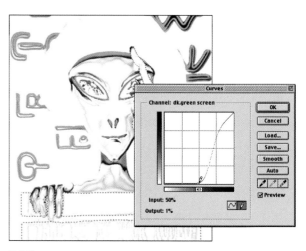

3.25

deselect and curve the image, you'll get an undesirable fringe dot along the selection edge. In the new green channel I used Curves to change the highlight and shadow, leaving mainly a midtone area (3.21). Here is the final image after adjustments (3.22)."

THE DARK GREEN CHANNEL

"In the dark green channel, I copied areas from all elements except for the background. The areas were copied from the original process yellow channel and placed into a new dark green channel. When I curve this information, I'll leave the image's shadow areas. This second green channel allows some latitude when printing, guaranteeing an extended green gradient in the skin areas and making printing easier. This channel was curved in segments. The first segment curved

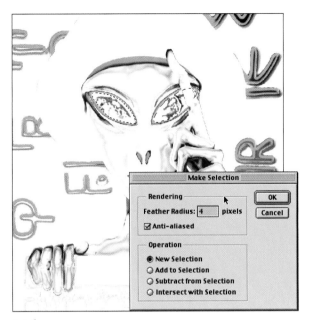

3.26

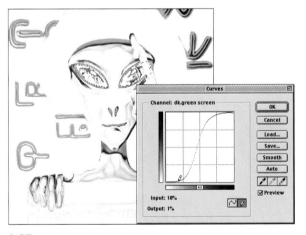

3.27

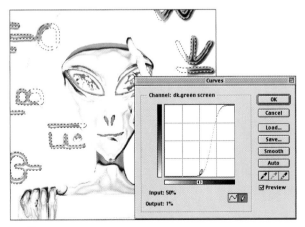

3.28

only the alien's skin information (3.23). Then I curved the hat information (3.24), and then the fence and type (3.25). The eyes were first selected and a feather radius applied to give a softer edge (3.26 and 3.27). The brand graphics were then curved (3.28). Finally, we see the dark green channel after all of the segment adjustments (3.29)."

THE RED CHANNEL

"This channel is a copied selection of the whole image, excluding the background from the process magenta channel. The selection is pasted into a new red channel. This image needs to be curved separately. I adjusted the curves on the skin area (3.26),

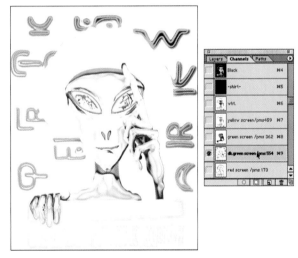

3.29

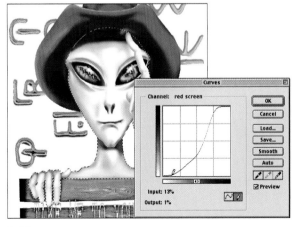

3.30

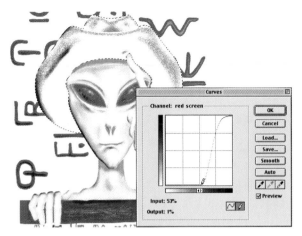

3.31

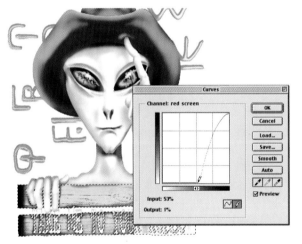

3.32

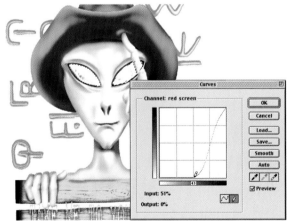

3.33

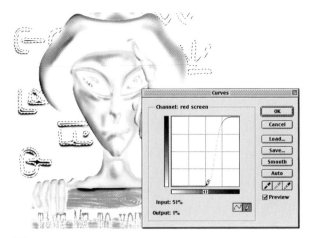

3.34

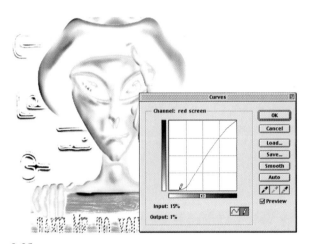

3.35

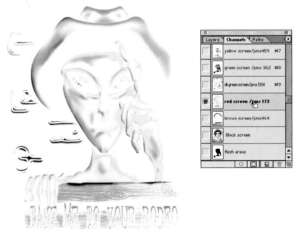

3.36

the hat (3.31), the fence (3.32), and the eyes (3.33 and 3.34). With the eyes again, I used the feather radius to give a softer edge. I finished off the red channel by curving the brand graphics (3.35) and the type. The final red channel has more depth (3.36)."

THE BROWN CHANNEL

"In the brown channel I used information from the hat, fence, and background branding symbols. The hat and the fence image were copied from the process yellow channel and curved (3.37). The background branding graphics were copied from the process cyan

channel and, along with the hat and fence, they were adjusted using the Curve command while still selected (3.38). Here is the final brown channel (3.39)."

THE BLACK CHANNEL

"Last, but not least, the black channel is curved. In this selection, I used the entire image except the background from the black channel. In this case I curved the whole selection together (3.40). The fence and brand information wasn't curved back far enough, so

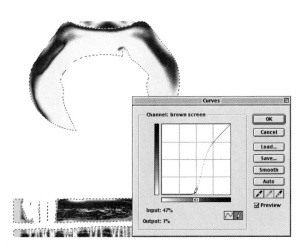

3.37

3.39

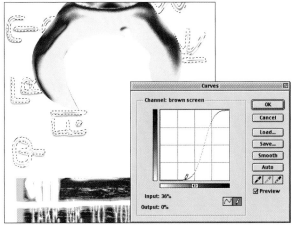

3.38

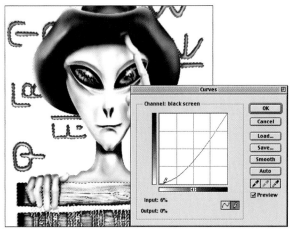

3.40

I curved them a second time (3.41). If you know that you are only printing on black, then you have no need to create this screen. This image shows the final black channel (3.42).

"In addition, I made a selection of the new spot red channel by holding down the ⌘ [Ctrl] key and clicking the red channel. I deleted the selected information out of the new green, dark green, and black channels. This keeps the reflected red lit areas from getting muddy (3.43)."

FINAL TOUCHES

"In the next six images I show the separation color channel turned on in the order as it would print (3.44–3.49)." The next image shows what the image

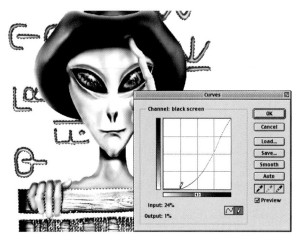

3.41

3.42

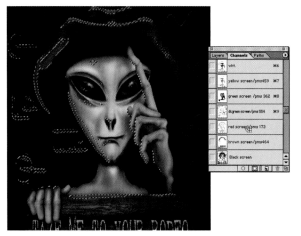

3.43

3.44

3.45

3.46

3.47

3.48

3.49

3.50

would look like printed on a black background (3.50). You wouldn't want to print the black so the black shirt would show through in these areas, leaving a lighter-weight print. This makes it more breathable and gives you a softer hand. Figure 3.51 shows the image printed on a colored shirt (3.51).

This separating process enables you to print on lights and darks, although (there's always an although) printing on black gives you the best contrast, making it more dramatic. When printing regular four-color process and dealing with out-of-gamut colors, you can use this method to create your own spot-color screens. You can even use this method to add special-effect screens to your image such as puff ink, fluorescence, glitters, and so on.

3.51

CHAPTER 4
CREATING BUDGET 3D CHARACTERS

From your computer's perspective, 3D artwork is the pinnacle of artistic achievement. Armed with the proper software, you can set up an intricate 3D landscape, toss in a hundred or so wireframe objects, apply surface textures and patterns, shine a few lights on your subjects, and render the whole thing to a high-resolution image file. The result is so intensely realistic — you swear you can hear your computer clap its hands and scream "It's alive!" as it writes the final kilobyte.

But while 3D is a big thrill for your processor, its effect on your brain is distinctly less agreeable. You have to master an entire glossary of new terminology, learn to work in a 3D environment on a 2D screen, and put up with incessant computational delays that make Photoshop look like a raging speed demon.

When push comes to shove, learning a new 3D drawing program may be more hassle than it's worth. The solution is to fake it in Photoshop.

MIKE'S FIRST ENCOUNTER WITH 3D

At least, faking it in Photoshop was the verdict of artist Mike Strassburger, cofounder of Modern Dog, a Seattle-based graphic design firm. His job was to jazz up a collection of the studio's cartoon characters that had appeared on a line of K2 skis sold in Japan. By all accounts, Modern Dog's creations were already a hit overseas, helping to distinguish K2's tips from those of its competitors. K2 even went so far as to commission a comic book that explained where the characters came from and how they ended up on the skis (4.1). But as other manufacturers populated

I'm all for automating the process, particularly when it's as easy as applying a filter.

MIKE STRASSBURGER

4.1

Tokyo's sporting-goods showrooms with copycat cartoons, Strassburger looked for ways to remind skiers that his critters were the ones that started the trend.

"The K2 characters have been going on for about three years," recalls Strassburger. "They started out really flat (4.2). Every year, we developed them a little more to compete with the rip-off skis. At first, we just put drop shadows behind them, but they still looked pretty flat. So we decided to go fully 3D."

Adept at using Photoshop, Illustrator, and QuarkXPress, Strassburger's first inclination was to boldly venture into yet another category of software

4.2

by investing in a 3D drawing program. After asking a few friends which program they used, he forked over $900 for StrataStudio Pro.

But things didn't go according to plan. "I had never worked in 3D, so I didn't understand any of it. I tried drawing a character's head, but I didn't know how to subtract one shape from another, or, well, anything. All I could do was make a sphere and push little parts in and out — that was totally out of control. So I just said, 'Ah, forget it.'"

THE BUDGET APPROACH TO 3D

Strassburger reckoned he could achieve the effects he wanted in Photoshop without going to the trouble of learning a new program. By segregating the illustration into layers and painting in shadows and highlights with the airbrush tool, he developed a technique virtually identical to applying a traditional airbrush inside a frisket. All it took was a bit of forethought and organization.

For starters, members of Strassburger's team sketched trial versions of the characters in Illustrator (4.3). "Sometimes I design the character, sometimes someone else designs it. But I always end up doing the 3D finishing work."

After culling the best characters for the ski logos, he rasterized the artwork inside Photoshop (using

ARTIST:
Mike Strassburger

COMPANY:
Modern Dog
7903 Greenwood Ave. North
Seattle, WA 98103
206/789-POOP
mike@moderndog.com

SYSTEM:
PowerBook G3 500 MHz
20GB hard drive

RAM:
256MB total
60MB assigned to Photoshop

MONITOR:
14.1-inch LCD

VERSION USED:
Photoshop 5.5

OTHER APPLICATIONS:
Adobe Illustrator, QuarkXPress, Adobe After Effects, StrataStudio Pro, Flash

WORK HISTORY:
1981 — Entered graphic design field right out of high school.

File➤Open), sizing each character 5 to 6 inches tall at 300 pixels per inch. "The final characters are only about 3 inches tall, but it's always a good idea to work large and downsample later."

FRISKETS FOR THE AIRBRUSH

At this point, you might assume that Strassburger would dive right in and start airbrushing his brains out. However, as with its traditional counterpart, Photoshop's airbrush by itself doesn't provide sufficient control. The airbrush needs a frisket. "Every single element has to be on its own layer so it can mask the airbrush. Eyes, eyelids, eyebrows — they're all separate.

"I use the original character just as a template layer in Photoshop. Then I create my new layers on top of that." Because these are high-contrast characters with lots of smoothly curving edges, Strassburger creates the new layers by tracing the character with the pen tool."

DRAWING PATHS

But why redraw the paths when they already exist in the original Illustrator file? Can't you simply port the paths over from Illustrator?

"I actually do bring in all the paths from Illustrator just in case. But most of them are no good. When we draw the characters in Illustrator, we do it in the cartoon style where the outlines are fat in some areas and thin in others. As a result, neither the inside nor the outside line is correct."

As we've demonstrated using the head from the scorpion (4.4), the 3D character doesn't share the flat character's heavy outlines.

(For the sake of comparison, the bottom head shows the original Illustrator paths superimposed on the final 3D character.) Strassburger was also free to make creative modifications as he redrew the paths. You can see his adjustments to the scorpion in the angle of the cheek, the placement of the right eye, and the size of the pupils.

1987–present — Founded Modern Dog with college pal, Robynne Raye.

1992 — First computer job revising annual report in PageMaker on borrowed Macintosh SE.

FAVORITE MOUTHWASH:

Drug Emporium house brand version of Listerine, mint flavor ($2 compared with $7).

4.3

4·4

MAKING THE LAYERS

Strassburger drew the paths and saved each one independently of the other. This made for what amounts to the tidiest collection of paths we've ever seen in a Photoshop document (4.5). He then created a separate

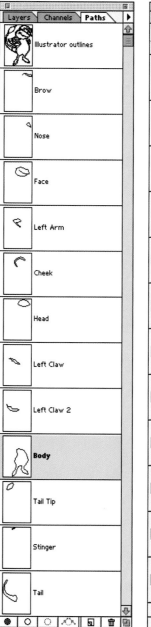

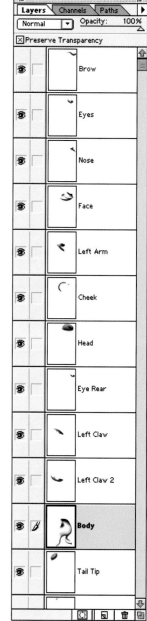

4·5

layer for each path, converted the path to a selection outline (by pressing Enter on the keypad), and filled the selection with the colors specified in the template.

In most cases, there's a one-to-one correlation between the paths and the layers. But as you can see in 4.5, a couple of layers — Eyes and Eye Rear — seem to have sprung up out of nowhere. The eyes are made up of angled ovals that Strassburger drew with the elliptical marquee tool and rotated in the quick mask mode (4.6). Clearly, there's no sense in using a complicated tool when a simple one will do.

PAINTING THE HIGHLIGHTS AND SHADOWS

From here on out, Strassburger applied the tools of traditional shading. He used the dodge tool to paint in highlights and the burn tool to paint in shadows. Because he was shading flat colored areas to begin with, he spent a good deal of time messing with the controls in the Toning Tool Options palette. "When shading the yellow area in the bee's face, I had to set both dodge and burn to the Highlights setting (4.7). Otherwise, the tools wouldn't produce any shading at all."

But Strassburger's favorite shading tool is the airbrush. "I ended up doing more airbrushing than dodge and burn. Using the dodge tool and choosing Highlights or Shadows gave me different looks depending on which color I was painting. It made it look like there was weird lighting going on (as 4.7 illustrates). I realized if I used the airbrush with the foreground color set to black, the effect looked more consistent."

Before applying the airbrush tool, Strassburger was always careful to turn on the Preserve Transparency check box in the Layers palette. Keep in mind that you have to activate the check box for each and every layer in the stack. (Because this gets a little tedious, you can quickly toggle the check box from the keyboard by pressing the / key.) With Preserve Transparency active, each layer acts as a mask for the airbrush — you can't paint where there aren't already pixels.

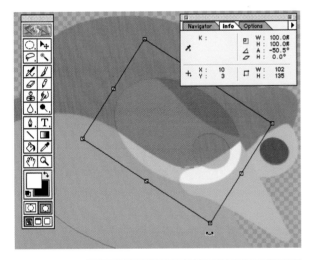

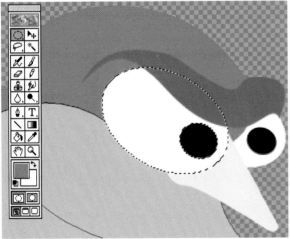

4.6

4.7

After shading the individual layers, Strassburger painted the cast shadows, in which one layer appears to shade the layers behind it. "You can airbrush all the parts and have them looking exactly right by themselves. But then when you place, say, the head on the body, you need to make sure the head casts a shadow on the body to make the effect believable."

In the flame character, for example, Strassburger painted a large shadow on the red face layer to create the appearance of a shadow cast by the eye (4.8).

"When painting the characters, I always imagined the light was coming from the top left. But as long as you're consistent, it doesn't matter."

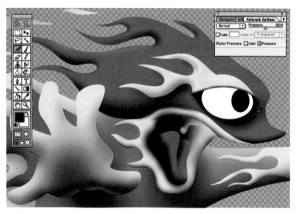

4.8

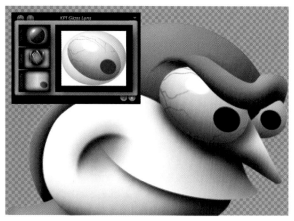

4.9

THOSE GLASSY EYES

Again, you have simpler ways to create shadows inside a sphere. "Sometimes I painted the eyeballs and bellies with the airbrush tool. But most of the time, I used the Glass Lens filter from Kai's Power Tools (4.9)." If you don't own Kai's Power Tools (KPT), you can achieve similar effects using Photoshop's own Lighting Effects filter. You may even be able to achieve the effect you're looking for with a simple radial gradation. "I'm all for automating the process, particularly when it's as easy as applying a filter."

SOMETIMES, IGNORANCE REALLY IS BLISS

"The whole reason we came up with this technique was we didn't know how to use the proper tools," confides Strassburger. "But even if we had, I'm not sure if we would have attempted something as intricate as the bee or the flame character. I mean, I don't know how hard of a time other people have with computers, but for most artists, I imagine this is an easier way to achieve 3D effects. And for us at least, it ended up delivering a better effect than if we had gone with a real 3D program (4.10)."

Does this mean Strassburger has decided to call it quits on 3D software for good? "No, I eventually figured out how to extrude type in StrataStudio Pro. And recently, I learned how to do much more with it. I probably understand 70 percent of the program. In fact, I just finished rendering the Comedy Central logo in real 3D, so I'm pretty comfortable with it now."

It just goes to show you, sometimes it's a good idea to buy an application and let it molder on your shelf for a while. It can be quite invigorating to curse yourself for not having the time or energy to learn a new piece of software. Stress sometimes leads to ingenuity, and frustration can fire the creativity of the clever mind. So go for it — buy that 3D drawing program you've had marked in the catalog for the last five months. You'll be back in Photoshop inventing workaround techniques in no time.

4.10

TYPOGRAPHIC
EFFECTS

PHOTOSHOP

CHAPTER 5
SPECIAL TYPE EFFECTS

W hether a picture is really worth a thousand words is a subject for debate. Take a masterwork by Eugène Delacroix and display it within sight of countryman and contemporary Victor Hugo, and you can count on 1,000 words minimum. But flash an Easter card in front of the character Lenny in *Of Mice and Men,* and about the best you can expect is, "Duh, dat's a pretty bunny, George!"

Even so, there's clearly some magic that occurs when you combine pictures and words into a single element. In his cover art for *Sports Illustrated*'s baseball and football calendars (5.1), Brooklyn-based artist Eric Reinfeld proves that text can both tell and show its message. "Photoshop's not the kind of program where you set some type, kern it a little, and say 'Gee, nice headline.' I mean, you can do that, but if you do, you're not bringing any creativity to bear; you're just plopping words together. Photoshop gives you an opportunity to distort type, add dimension, and hopefully infuse it with a little of your own aesthetic energy."

Reinfeld should know. The artist derives a significant part of his income from turning type into full-fledged artistic elements with genuine form and substance. From the raised lettering of the Sports Illustrated cover art (5.1) to the waxy edges of the Marét logo (5.2), Reinfeld gives us the sense that his type is actually made of something. Even the corporate-cool letters in Time-Warner's empire ads (5.3) convey a subtle presence of depth.

In this chapter, Reinfeld shows you how to mold matter into abstraction. After all, when working in

Photoshop gives you an opportunity to distort type, add dimension, and hopefully infuse it with a little of your own aesthetic energy.

ERIC REINFELD

5.1   Artwork by Eric Reinfeld

Photoshop, your goal is not so much to create real-world type as it is to build letters from the essence of life. You know the photograph is an image. We can plainly see that the artwork is an image. But lest we forget, the type is every bit an image as well.

THE BASIC APPROACH

Reinfeld uses two programs to make his text. "Photoshop is a heck of a program for stylizing type, but I think everyone agrees that it's not the best program for creating the letters in the first place. There's a plug-in from Extensis called PhotoTools that improves Photoshop's type capabilities. I use it when I'm making quick comps, just to get ideas across and see how they

look. But when I start on the final artwork, I create the type in Illustrator and then bring it into Photoshop. The antialiasing is much better that way."

Now Photoshop 6 has really expanded in its way of dealing with type. No longer do you have to use the Layers palette to edit type; you can use the Type tool as you do in most other programs to change type. Type is now created as Bézier type, meaning it is vector-based, which enables you to view smoother letters and gives you the ability to apply layer effects or anything else for which you would normally use Illustrator. Character and Paragraph palettes are new to Version 6 and let you do much of the type effects you would have used another program for. The type even remains editable while you apply warped effects to it.

5.2

5.3

ARTIST:
Eric Reinfeld

STUDIO:
MacSushi, Inc.
87 Seventh Avenue
Brooklyn, NY 11217
718/783-2313
reinfeld1@aol.com
macsushi@earthlink.net

SYSTEM:
Mac G4 450
18GB storage (including Quantum Atlas and Micronet HotSwapable arrays)

RAM:
300MB total
275MB assigned to Photoshop

MONITORS:
Apple 17- and 20-inchers

EXTRAS:
Targa 2000 Pro video-capture board

VERSION USED:
Photoshop 5.5

OTHER APPLICATIONS:
Adobe Illustrator, Adobe After Effects, QuarkXPress, ElectricImage Broadcast, Form·Z

Reinfeld saves his type in the native Illustrator (ai) format, and then he opens it up in Photoshop. "Note that I don't Place the file (with File ➤ Place), I open it. That way, I can enter the resolution I want to use, specify RGB or CMYK, and so on. Then, I increase the canvas size by an inch or so all the way around to give myself room to work."

At this point, Reinfeld might import a background. "Because I opened the type from an EPS illustration, the background is transparent. Just as an example, I took in a generic stock image of some clouds and dragged it in as a new layer behind the text (5.4).

"Now, what I'm about to show you is the simplest kind of type treatment you can do in Photoshop — type filled with an image surrounded by a shiny halo. Of course, it could just as easily be a drop shadow or a color fringe or whatever. Try it a couple of times and you'll see that this basic approach works for a dozen different effects. A clipping group here, some expanding and blurring there, and you're done."

CLIPPING IMAGE AGAINST IMAGE

"The clouds were a little muddy, so I went ahead and added a Levels adjustment layer on top of the cloud layer to brighten it up a bit. I didn't apply the Levels command directly, I used an adjustment layer because I still wanted to have access to the original dark clouds. My feeling is, always use adjustment layers when you

can. No sense in applying the effect for good until you get everything exactly the way you want it."

Reinfeld's next step was to fill the type with the darker clouds. "I made a copy of the clouds by dragging the layer onto the little page icon. (By the way, I have to say, I hate the way the page and trash icons are right next to each other at the bottom of the Layers palette. I'm constantly throwing away a layer when I mean to copy it.)

"Anyway, I dragged the cloned clouds to the top of the layer stack. Then, I grouped the cloud layer with the type below it to make a clipping group." You can do this by targeting the cloud layer and pressing ⌘/Ctrl+G. The result is a darker patch of clouds masked by the type (5.5).

EXPANDING THE TYPE FOR THE HALO

"Even though I've got this clipping group, my text is unharmed, same as it ever was. The great thing about this technique is that I can get to my original text any time I need it. Like now."

To make the halo, Reinfeld started by duplicating the text layer. "The weird thing here is that Photoshop makes the duplicated layer part of the clipping group and releases the original. It doesn't matter, of course — it just affects how the layers are named — but I've seen it confuse people."

WORK HISTORY:

1985 — Opened up independent branch of father's dry cleaning business.

1987 — Purchased color Mac II system, learned to use PixelPaint and Illustrator.

1990 — Designed belts in Photoshop for New York fashion company.

1992 — Converted *The American Kennel Club Gazette* from traditional to electronic publishing.

1993–present — Left job as Senior Desktop Color Technician at high-end service bureau to start up MacSushi, Inc. Clients include *Time*, Sony, Paramount, and others.

1997 — Authored *Real World After Effects* (Peachpit Press).

FAVORITE COLLECTIBLE:

Antique advertising signs ("If you have old signs in the house, contact me immediately").

To make the cloned type thicker, Reinfeld applies Filter ➢ Other ➢ Minimum. "When working with a layer like this, the Minimum filter shrinks the transparency mask and expands the letters. It's a little counterintuitive—seems like Maximum would do the expanding. If you can't keep Minimum and Maximum straight, just try one. If it's wrong, undo and try the other. You've got a 50/50 chance.

"I entered a Radius of 6. But you can do less or more—whatever you want. It just tells Photoshop how far to blow up the text (5.6)." Incidentally, if you create your text directly in Photoshop instead of importing it from Illustrator, make sure you turn off the Preserve Transparency check box before choosing Minimum. Otherwise, the letters are immutable.

BLURRING AND DODGING

"Next, I applied a nice Gaussian Blur so the type spreads out. Some folks like to match the Gaussian Blur radius to the Minimum radius. I usually take it a few notches higher. You just want to get a gradual separation between type and background." At this point, Reinfeld ended up with a drop shadow. To turn it into a halo, he filled the layer with white by pressing ⌘/Ctrl+Shift+Delete (5.7).

"From here, you can do a million different things. Apply blend modes, change the Opacity, modify the other layers. Knock yourself out." To demonstrate, Reinfeld selected Color Dodge from the blend mode pop-up menu in the Layers palette and reduced the Opacity setting to 70 percent. This setting resulted in

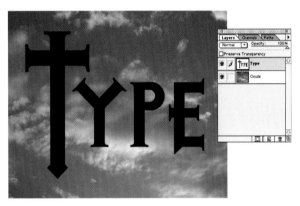

5.4

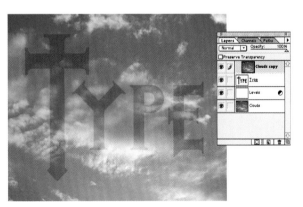

5.5

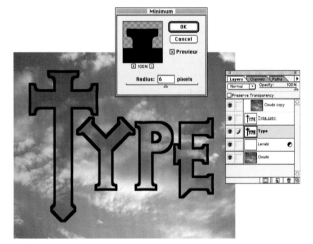

5.6

5.7

a more dramatic halo with hot, glowing edges. Then, he selected the text layer inside the clipping group and applied the Motion Blur filter at a 90 degree angle and a Distance value of 30 pixels. This action blurred the halo into the tops and bottoms of the characters without harming the cloud pattern (5.8).

CREATING SOURCE VARIATIONS

"Okay, that was easy. If you want more sophisticated effects (5.10), you have to do a little more work." Reinfeld marries the old-school approach of building depth via channel operations with some of Photoshop's newer layering functions. "Whenever I create serious type effects, I work in two files. One file is a source file, the other is the target. The source contains the original type and a few layers of simple variations; the target's where I build the actual composition. Then, I use the Apply Image and Calculations commands to bounce back and forth between these two files.

"I start off the source file by opening type I've created in Illustrator and flattening the image so I have one background layer—black type against a white background (5.11). This layer is sacred. I will never, ever, ever, touch it, except to duplicate it. Every text effect I create stems from this one background layer."

THE BENEFITS OF LAYERED TYPE

By keeping your effects and text variations on separate layers, you ensure absolute flexibility. "Here's where things become interesting. Try linking the two type layers with that chain icon in the Layers palette. Then, you can move the type mask and halo together. I can even apply Free Transform and flip or distort the two text layers without affecting the cloud patterns at all (5.9). I might also link the top cloud texture with the type to get yet another look."

5.9

5.8

5.10

CHANGING THE WEIGHT

Reinfeld then duplicated the layer twice and created two weight variations using the Minimum and Maximum filters. "Because this is black type against a white background—no transparency—you use Minimum to expand the weight of the type and Maximum to contract it." Reinfeld created a thinner variation with Filter ➤ Other ➤ Maximum set to a radius of 6 pixels, and a fatter version using Minimum and a radius of 9 pixels (5.12). As you'll soon see, these define the inner and outer edges of his embossed text effects.

MAKING OUTLINES

Next, Reinfeld duplicated his existing base layers—Background, Thin by 6, and Fat by 9—and applied a trio of effects to each. "First, I apply outline effects. You think, 'Oh, the Find Edges filter,' right? No way, not enough control. I use a layering trick that involves Gaussian Blur and the Difference mode. It's really easy.

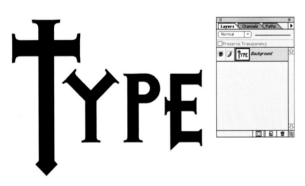

5.11

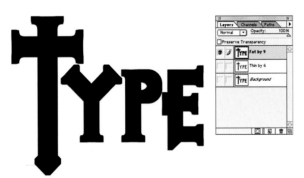

5.12

"Say I want to start with the original type. I duplicate the background layer and apply the Gaussian Blur set to 1.5 pixels. This gives me a subtle soft edge that will determine the thickness of the outline. Then, I duplicate this new layer, invert it (⌘/Ctrl+I), and apply the Difference blend mode. Then, I do a ⌘/Ctrl+E to merge the two outline layers into one." The result is a soft outline about 3 pixels thick (5.13). Reinfeld repeated this operation on the Thin by 6 and Fat by 9 layers as well.

SOFT EMBOSS EFFECTS

"I use the Emboss filter to give the text depth. But before I can do that, I have to blur the type. Emboss doesn't like hard edges." Reinfeld duplicated the three original type layers—our friends Background, Thin by 6, and Fat by 9—and applied the Gaussian Blur filter to each with a Radius value of 6. Then, he duplicated each of the blurred layers and applied the Emboss filter. "The settings you use are totally up to you. But you'll probably want to be consistent." For this example, Reinfeld used an Angle value of –60 degrees, a Height of 6 pixels, and an Amount value of 150 percent (5.14).

THE SOLID BLACK LAYER

"Last and certainly least, I create a new layer at the top of the stack and fill it with black. It's nearly always a good idea to have a black layer handy when using channel operations. Many of the layers I've created I'll use as masks, and I'll need to fill the masked areas with black or white. So long as I've got this black layer sitting around, I can make black, white, or any shade of gray."

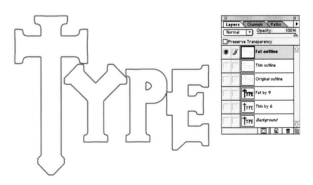

5.13

ASSEMBLING THE ACTUAL COMPOSITION

"When creating your target image, you need to make sure it's the same size as the source." After you choose the New command, select the name of the source file from the Window menu. This ensures a pixel-for-pixel match. "Then, import the image that you want to use as a background for your type. You can use the Place command, or just drag and drop an image from an open file." For the example described here, Reinfeld used another cloud image.

THE FIRST EMBOSS EFFECT

After dropping in the cloud background, Reinfeld created a new layer for his first emboss effect. "As I mentioned earlier, the Emboss filter works best with blurry edges. But that doesn't mean you want your type to be blurry. The solution is to mask the emboss effect."

Reinfeld chose Image ➤ Apply Image to display the Apply Image dialog box. He selected his source image from the Source pop-up menu, and then selected the standard-weight emboss layer from the Layer pop-up menu. The Blending options were set to Normal and 100 percent. "Be sure to turn the Preview check box on when you're inside this dialog box so you can see what you're doing."

To define the edges of the emboss effect, Reinfeld turned on the Mask check box and again selected the source image from the pop-up menu. This time, however, he selected Background from the Layer pop-up, and turned on the Invert check box. The result is embossed text inside a precise text mask (5.15).

Some may wonder why Reinfeld didn't convert the type to a selection outline and use that to drag and drop the emboss effect. "Hey, try it. It works, but it isn't any easier. You have to hide everything but the background layer and then go to the Channels palette and retrieve the selection. Then, you have to switch to the emboss layer — it's a lot of busy work. I prefer to just send everything through masks, as I did here. The Apply Image dialog box may look tough at first, but once you become familiar with it, it's quite easy to navigate."

After creating the new emboss layer, Reinfeld applied Hard Light from the blend mode pop-up menu in the Layers palette. This etched the type into the cloudy background (5.16). "See, now that alone is a pretty good type effect. Thank you folks, and have a nice day." But Reinfeld has no intention of stopping there.

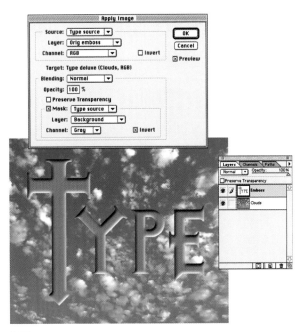

5.14

5.15

THE RED INNER EMBOSS

Reinfeld then set about creating another level of emboss inside the first. As before, he created a new layer and chose Image ➤ Apply Image. The dialog box came up with the same settings he applied before. All he changed were the two Layers settings. He selected the layer that contains the thin emboss effect from the top Layer pop-up menu. Then, he set the lower Layer pop-up to Thin by 6. This masked the thin emboss effect with the thin type (5.17).

Reinfeld could have applied the Hard Light mode to this layer as well, but he didn't. "My intention is to give the new emboss layer some additional definition by adding outline effects behind it. This means the

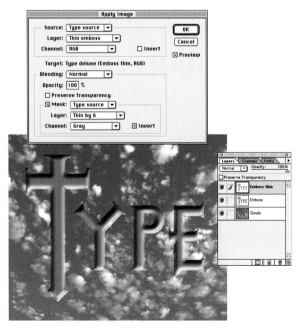

5.16

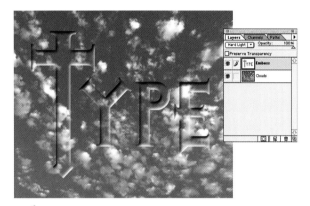

5.17

new layer has to be opaque." To blend the clouds into this opaque layer, Reinfeld duplicated the cloud layer, dragged it to the top of the Layers palette, and grouped it with the thin emboss effect by pressing ⌘/Ctrl+G. Then, he applied the Overlay mode, which is the exact inverse of Hard Light. As a result, the thin emboss layer appeared to blend in with the clouds exactly like the original emboss effect (5.18).

Just for the heck of it, Reinfeld added a layer to colorize the thin emboss effect with red. After adding yet another new layer, he filled the whole thing with 100 percent red and added it to the clipping group below by pressing ⌘/Ctrl+G. Then, he applied the Hue blend mode. This made the clouds inside the thin embossed type red while leaving both the luminosity and saturation values of the underlying pixels intact (5.19).

"When you have embossed text that's on its own layer and you're using it as the parent of a clipping group, you're ready for anything. If you work much with art directors, you know they like to see stuff really quick. If the art director wants me to try out a new color, I just go to the red layer and press Option/Alt+Delete. Bang, there it is: No work, new color. Everyone can visualize what's going on really easily."

INNER EMBOSS HIGHLIGHTS

Reinfeld's next step was to trace around the red emboss effect using the outline layers from the source file that he had created earlier. Again, he added a new layer, and again he chose the Apply Image command. This time, he switched the top Layer option to the solid black layer, and then he set the bottom Layer option to the

5.18

thin outline layer. This instructed Photoshop to use the thin outline as a mask and fill it with black (5.20).

Reinfeld moved the new black outline layer to behind the inner emboss clipping group. Then, he pressed ⌘/Ctrl+down arrow and ⌘/Ctrl+right arrow to nudge the outline one pixel down and to the right. He set the Opacity of this layer to 70 percent. This made a subtle black outline underneath the red text.

Naturally, Reinfeld needed a white outline to complement the black one. So he duplicated the outline layer, inverted it to white by pressing ⌘/Ctrl+I, and nudged the layer two pixels each up and to the left. We've zoomed in on this effect so you can see it in detail (5.21).

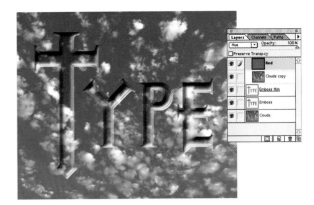

5.19

THE BIG BACKGROUND EMBOSS

Finally, Reinfeld set about denting the letters into the background sky, as if the type were resting on cloud-patterned fabric. As is his habit, he made a new layer and chose Image ➤ Apply Image. But this time, he did things a little differently. He selected the emboss effect applied to the fat letters from the first Layer pop-up menu. Then, he selected the accompanying Invert check box. The idea here was to switch the highlights and shadows in the emboss effect to better set off the existing emboss layers. For the mask layer, he selected the fat blurry layer from the source image, giving the type soft edges (5.22).

As the coup de resistance, Reinfeld dragged the new layer to the bottom of the stack, just above the clouds. He applied the Hard Light blend mode and set the Opacity to 80 percent. The end product is a sight to behold (5.23).

"What you've got here is an infinitely flexible composition, with a full set of source layers to go along with it. You'll notice, I didn't use all the source layers — hey, that's my prerogative. But later, maybe I will. The point is, I can go back and change my mind any time I want. This leaves me free to learn new effects and explore fresh territory."

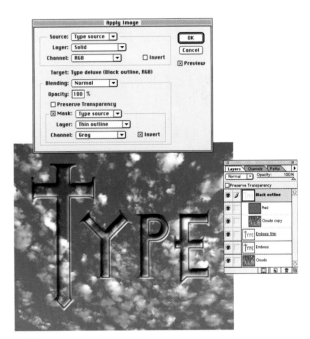

5.20

ROUGHING IT

"By now, you're probably starting to get an idea of what I do. The specific steps aren't all that important. It's the approach that really matters. Put together a

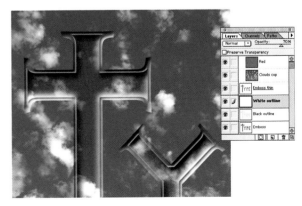

5.21

source file full of outline, Gaussian Blur, and Emboss variations, and you can experiment for days."

If you harbor any doubts about this, Reinfeld's next demonstration puts them to rest. Starting with a copy of the same gothic text that he's used in previous examples, Reinfeld applied Filter ➤ Brush Strokes ➤ Spatter. "I don't care for most of the Gallery Effects filters that were added to Photoshop 4, but this one's very handy." The filter roughs up the edges of the type, giving the letters a frayed appearance (5.24).

"That one simple modification makes a tremendous difference. From here on out, it's just a matter of repeating the thin, fat, outline, blur, and emboss stuff that I did earlier (5.25). Then, when you go into your composition file, you can have a field day." Reinfeld isn't exaggerating. The berry images feature three different adaptations of Reinfeld's technique, one of which he created (5.26) and two of which Deke designed (5.27 and 5.28). Every nuance is the result of retrieving outlined, blurred, and embossed layers from a source file and sending them through thin, fat, outlined, and blurred masks. Speaking from personal experience, it's a lot of fun.

ERIC'S CLOSING PEARLS OF WISDOM

"Before you go, I have to pass along a few parting shots here. First, if you decide to work in RGB, that's fine. Just be careful to pick the colors for your type properly. And by that, I mean set your color picker to CMYK. Even in the RGB color space, this ensures that while you may get an ugly color, you won't get a color that won't print.

"Second, the beauty of this whole approach is that you can take a composition you've applied to one background and substitute in a whole different background. For example, in a matter of seconds, I could

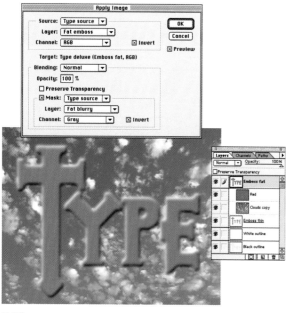

5.22

5.23

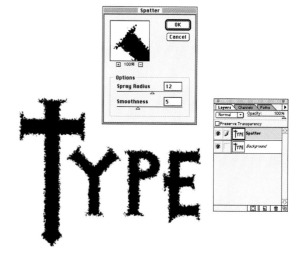

5.24

replace the clouds or the berries with a new image and completely change the look of my type.

"Third, a lot of folks have asked me my impression of Photoshop 5's layer effects. For the most part, I just use them for comping. They help me to add quick lighting effects, toss together some glows and shadows, things like that. But I've also experienced some banding issues. When you use layer effects on their own, you can run into artifacts and weird blends. So when I finish roughing out a layer effect, I'll choose Layer ➤ Effects ➤ Create Layer to break up the effects onto their own layers. Then I'll rebuild the effect by hand, or modify it with an adjustment layer, whatever. The point is, don't just accept the first thing Photoshop spits out. You can edit the effect to get exactly what you want.

"And last, if nothing else, this little exercise proves that text in Photoshop can look awesome. Zoom in on your type and check out how sharp your edges are. Some people say that you can't get sharp type out of Photoshop, but they're wrong. At 300 pixels per inch or better, you can count on your text looking great. Take my word for it — this stuff works." And now with the vector type features in Photoshop 6, the type is as clear as in any other program out there.

5.26

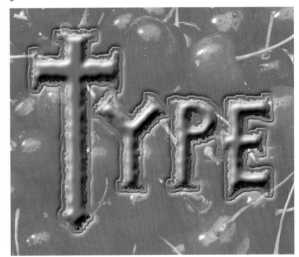

5.27

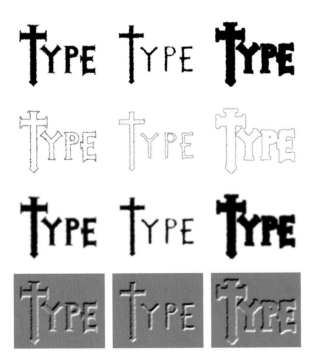

5.25

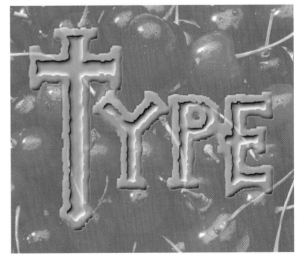

5.28

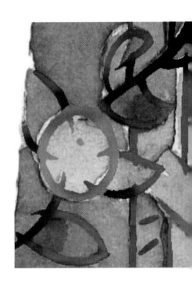

CHAPTER 6
INTEGRATING NATURAL MEDIA INTO DIGITAL ART

This book devotes a lot of space to ways that a computer, together with Photoshop, can broaden your creative range and make you more productive. But we would be lying if we characterized any computer — Mac, PC, or otherwise — as the ultimate achievement in artistic machinery.

Probably the most irritating aspect of a typical computer is that it doesn't begin to give you the same tactile feedback as a 25¢ pencil against a nickel sheet of paper. You move your mouse or stylus on a horizontal surface and observe the results a foot or more away on a vertical screen. Meanwhile, the screen provides you with a relatively tiny window into your artwork. As a result, it can be extremely difficult to sketch in, say, Photoshop and accurately gauge issues such as form and composition.

Simply put, you can expend less effort and create better artwork if you draw or paint directly to paper and then scan your artwork into Photoshop for further processing.

BUD'S NATURAL MEDIA EPIPHANY

Veteran freelance illustrator Bud Peen learned this lesson the hard way. "I struggled for weeks trying to create simple watercolors in Fractal Design Painter. I came to hate that program. I really hate it with a passion. It's just so awkward and annoying to work with. Finally, it occurred to me, why am I doing this? Why don't I just paint with real watercolors, and then scan in the artwork and modify it in Photoshop? It was like an anvil dropped on my head.

The key is to recognize the inherent purpose and limitations of your tools.

BUD PEEN

6.1

ARTIST:
Bud Peen

COMPANY:
Bud Peen/Cubit
2720 Madeline Street
Oakland, CA 94602
510/482-8302
www.budpeen.com
bud@budpeen.com

SYSTEM:
Power Mac G4 400 MHz
20GB storage

RAM:
128MB total
30MB assigned to Photoshop

MONITOR:
21-inch Sony Trinitron Multiscan 500PS
and a 13-inch Apple Color Monitor

EXTRAS:
Epson 1200e scanner with transparency
adapter

VERSION USED:
Photoshop 5.5

"It seems so obvious now. But I think the reason I never really considered it before is that there's a stigma associated with working outside the computer. It started when magazines such as *Macworld* required that their artists work on a Macintosh. It built a dividing wall between traditional and nontraditional materials. Nowadays, it's almost like there's this religion where everything has to be created digitally."

If such a religion does exist, Peen has plainly left the fold. In fact, looking at Peen's playful, perspective-irreverent artwork (6.1), you would swear he had never touched a computer in his life. The watercolor effects were obviously created using real brushes dipped into real water-soluble pigments and dabbed onto real pieces of paper. (Shocking, really — we can hardly believe our editor lets us relate such appalling news.) But in truth, these are layered Photoshop files scanned in multiple passes and finished with the airbrush tool. As you discover in this chapter, Peen could not have achieved these effects without the aid of a computer. Now, in Photoshop 6.0, Peen can take full advantage of the evolved Layers incorporating Layer Sets and fill layers. Gradient Map also joined the list of adjustment layers.

"The key is to recognize the inherent purpose and limitations of your tools." Photoshop, for example, easily outperforms the $30,000 stat camera, but doesn't hold a candle to the $3 pen nib. By contrast, conventional illustration tools permit you to quickly create elements, but compositing and production are nothing short of tortuous. By merging natural media with digital tools, Peen has learned to command both ends of the process. The result is a style that favors efficiency and control without wearing its method on its sleeve.

PART I: A CONVENTIONAL BEGINNING

Peen's illustrations typically comprise a series of calligraphic outlines laid against a brightly colored watercolor background. After getting the client's approval for his rough pencil sketch — which he draws meticulously on ledger paper — he traces the sketch onto five-ply bristol using graphite paper (it's like carbon paper except with graphite on it). "It's a very primitive method, but I don't know of any better way." He then paints the watercolors over the graphite lines on the bristol board (6.2).

After the watercolors dry, Peen draws to registration dots on the bristol board. He then places a sheet of translucent Duralene on top of the bristol and copies the registration dots to ensure proper alignment. Finally, Peen traces along the graphite lines using a Gillot Extra Fine quill pen. "Once the line work dries, I'll go in with a single-edged razor and scrape away mistakes and sharpen up some of the lines."

Isn't it a little unusual to apply the watercolors before the line work? "Yeah, it's completely opposite

OTHER APPLICATIONS:
Adobe Illustrator, Adobe Streamline, Macromedia Director, QuarkXPress, Strata StudioPro (still learning)

WORK HISTORY:
1977 — After graduating from college, set up silk screening department in Santa Rosa print shop.
1979 — Worked for New York advertising agency.

1983 — Spent a year in Paris studying fine art and sculpture.
1989–present — Started up Bud Peen/Cubit. Commissioned by *PC World* to create five illustrations in CorelDRAW; work came out flat and lifeless.
1995 — Gave up trying to create natural effects on computer and purchased scanner to integrate traditional media into digital workflow.

FAVORITE MOVIE GENRE:
Submarine flicks ("I often shout 'Dive! Dive!' when the phone is ringing off the hook and work is piling up.")

the way most people do it. But I found that most artists are a little sloppy with the watercolors if they apply them second. The background becomes an afterthought. By painting the watercolor first, it makes me spend more time and get the colors just right. For me, the watercolor is the most important part of the illustration.

"At this point the line work is all black (6.3). Now, in the old days, I would submit the bristol and Duralene as a composite mechanical and specify a flat process color for the line work. But the lines just sat there like lumps on top of this very expressive watercolor background. I was never really happy with that."

PART II: SHIFTING INTO DIGITAL

This sounds like a job for Photoshop. "There's something liberating about having a scanner hooked up to a computer. Once I crossed that threshold and decided that I could create things outside the computer and bring them in, everything started falling into place. I discovered I could do things that I never could before."

To prepare the watercolor and Duralene for scanning, Peen carefully aligns the registration dots and slices a common straight edge along the tops of both sheets. "This way, I can place the top of each page flush with the edge of the scanner to ensure vertical alignment inside Photoshop." He scans the watercolor

6.2

6.3

in 24-bit color at 300 pixels per inch. Then he scans the line art in black and white at the same resolution.

COMBINING THE ARTWORK

Peen opens both images in Photoshop. Using the Canvas Size command, Peen crops the taller of the two images to match the shorter one, making sure to crop away from the bottom. Then he drags the line art and Shift+drops it into the watercolor image, resulting in a new layer. Pressing the Shift key during the drop confirms that the two images are aligned vertically.

As things stand, the black-and-white line layer hides the watercolor background. To get rid of the white pixels, Peen goes to the Channels palette and ⌘/Ctrl-clicks the RGB composite channel. This selects the

white pixels and leaves the black lines deselected. Pressing the Delete key makes the white go away. Then Peen deselects the image (⌘/Ctrl+D) and ⌘/Ctrl+Shift drags the lines into horizontal alignment with the watercolor background (6.4).

COLORING THE LINES

Now for the fun part. Peen turns on the Preserve Transparency check box in the Layers palette so he can paint exclusively inside the quill lines. Then he uses the airbrush to add colors at will (6.5). "I'll use the eyedropper to lift colors from the watercolor layer. Then I'll adjust the color to darken it up in the Colors palette. The colors in the lines are always related to the colors in the background (6.6).

6.4

6.5

"If I wanted colored lines before Photoshop, I had to resort to dipping a brush into as many as 20 colored inks. It was incredibly complicated. Now it's not only easier and less messy, but I have much more control." One look at Peen's colored lines by themselves (6.7) illustrates just how much better Photoshop handles coloring functions than traditional media. "And I can go back and change colors with complete flexibility."

Does Peen experiment much with the Layer palette's blend modes before flattening the line art into the watercolor? "If the line work is really defining, I'll leave the blend mode set to Normal to make the lines opaque. But if I'm doing more subtle work,

I'll apply the Multiply mode to burn the lines into the watercolor."

WHEN YOU FIND A GOOD THING . . .

Just for the sheer heck of it, we've included additional examples of Peen's artwork showing the progression from scanned watercolors (6.8) to black line art overlay (6.9) and final airbrush-colored lines (6.10). "What I love about this technique is that I can place the lines on the watercolor work and see right away how the lines react to the watercolors. There's a degree of immediacy that you simply can't get with conventional mechanicals."

6.6

6.7

VECTOR VARIATIONS

Although flexible, Peen's watercolor approach isn't right for every job. Sometimes Peen wants a more synthetic look; other times the Photoshop approach simply isn't practical. "I originally wanted to create the Antiquarian Book Fair poster (6.11) using watercolor and quill pen. But it was such a large piece — more than 30 inches tall — that I simply couldn't make it work inside Photoshop. I tried to airbrush one of the lines and it took like five minutes. So I was forced to turn to Illustrator instead."

In this case, Peen scanned his quill-pen illustrations — one for the title, another for the reading minstrel — and converted it to vector objects using the automatic tracing program Adobe Streamline. Peen then positioned the quill paths on a layer inside Illustrator and created the color paths on a separate layer in the background.

PATHS INSTEAD OF WATERCOLOR

Why discuss a piece of Illustrator artwork inside a Photoshop book? Because this poster was a step in discovering additional ways to color lines inside Photoshop. "I began to experiment using Illustrator paths as a background element instead of watercolor."

For example, in the case of the Emale graphic (6.12), Peen started as usual by inking in the line art,

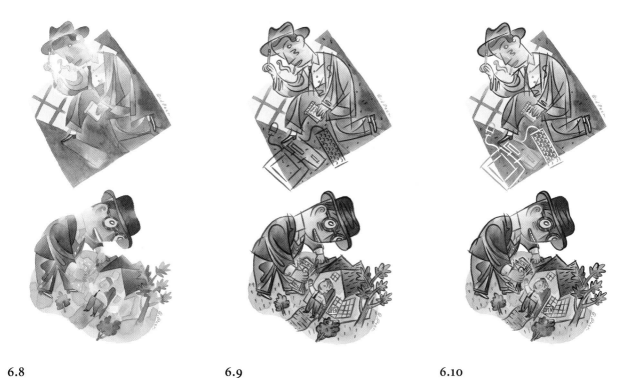

6.8   6.9   6.10

scanning it, and converting the lines to paths with Streamline. Then he used Illustrator's brush tool to paint in color on a separate layer behind the line art. "Generally, I don't like Illustrator's brush tool. But it came in handy here."

After saving the background paths and line art as independent files, Peen opened the background paths in Photoshop and airbrushed in a few dollops of color to add a hint of depth to the flat fills (6.13). He then opened the line art and dragged it over as a separate layer. And finally, he turned on the Preserve Transparency check box and painted color inside the lines (6.14).

In case you're wondering what font Peen used for Emale, the answer is none. "The type was a piece of quill pen artwork. I introduced it as a separate layer inside Photoshop."

EMBRACING SYNTHETIC MEDIA

"I think the Predicting Doom piece I did for *InfoWorld* (6.15) is a really nice one because it enabled me to

6.12

6.13

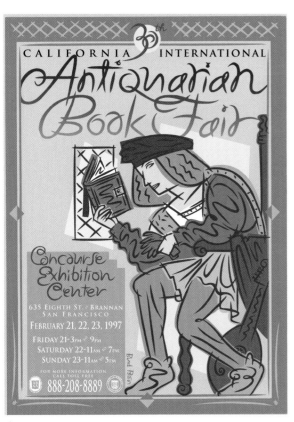

6.11

6.14

really push the synthetic aspect of the artwork. I used Illustrator blends to feather the sky and ground. You can even see the banding—it doesn't even remotely resemble watercolors, which is the way I wanted it."

As usual, Peen brought in the line art through Streamline. But when processing more complicated artwork such as this, Streamline has something of a problem. "The program traces paths from the outside in. It actually stacks on top of each other areas of black and white. This means the white areas are opaque, which prevents the colored fills from showing through.

"To fix this in Illustrator, I go ahead and slip a dark box behind the traced paths so I can see which areas are opaque (6.16). Then I start selecting paths from the outside in and convert them into compound paths until all the interiors become transparent (6.17). It sounds like a lot of work, but it usually ends up being only about eight or nine paths that have to be converted."

YOU USE *WHAT*-PEG

Peen's colors are so vivid, you might think he spends a lot of time worrying about CMYK conversions and color matching. "I stick with RGB for the sake of e-mail. My colors are bright, but I'm not that concerned about specific color palettes. I just want small file sizes."

And with commercial printers urging their clients to submit printer-ready EPS files, what format does Peen use? "JPEG, actually. I've been using JPEG files for years without any problems. And they take far less time to e-mail to my clients." Chalk up another one for the independent-minded artist.

SO MUCH MEDIA, SO LITTLE TIME

"Illustrating is all about solving problems within a framework of equations that you use on a regular basis. That's why I like the computer; it gives you so many different chances to exercise your options. With traditional art, the closer you get to the end, the fewer options you have. But with a computer, you never reach a dead end. You can always strip out elements or undo steps. You have this incredible freedom to experiment, from the beginning all the way to the end."

THE WORLD OF THE TACTILE

Lately, Peen's artistic interests have been leading him into still other traditional and nontraditional media.

6.15

6.16

6.17

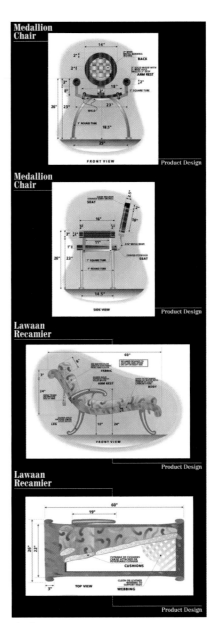

6.18

"I'm a sculptor by training. So in addition to my illustrations, I've been dabbling in furniture design (6.18). It started a couple of years ago when I sent off a few drawings of lamps and clocks to a Dallas-based furniture artist named Lam Lee. I didn't expect much, but he just went nuts. He told me, 'Your work fills my heart with great joy.' It was wonderful! I've never had a client tell me that before. So he asked me to design a whole line of furniture. I use Photoshop to prepare the mechanical sketches for the factories, which lets me integrate different colors and materials very quickly. The frames are made of wood, and then they cover it with these little tiles of beautiful stone. It looks great, but it's incredibly heavy."

THE WORLD OF THE SCREEN

If you're more interested in something that you can bring into your house without the help of three hardy workmen, then you can find Peen's illustrations in the National Geographic online Fantastic Forest project (6.19). Designed by multimedia artist Brad Johnson, this award-winning site is definitely worth a visit — especially if you have kids. In addition to Peen's forest elements — each created as an independent watercolor — Fantastic Forest offers excellent examples of Shockwave sounds and objects. Of particular interest, you can build your own forest using a few of Peen's watercolors (6.20). To see it for yourself, go to *www.nationalgeographic.com/modules/forest.*

6.19

6.20

CHAPTER 7
FROM ILLUSTRATION TO PHOTOREALISTIC IMAGE

In this chapter, artist Jon-Paul Fay discusses how he initially uses Illustrator to create an illustration, and then takes the illustration into Photoshop for further realistic enhancements. He uses channels and lighting effects to create a more natural realistic texture of a house. By using filters and lighting effects with alpha channels, he creates a naturalistic three-dimensional look to his images. Many artists use this approach with their images: Start with a sketch and use Illustrator to get the basic form and paths drawn. Then use Photoshop to add the realistic effects and bring the sketch to life. Not many artists use only one program to create their artwork. Photoshop is the glue that holds all the other programs and artwork together.

As an artist, you must evolve with the media.

JON-PAUL FAY

THOUGHTS BEHIND THE ARTIST

Fay says, "The digital field strikes great interest in me. I have been working with this media seriously for over a year. My first introduction to computer imaging was in 1995 with Photoshop 3.0. I had fun with Photoshop, but I felt constricted. Maybe the lack of my experience led to this feeling. Now that I've been using Adobe Photoshop 6.0 and Adobe Illustrator 9.0, I see endless possibilities. I love the detail that I can get in my traditional illustrations, but I can't pass up what Photoshop 6 has to offer."

INITIAL CONCEPT

The image used for the chapter opener shows Fay's finished house image. He used a combination of

Illustrator and Photoshop to make this photorealistic-looking house with landscaping. With this piece, Fay started off with the idea of creating a realistic-looking house and surroundings using Illustrator and Photoshop. He started in Illustrator to build the basic blocked-in shape of the house without using any perspective, making it one-dimensional. He wanted to use the tools and filters of Photoshop to create the

realistic aspects of the illustration. Photoshop offers many options in creating special effects such as textures, lighting effects, perspective, and blurs that can create an atmosphere. He used the base Illustrator and Photoshop programs without any fancy extra extensions. Fay stayed away from any scanned images because he wanted to achieve a three-dimensional look using only Photoshop.

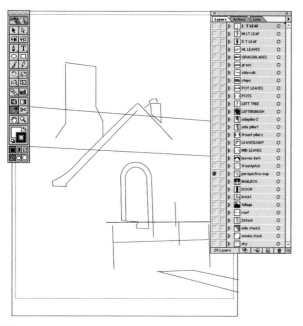

7.1

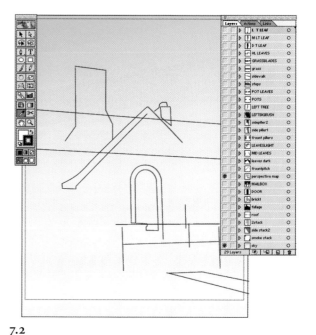

7.2

ARTIST:
Jon-Paul Fay

STUDIO:
Rocky Mountain College of Art & Design
6875 E. Evans Avenue
Denver, CO 80224
1-800-888-ARTS
jon-paul@dzinescienve.com

SYSTEM:
Power Mac G4
20GB storage

RAM:
256MB total
180MB assigned to Photoshop

MONITOR:
21-inch View Sonic A90

EXTRAS:
Epson STylus Color 880 printer

VERSION USED:
Photoshop 6.0

OTHER APPLICATIONS:
Adobe Illustrator 9.0

WORKING IN ILLUSTRATOR

Fay initially starts his illustration in Adobe Illustrator so he can get the vector work prepped and accurate before taking it into Photoshop. He uses a perspective layout of the house as a guide. The perspective shapes show the basic layout of the final product (7.1). Next, he fills the whole page with a gradient for the sky background. Fay, as in traditional painting, likes to cover up the canvas as quickly as possible (7.2). He built the shapes off the roof and the front façade of the structure. Using the Pen and Shape tools, he created the basic shapes of the house. At this point, Fay is not worried about putting the shapes in perspective—that will come later. To prepare for this, he extends the horizontal edges just beyond the perspective map lines (7.3).

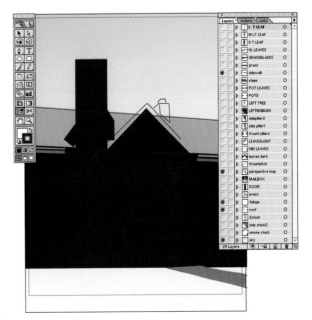

7.3

BUILDING WITH COLOR AND TEXTURE

At this point, Fay puts in the trim of the house using high-contrast colors (7.4). These contrasting colors show where the shadows in the trim will be. The reason for creating the contrast is because, when he brings the image into Photoshop, the Lighting Effects will have a stronger effect with contrasting colors.

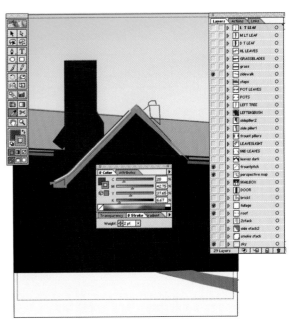

7.4

WORK HISTORY:

1995–2000 — Waiter and muralist while in college

2000 — Received a BA in illustration

FAVORITE SPORT UTILITY VEHICLE:

Jeep CJ5 from 1976 to 1983. That was back when they made real Jeeps!

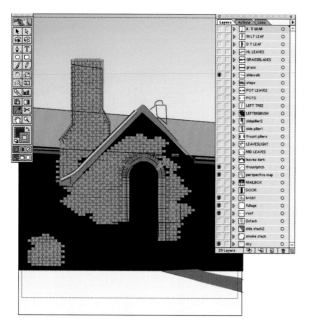

7.5

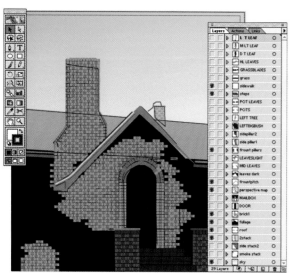

7.6

The bricks are then added. Fay approached the bricklaying as if he were actually building the house with real bricks. He took twelve different brick styles and put them in small groups until he covered up the space that was visible (7.5). Each brick has distinct lines and spots that show up as cracks and bumps in the Lighting Effects area of Photoshop. To finish up the rest of the brick areas, he put each group of bricks on different layers so they could be distorted separately (7.6). The Value of the color rather than the color itself is crucial here. The actual color of the bricks will be adjusted in Photoshop later.

ADDING BUILDING STRUCTURES

Fay added the pillars and chimney to the house design. The easiest way to make the sides of the walls that are at an extreme angle is to build them as if you are looking at them in a straight-on view (7.7). It looks kind of funny in this area, but in Photoshop, the perspective will make the walls look realistic.

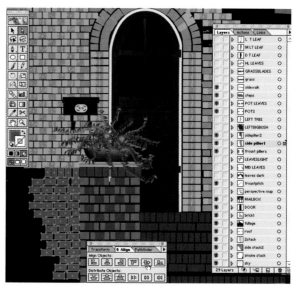

7.7

CREATING THE GREENERY

The vines are created using a Pattern brush in
Illustrator. He creates the vines in layers to simulate
the depth and give a three-dimensional quality to the
plants. The first layer is the darker leaf (7.8). He
applies this Pattern brush, enabling some of the dark
areas underneath to show through. The next layer is
the midtone leaves. He again uses the Pattern brush
to stroke the vines in areas that are exposed to light
and around a focal point (7.9). Finally the highlight
leaves are painted in the direct sunlight (7.10). He
will later create more depth using a shadowing technique in Photoshop.

7.9

7.8

7.10

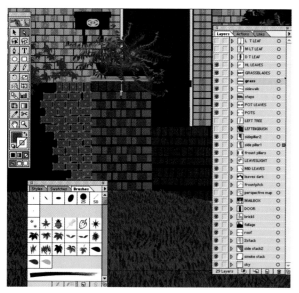

7.11

7.12

The grass is created using a Scatter Brush with at least twelve different blades of grass. He applies the paintbrush strokes in a wavy horizontal direction, changing the size of the brushstroke from front to back (7.11). The front strokes being longer than the back strokes gives the grass a perspective and three-dimensional feel. The bushes and tree limbs were added to create a more fully landscaped yard (7.12). The bushes were created using the Scatter Brush tool. Fay used two values of light and dark in the bush to simulate a bit of depth for the bushes. To create the tree limbs, he used the Pen tool. The tree limbs were then filled with a color to look like the tree is in a dark shadow. To finish off the tree, he'll add the highlights in Photoshop.

To finish up the greenery, Fay added leaves to the tree. Using the Scatter Brush tool, he creates the leaves on the tree in three different shades of leaves in light, medium, and dark (7.13). Adding the door, mailbox, smokestack, and the pots with flowers (7.14) completes the final details on the house. To continue this illustration in Photoshop, Fay exported the file to Photoshop with layers intact.

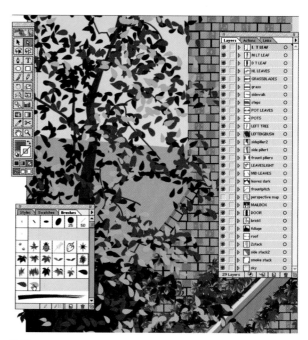

7.13

ADDING DEPTH AND REALISM IN PHOTOSHOP

After he brought the Illustrator file into Photoshop, Fay turned off all layers except the brick and sky layers. He then created a new layer for the finished bricks. With the Pen tool, he drew the shape of the bricks he was going to use (7.15). Converting the path he drew into a selection, he filled this area with color (7.16). On the bricks, he created an alpha channel for a texture map. He used a slight Gaussian Blur

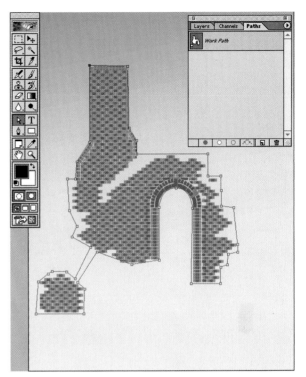

7.15

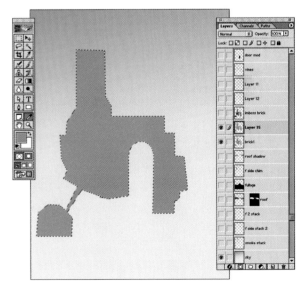

7.16

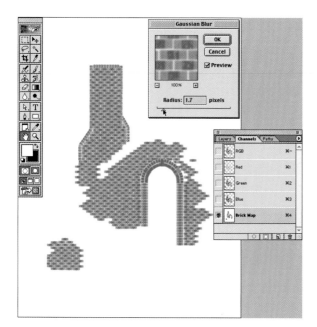

7.17

to add some texture to the brick (7.17). On the finished brick layer, he applied the Lighting Effects to give the depth to the bricks (7.18). The Noise filter adds more texture to the bricks (7.20). By selecting the negative space on the brick, he created a mask for the grout. He then placed the grout selection over the finished bricks, and then airbrushed in the grout color (7.19). The final touch was to set the bricks in place using the Distortion tool (7.21). The old brick layer was then discarded.

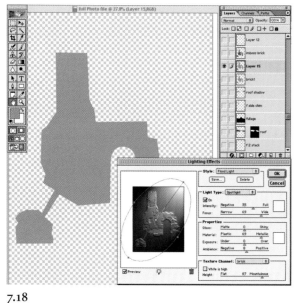

7.18

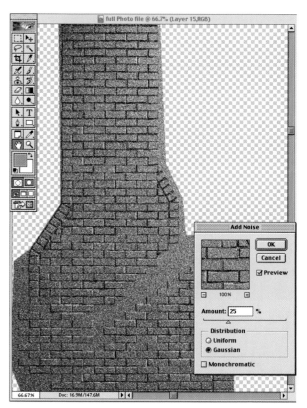

7.19

TEXTURIZING THE ROOF

The roof of the house was created using a simple four-dot pattern. He then made a selection and chose Edit ➢ Define Pattern (7.22). On a new layer, he filled the defined pattern over a roof selection (7.23). A Motion Blur was then added to create the lines and

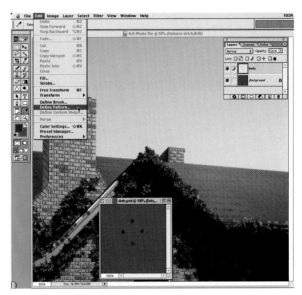

7.22

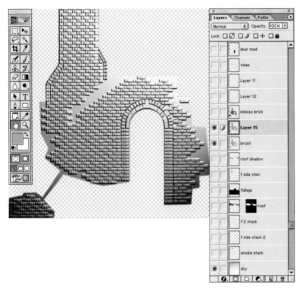

7.20

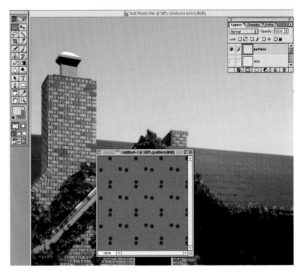

7.23

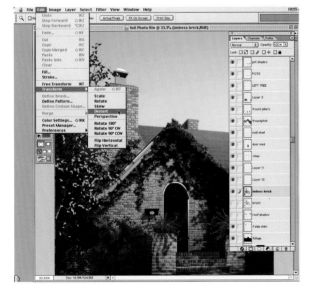

7.21

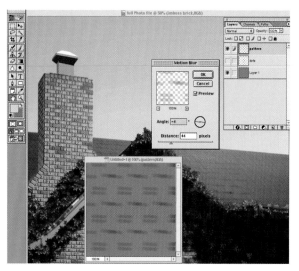

7.24

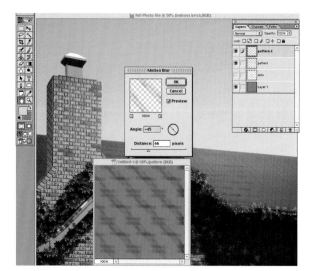

7.25

shadows on the shingles (7.24). Next, he applied the same defined pattern on a new layer and used a Motion Blur at an angle to fit the perspective of the vertical shadows and lines on the shingles (7.25). Lighting Effects were used on an alpha channel the same way he did the bricks on the finished shingle layer (7.26). Fay added atmospheric effects using a Gaussian Blur (7.27).

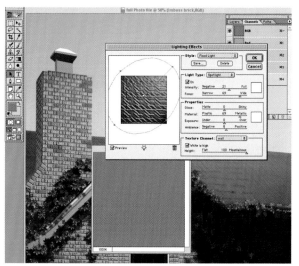

7.26

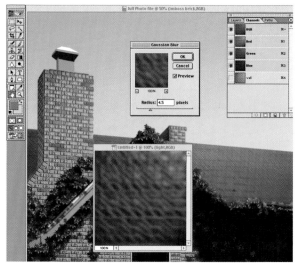

7.27

ADDING SHADOWS

To create shadows, Fay used his layers from
Illustrator to make selections. He first selected the
layer with vine leaves. He next created a new layer
directly below the vine leaves layer. He filled that layer
selection with a built black color (7.28). To see the
shadows, he moved the shadow layer away from the
leaves on the bricks and changed the opacity slider in
the Layers palette to show the shade on the bricks
(7.29). To soften the edge of the shadows, a Gaussian
Blur was applied (7.30). To make the shadows more

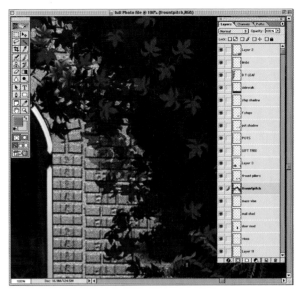

7.29

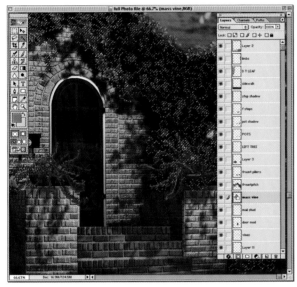

7.28

7.30

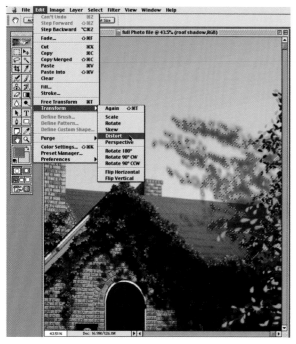

7.31

realistic, he distorted the shadows to fit into the perspective of the image. He repeated the shadow process on the rest of the greenery and used the Distortion feature to set the shadows in place (7.31). The final image (7.32) shows the shadows completed, making this illustration seem almost photo-quality.

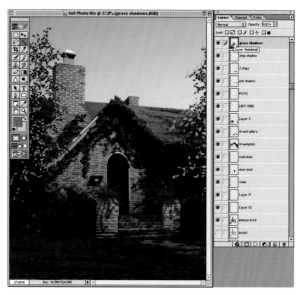

7.32

CHAPTER 8
MERGING PAST AND PRESENT WITH SUMI BRUSHSTROKES

The tools artists, photographers, and designers use influence how they work and what they produce. This is equally true for digital, as well as conventional, tools. All too often, software features, the latest plug-ins, or trendy special effects carry a digitally produced image as much as (or more than) the skill or sensitivity of the artist. We need only remember the morph, fractal, or KPT phases that have passed over us in the past few years to see how quickly a fad comes and goes. It's certainly rare to find an artist working with Photoshop who draws deep inspiration from studying the masters, artisans, and diverse century-old art forms. Enter Hiroshi Goto.

Hiroshi Goto — illustrator, artist, and president of the successful design firm HI! Seisaku-Shitsu — lives and works in Tokyo, Japan. Goto blends the old and the new in a fascinating and seductive manner. His passion for the modern world of computer graphics and design is balanced by a profound appreciation for the history of his native culture. Spending much of his time in the tea establishments of the historical city of Kanazawa, playing the shamisen stringed instrument, and singing the Naga-uta, the world of the geisha is strongly reflected in Goto's art.

Goto did not follow a direct path into the fields of art and graphic design. "After graduating from junior high school, I went on to become a hair designer, studying hair design at night and working as a stylist during the day. I began to doubt my choice and, thanks to an introduction arranged by my mother, I was able to find a job at a design office. I went on to study graphic design through practical work experience, visiting as many design offices as I could to gain knowledge about the industry. Ten years ago I established my own

Working with Photoshop enables me to accomplish what was previously achieved through tedious hand-craftsmanship, copy machine work, film processing techniques, and a touch of luck.

HIROSHI GOTO

8.1

design office, HI! Seisaku-Shitsu, and two years after that I first came in contact with the Macintosh computer. At that time it was still unusual in Japan to do graphic design work on a computer, because its

compatibility with the Japanese language was quite insufficient (to put it politely). Every day of work was a constant trial-and-error process, requiring infinite patience."

Goto's images combine traditional drawing and painting techniques with Photoshop, which he uses to color drawn image elements and merge them with scanned backgrounds. "Working with Photoshop enables me to accomplish what was previously achieved through tedious hand-craftsmanship, copy machine work, film processing techniques, and a touch of luck. Most importantly, when I work with Photoshop I can see the results immediately. Looking back, I began to see the emergence of Photoshop as a revolution in art and design and became hooked on using it to produce original pieces of art. It has taken me three or four years to develop my own personal style, and I am still fascinated by working with the latest technology to create traditional yet modern images."

INSPIRATION AND PROCESS

Twentieth century Japan is a country of contrasts, where tradition and cutting-edge technology mingle at will. Goto's work reflects this and speaks of a place where the digital and the traditional balance one another. The *Morning Glory* image is a perfect example. "This image was created specifically for the *Photoshop Studio Secrets* book, and I might say that it

ARTIST:
Hiroshi Goto

ORGANIZATION:
HI! Seisaku-Shitsu
404 Kagurazaka Heights
Tsukiji-Cho 15
Shinjuku-ku, Tokyo, Japan
(011) 81-3-5227-6720
www.haili.com/gallery
Goto@c-engine.co.jp

SYSTEM:
Power Mac 7200/166 with G3 Card
Mac OS 8.1
2GB storage

RAM:
272MB total
150MB assigned to Photoshop

MONITOR:
Sony 17-inch Multiscan

EXTRAS:
Nikon Coolscan 600 dpi flatbed scanner

VERSION USED:
Photoshop 5.0

PRIMARY APPLICATIONS:
Adobe Illustrator 8.0, FreeHand 8,
QuarkXPress 3.3

is my favorite of all the pieces I have created so far (8.1). I like to go out drinking in the old part of town, sometimes until the early morning hours. One morning as I came home at around 5 a.m., the morning glories (hence the name) were in full bloom. Because they droop and wilt as soon as the summer heat finds them, I had never seen them in this richness before. After looking at the blue flowers in full bloom covered in morning dew, I was inspired by the feeling of freshness that they gave me to create a new painting."

Goto starts every painting with a pencil sketch of the image (8.2). The sketch then serves as a template, which he places on a light table. He then paints over the sketch on watercolor paper with ink and paint (8.3). "At this point I am already thinking about the Photoshop aspect of the work and am considering which parts of the image need to be on their own Photoshop layer. I make a separate painting for each layer to be. For example, when I painted the Morning Glory image, I broke the flower up into blossoms, buds, and leaves, and painted each one of these pieces separately (8.4, 8.5). Later, each piece became an individual Photoshop layer. It's more practical for me to paint each layer individually with ink and paint than it is to try to separate the elements later in Photoshop. This is an original technique and not a traditional one, reached simply through experimentation." Goto's method of brushwork is also self-taught and he is still refining techniques as he experiments with

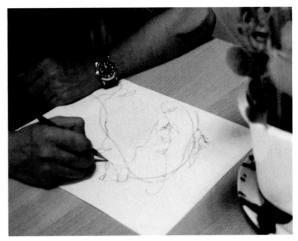

8.2

8.3

WORK HISTORY:

<u>1988</u> — Established HI! Seisaku-Shitsu, a graphic design office.

<u>1990</u> — Purchased first Macintosh Ilcx.

<u>1992</u> — Received the Adobe Design Contest Adobe Award and started to get serious about creating art on a computer.

<u>1993</u> — Group exhibitions. First work featured in Japanese magazines and books.

<u>1994</u> — Selected to create the yearly New Year's card for Japan's National Ministry of Posts.

<u>1996</u> — Created numerous illustrations for magazine and book covers, and other media forms.

<u>1998–present</u> — Keeping very busy creating cover illustrations for magazines and novels, advertisement posters, record jackets, calendars, and a variety of other projects.

FAVORITE MUSICAL INSTRUMENT:

The *shamisen*, which is a three-stringed instrument. "This traditional Japanese art form is not commonly studied today and I find it infinitely interesting. My group has no other 'youngsters' so I am a bit spoiled and coddled by my elders."

8.4

different types of paper and brushes, and amounts of ink, paint, and water.

SKETCH TO MASK

After the sketch and paintings are done, the image is two-thirds of the way to completion. Goto scans each painting at 300 dpi in grayscale mode with his flatbed scanner and brings each file into Photoshop. "The next step is a bit tedious but very important." Goto proceeds to mask out each image element with a high-contrast luminance mask. He starts by duplicating the entire grayscale image file as a new channel (8.6). He then uses Curves to increase the contrast, forcing the background paper to white and darkening the flower itself (8.7). Due to the tonality in the image, light areas often remain in the dark flower, so Goto cleans up the mask with the Dust & Scratches filter (8.8). By inverting the mask he can easily see where the Dust & Scratches filter left artifacts (8.9), which he can erase with the block eraser (8.10).

After the initial mask is complete, extrapolating additional masks for each image element (8.11–8.14) is easy. "However, I must be careful not to leave any jagged edges. Sometimes I have to carefully apply the blur filter or use the blur tool to selectively eliminate them."

8.5

8.6

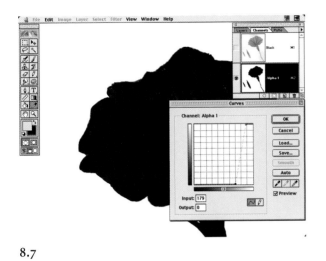

8.7

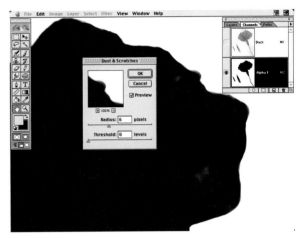

8.8

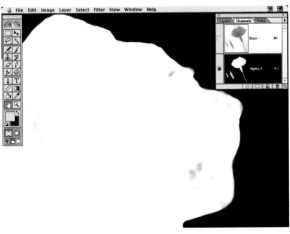

8.9

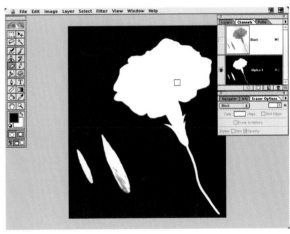

8.10

8.11

8.12

8.13

8.14

MASKS TO COLOR

Before adding color to the image, Goto experiments with the Solarize filter to highlight the shadowy areas of the grayscale image. This adds a unique effect reminiscent of traditional woodcut prints (8.15). He then inverts the image. Sometimes this leaves the piece with insufficient tone, so he darkens it using Brightness/Contrast.

The next step is to add color to the image. First he converts the grayscale image to RGB mode. "Often in the final stages I must convert the file to CMYK mode, but I initially work in RGB because CMYK does not provide the color palette that I need. Because I take my files out to different output devices, some of which require RGB data while others work with CMYK data, I keep the files in RGB as long as possible and check them with CMYK preview in Photoshop (⌘/Ctrl+Y) to see how the CMYK transform will affect my color palette. If the change is too extreme, I use Select Color to select the out-of-gamut colors and then use Hue/Saturation to desaturate those colors."

By loading the individual alpha channels and working with image adjustment layers, Goto can add color piece by piece and is able to return to each adjustment layer to fine-tune the color and tonality. He starts with Color Balance to get the initial color (8.16) and then uses Hue/Saturation (8.17) to fine-tune the intensity of each piece, as you can see in the final flower (8.18).

"Although I create the image in pieces, I visualize the complete piece as a whole. I find that a real living object is far more unique and intricate than anything that springs from my imagination. Referring back to my original concept of the *Morning Glory* image (still residing in my head), I turn to the computer. I try to think of my own mind as another filter for the image." Notice how Goto has separated the leaves from the blossom (8.19). Although many people would overlook the common green leaves and tendrils, he has composed and colored them beautifully so they become supporting vines for the rich blue blossoms (8.20).

MAKING THE BACKGROUND

After all the image elements have been masked, toned, and colored accordingly, Goto creates a unique background for the image. He has different ways of doing this. "Sometimes I try to find a section of the image in which nothing is drawn and which may contain scan irregularities or show the texture of the paper. I enlarge these areas, heighten their contrast, add texture with the Noise and/or Motion Blur filters, and finally add color with the previously mentioned technique."

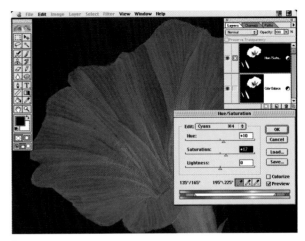

8.17

8.15

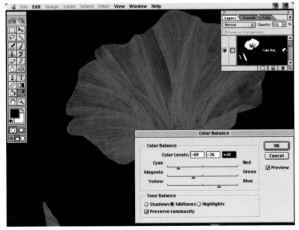

8.16

8.18

8.19

For the *Morning Glory* piece, Goto created a pattern from the painting of the branches and leaves of the plant (8.21). Working intuitively, he used the Transform function to distort the shape of the image, applied the Motion Blur filter (8.22), and heightened the contrast of the image (8.23, 8.24).

Eventually, the image is broken down enough to become an abstract pattern (8.25). "By loading the luminosity of this abstract pattern (⌘/Ctrl+Option/Alt+~ [tilde]) and creating a new alpha channel, I can use the pattern as an alpha channel for the background layer. After loading the selection, I continue to experiment with inverting colors, using the Solarize filter as I go (8.26). Most importantly, I have no fixed technique for backgrounds and often simply go with the creative flow to make them. If you can believe it, sometimes I even end up using scans of my own fingerprints for backgrounds!"

8.20

8.21

COMPOSITING

"Once the background is ready, I select each piece of the painting and bring it to the background file as a new layer. I align the pieces with prepared guidelines to bring everything into position, and the piece is finished. Because I have sketched, painted, and scanned the pieces to scale, the compositing aspect of my images is rather straightforward (8.27–8.32)."

To finish an image, Goto signs each piece with the traditional Tenkoku seal. Traditionally, it has been applied to Nihon-ga paintings and written materials in Japan as a simplified pen-name for an author or artist. It features the name "Hiroshi" written in a typestyle called Tensho. Goto actually carved this stone seal and uses a scanned version of the seal's impression to sign his artwork (8.33). Interestingly enough, the layer with the seal on it is the only time

8.22

8.23

8.24

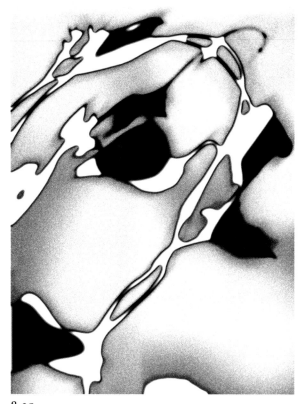

8.25

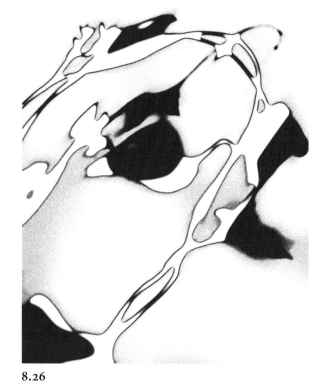

8.26

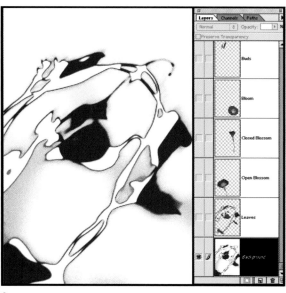

8.27

8.28

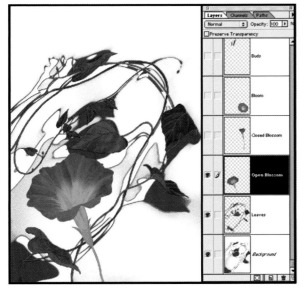

8.29

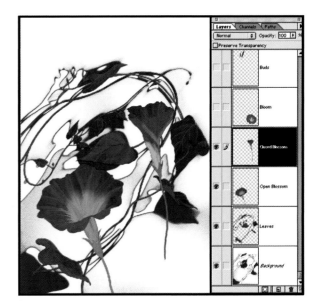

8.30

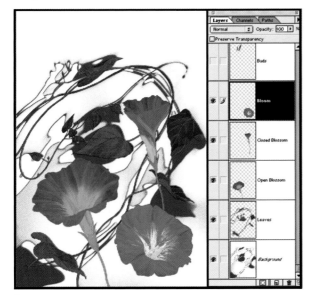

8.31

8.32

8.33

that Goto uses a blend mode other than Normal. He uses Multiply to darken the seal to make it look as if it was actually printed onto the paper.

Here you see the final composited painting (8.34) with a detail view that reveals the fine color and textured tonality contrast between the background and subject (8.35).

GALLERY CONVERSATIONS

One of the images that we were most taken by is the hauntingly beautiful image of a light lily on a very dark background (8.36). This piece was used for the cover of a Japanese novel entitled *Yogare. Yogare* is a sorrowful word from the Heian period that describes a situation in which a man promises to meet his lover at nighttime, but grows tired of the woman and decides not to meet her. Goto wanted this image to express the painful nighttime longing of a woman for her man,

and this led to a piece featuring the contrast of a white lily floating in the depths of a dark background.

"It is not often that I find work in which a black background is required. It depends on the work in question, but generally Japanese clients seem to dislike dark backgrounds. I myself have a preference for them."

THE FISH

The ornamental fish is another icon of traditional Japanese culture. "You can find this fish in people's aquariums all over Japan. It is black, has eyes that bulge out of its head, and is described by the Japanese name *demekin* (8.37). The tail of the demekin is truly beautiful, and to accent it I used a softly curving image of water in the background. To create the background, I drew a series of curved lines in FreeHand, imported them to Photoshop, and then used the Shear and Blur filters to mimic the graceful motion of flowing water. I pasted this shape into an alpha channel, loaded the channel to the image, inverted it, and added color with the Color Balance and Hue/Saturation technique described earlier."

CHERRY BLOSSOMS

The cherry blossoms that bloom in spring are an integral aspect of traditional Japanese culture, annually awakening the country with festivals, concerts, and celebrations. As Goto explains, "The theme for this

8.34

8.35

television station poster was 'Spring in Japan' (8.38). I tried to attain light and airy colors to match the feeling of spring. The blue background represents the color of the Japanese spring sky. By using a pale pink color blending into the sky background, I tried to express the gentle, bright, and cheerful feeling of spring. Finally, I used the noise filter to imitate the pollen in a natural cherry blossom (8.39). Expanding the texture of paper from the scanned painting and adding color and shadows created the background. Each flower petal required its own Photoshop layer and level of transparency."

THE PEONY

For the peony painting (8.40), Goto essentially used the same technique described earlier, although it may seem more complex because this oriental flower has a very complex shape and the petals are in multiple folds. "The work in Photoshop was not especially difficult but the original painting took most of a day. The background image is meant to remind one of a gold *byobu* folding screen."

PAINTING WITH WATERCOLORS

In interviewing Hiroshi, we were quite surprised to find out that he doesn't paint with Photoshop and, therefore, doesn't use a pressure-sensitive tablet for his work. "I am still considering studying traditional watercolor technique. When it comes to the use of color and composition, I refer to the traditional Nihon-ga paintings for inspiration and ideas. I make quite a few trips to museums and galleries to view the Nihon-ga and am constantly studying a variety of

8.37

8.36

8.38

books on the subject. The feature that strikes me most about traditional Nihon-ga is the bold sense of design style and that even though objects are not drawn in perspective, the viewer still gets a strong sense of depth from the paintings as a whole. One of my favorite painters is Kiichi Suzuki of the famous Rinpa Group, active in the latter half of the Edo Period (1615–1868). The Rinpa style arose in the Momoyama period (1573–1615) and was characterized by an emphasis on two-dimensional design, striking color patterns, and the previously mentioned bold sense of design style."

Goto uses the Tarashikomi (spilling ink) method characteristic of the Rinpa style to draw the branches and stems of plants. Before the first brushstrokes have dried, he lets more concentrated ink run through parts of the painting. So rather than mimicking paint with a computer, Goto paints with the real thing, enabling the serendipity of the flow of ink to add to the image.

Now, with Photoshop 6, Goto can go directly to the top of the screen under the menu bar to access paintbrush options while painting. Photoshop 6 has enhanced the Options palette and made it part of the top of the screen. Now, when you double-click the Brush tool, you can view all of its options underneath the menu bar.

8.40

THE FINAL PRINT

We were curious as to how Goto submits work to his clients, and his solution illustrates the conundrum that many digital artists experience. "I submit work in various forms, but when it is required to submit an image as data, I do so with a file converted to CMYK on an optical disk. Somehow it seems that every time I do this, responsibility for the color reproduction always comes back to me and this often becomes a hassle. So whenever possible, I submit a piece already output in the original RGB mode using a Fuji Pictography 4000 continuous tone, high-resolution printer. For my personal exhibition work, I print each piece on Japanese washi paper using the

8.39

IRIS 3047 printer. With this method I can create large poster size prints — but interestingly enough extremely high-resolution images are not necessary to create very good results. Because the washi soaks up a portion of ink, I get a slight blurring of the dots, and even a 150 dpi file offers remarkable quality."

IN CLOSING

In closing, we would like to extend a sincere thank you to Jade Carter for his accurate translations and extreme patience.

CHAPTER 9
GLASS, SMOKE, AND REFLECTIONS

W hen it comes to creating a photorealistic effect such as glass or smoke, Photoshop is the perfect tool. Eliot Bergman uses Photoshop as well as Illustrator and Alias Sketch! (a 3D modeling program) to design and implement a variety of effects on his artwork. Bergman's work was originally specialized in information graphics — as in charts, diagrams, and maps. He worked in the traditional method of technical pens, drafting film, and rubylith. With these tools he created preseparated artwork for his clients. Imagine Bergman's relief when he purchased his first Mac computer to automate many of the tasks he was laboriously doing by hand. Proficient in Illustrator (his samples were featured in Adobe Illustrator's software as well as other illustrator books and magazines), he was not really interested in Adobe Photoshop. His first Mac was a IICX with 80MB hard drive and 32MB of RAM and wasn't really capable of handling his more intensive work. With computers getting faster and bigger, his interest in Photoshop grew considerably.

Bergman prefers to build three-dimensional models rather than work with photography or stock photographs. In using his imagination, he isn't limited to what he can produce. By building a three-dimensional model, he can render and assemble them in a layered Photoshop file. Although he doesn't try to make his images look like a realistic effect, he creates very dynamic, poster-like images. Because of his traditional background — drafting, airbrush, photography — working with Photoshop has become much easier. All of these traditional skills can easily be used in Photoshop to create smoky, glass, and reflective effects.

It's satisfying to achieve what I had in mind.

ELIOT BERGMAN

"In figure 9.1 I created a bottle-at-sea image created as an advertisement for a trade magazine. Another image discussed in this chapter (9.2) shows artwork that I created for a CD cover." In both of these images, Bergman relies on Illustrator and Alias Sketch! to start the artwork. In the last image (9.3) Bergman shows a broken chain that shows a metallic effect as well as some great shadow work.

9.2

9.1

9.3

ARTIST:
Eliot Bergman

ORGANIZATION:
Eliot Bergman Digital Illustration
888-COOLPIX toll free
212-466-0300
212-645-0751
www.ebergman.com
ebergman@emedia.net

SYSTEM:
Power Mac G3
Mac OS 8.5.1
8GB storage

RAM:
256MB total
128MB assigned to Photoshop

MONITOR:
ViewSonic PF775

EXTRAS:
None

VERSION USED:
Adobe Photoshop 5.0

OTHER APPLICATIONS:
Adobe Illustrator 8.0, Alias Sketch! 2.0, Maya 3.0, Poser 4.0

CREATING A BOTTLE AT SEA

The advertisement for a trade magazine came with an initial concept. This piece was to stress that the magazine covers important stories that detail how multifunctionals manage the flow of materials, information, and funds across different channels. Using the classic note in a bottle creates this message.

"I combine all artwork using Adobe Illustrator, Alias Sketch!, and Photoshop. While you can draw two-dimensional artwork directly in a three-dimensional program, using Illustrator is much easier to do the initial drawing. Illustrator is perfect for drafting the precise sections, plans, and profiles in two dimensions, and then importing them to the three-dimensional program. Illustrator is also used to create quick color and bump maps that are then exported into Photoshop to retouch and save as a PICT file for later use. You can also create and render complete raster images in three-dimensional programs; it is much faster and easier to work with a layered Photoshop file than to change parameters and create multiple renders until the desired effect is achieved in a three-dimensional program."

WORK HISTORY:

<u>1979–1980</u> — The Cooper Union, New York, B.F.A.

<u>1979</u> — AGS, Basel, Switzerland

<u>1980–1983</u> — Designer, *Fortune* magazine

<u>1983–1985</u> — Partner, Bergman Hake Design

<u>1983–1990</u> — Instructor, Parsons School of Design

<u>1985–present</u> — Principal, Eliot Bergman, Inc.

Corporate clients include: Allied-Signal, American Express, AT&T, Bloomberg, Citibank, Disney, Du Pont, Fidelity Investments, Gray Advertising, Honda, IBM, Isetan, Keller International Publishing, Kraft, McGraw-Hill, MCI, Mead, Reebok, and Scitex.

Work has appeared in: *Architectural Record, BusinessWeek, Computer Shopper, Consumer Reports, Forbes, Fortune, Frequent Flyer, Golf, Life, Money, New York, Newsweek, PC, Popular Science, Sports Illustrated,* tele.com, and *Time*.

FAVORITE PASTIME:

Hanging out at the pool with my wife, Kiyono.

9.4

9.5

9.6

9.7

FLESHING OUT THE DESIGN

In Bergman's words, "For the bottle image, the first step was to draft the contour of the bottle in Illustrator (9.4). An initial stroke weight of 1 point was given to the outline of the bottle shape. The stroke weight was then changed to a 6-point rounded stroke (9.5). The stroke was then turned into an outline and the bottle cut in half (9.6). I did this to create an exact symmetrical bottle shape with a centerline guide to revolve the bottle around. The bottom or diameter of the bottle was created the same way as the contour. First I drew a line, a added a thick stroke, and then outlined the shape and cut it in half (9.7). Both the contour and the bottom diameter were imported into Sketch! and revolved to create a simple three-dimensional model."

In Illustrator Bergman created a color map for the priority note on the bottle and exported it for use in Photoshop. In Photoshop, he saved the Illustrator color map file as a PICT to be used later (9.8).

WORKING IN 3D

Alias Sketch! is Bergman's program of choice when rendering a three-dimensional model. In Alias Sketch! he used a stock image of water in a swimming pool for a color and bump map tile for the ocean (9.9). He also pulled a sky image to be used as a color and bump map tile (9.10). The tiles were put directly into the three-dimensional file, but the sky tile was rendered separately so it could be adjusted or enhanced later in Photoshop.

9.8

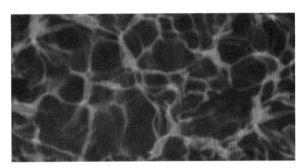

9.9

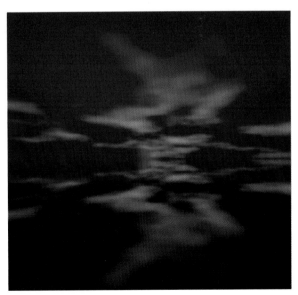

9.10

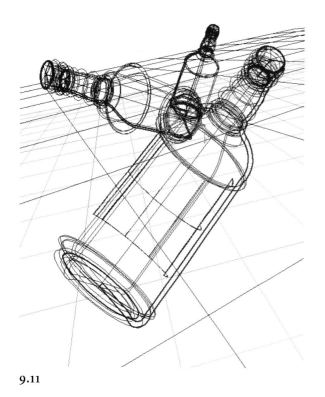

9.11

In the original composition, there were three bottles (9.11), but the design lacked impact and was quickly discarded in favor of the final composition (9.12). In the materials dialog box in Alias Sketch!, the model was assigned a color and a degree of refraction and reflection to simulate a glass look (9.13, 9.14). In addition to the bottle model, the color map for the note was imported and applied as well. Using the Phong quick render, he double-checked the model's geometry (9.15) before the final ray-traced bottle and label images were queued and rendered (9.16, 9.17). The note was rendered as a separate file for use as a Photoshop layer.

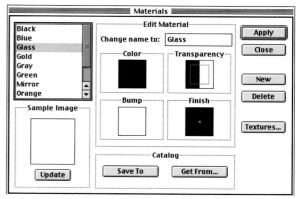

9.13

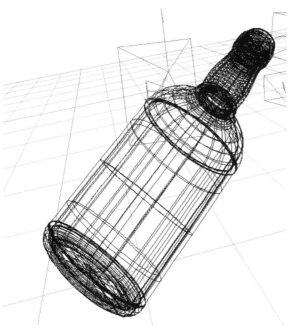

9.12

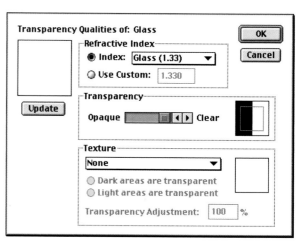

9.14

9.17

9.15

9.16

COMBINING AND APPLYING EFFECTS IN PHOTOSHOP

Bergman explains, "In Photoshop, the render of the foreground was color-corrected using hue, saturation, and contrast to sharpen the bottle and make the water look bluer (9.18). The sky render was copied from Alias Sketch! and pasted into Photoshop. Using the Free Transform function, the sky was scaled and distorted (9.19, 9.20). To perfect the note in the bottle, Bergman used separate layers to apply an airbrushed effect (9.21) and duplicated the note to enhance its legibility using saturation (9.22, 9.23). The first duplicated layer was set to Normal mode and 45 percent opacity. The second duplicated layer was set to Multiply mode and 60 percent opacity. The edge of the note was strengthened by a stroked subpath on a separate layer (9.24). The final note is much stronger than the original render (9.25, 9.26)."

9.18

9.20

9.19

9.21

9.22

9.23

9.24

9.25

9.26

FINISHING DETAILS

The details in this image were addressed in several ways. The foreground needed to blend seamlessly with the background (9.27). Bergman applied the Blur tool to create this seamless blending of the sky to the water. The Rubber Stamp tool was used to make the tiled pattern of the color and bump maps less regular and more natural (9.28). He used the Paintbrush tool to add a weathered look to the cork in the bottle (9.29). After retouching the image, Bergman merged the layers and applied lighting effects to further blend the foreground to the background, creating a more natural effect (9.30).

9.30

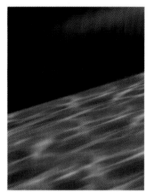

9.27

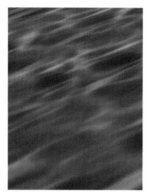

9.28

9.29

Bergman feels that Illustrator's type handling capabilities are much more exact than Photoshop's. In Version 6.0, it seems that Photoshop borrowed the type handling capability of Illustrator in that you can actually edit by using the Type tool to click and drag on the image. This is a much-needed improvement from using the Layers palette to edit your type. The headline (9.31) was set in Illustrator and then converted to outlines. The paths were placed into Photoshop and, using the Layer Effects dialog box, they were beveled (9.32). The body copy, also set in Illustrator (9.33), was placed in Photoshop and, in the Layer Effects dialog box, a drop shadow effect was applied (9.34). The logo for the publication was replicated with a simple radial marquee and the Gradient tool (9.35). The final image clearly depicts the initial concept with great beauty (9.36).

9.31

9.32

9.33

9.34

9.35

9.36

FEEL THE FUNK CD COVER

For this CD cover the client asked Bergman to interpret the dance music on the disc as he wanted. "I felt the idea of mixing a toaster and some old vinyl records would create a 'funky' image." He used Photoshop to put together and create the reflective surfaces of the toaster and to finish off the lighting effects of the image.

DRAFTING THE IDEA

The first step in creating the toaster image was to draft the parts of the toaster in Illustrator (9.37). This file was then imported into Alias Sketch!. In the three-dimensional program, the parts of the toaster were extruded and assembled to create a model. Illustrator was also used to create pattern tiles for the counter and the curtain (9.38, 9.39). These patterns were then exported into Photoshop and saved as PICT files to be used as maps in Alias Sketch!. The counter tile was eventually scrapped in favor of a solid green. Color and bump maps for the records were done in the same way as the curtain, using Illustrator to design the pattern and the three-dimensional program to render (9.40, 9.41).

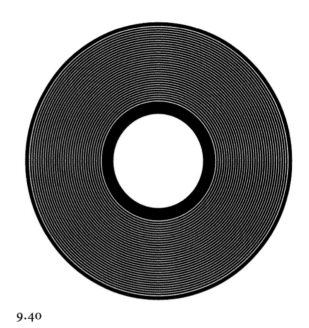

9.40

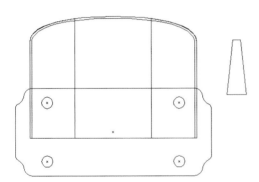

9.37

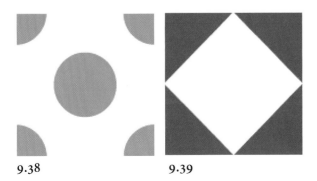

9.38   9.39

9.41

PUTTING IT ALL TOGETHER

The three-dimensional model was assembled (9.42) in Alias Sketch!. A rough preview showed the basic color and form. A smoother preview showed the highlights, shadows, and some details of the toaster (9.43). In the materials dialog box of Alias Sketch!, a degree of reflection was set to achieve the metallic look of the toaster. The other elements of the image were added together in Alias Sketch! and the colors and textures were mapped to create the final combined image (9.44).

ADDING THE FINAL TOUCHES

The image was close, but not perfect, so it was taken into Photoshop to add the finishing touches. Once in Photoshop, it was easy for Bergman to embellish the three-dimensional qualities of the image in several simple ways. "I used a Gaussian Blur for the toaster's cord (9.45) to create the perception that the cord was fading into the distance. To make the record look like it was popping out of the toaster, a motion blur was applied (9.46). I drew a doodle shape and applied the wave filter to it (9.47) to make the smoke effect.

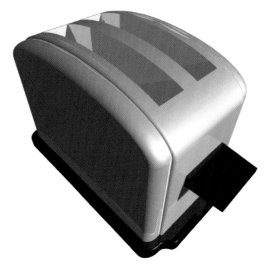

9.43

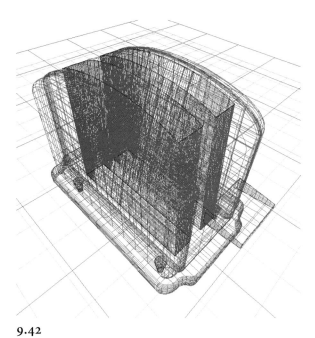

9.42

9.44

Highlights were added to the image using a combination of freeform paint strokes (9.48) and stroked sub-paths on separate layers (9.49). He used Lighting Effects to cast a blue glow on the whole scene (9.50)." Although Photoshop was used sparingly in this image, it is easy to see how important Photoshop is in bringing the image to life. If you compare the raw render from Alias Sketch! to the final piece, it is evident that Photoshop is the "glue" program holding the image together.

BREAKING THE CHAINS

Bergman's client for the next illustration was Keller International Publishing. He designed this cover for a trade magazine. This assignment was an illustration for a magazine article detailing the impact of the Internet on traditional supply-chain strategies. Rather than use a more prosaic approach depicting a Web, Web site, or network of computers, it was decided to use a visual metaphor. The power of the Web was represented by the @ mark bursting through the old ways of doing supply-chain business, which was represented by the chain.

9.49

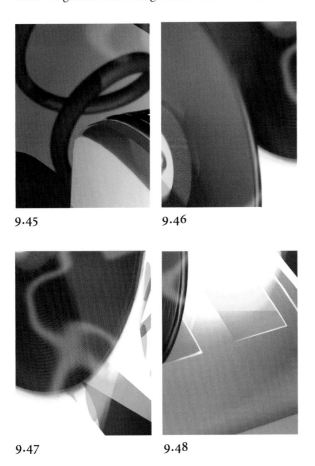

9.45

9.46

9.47

9.48

9.50

CREATING THE LAYOUT OF THE DESIGN

In Adobe Illustrator, Bergman drafted out the basic link in two ways. He first drew a path (9.51) for the chain, and then made the path into an outline (9.52). Both pieces were used to flesh out the chain in the three-dimensional program. You have different ways to create a torus, or doughnut-like loop, in a three-dimensional modeling program, so by creating two different files, he can compare the two. A loop can be modeled by sweeping a section along an extrusion path, lofting a series of sections, or by extruding a plan. In this case, a sweep was sufficient. The @ mark was typeset in Illustrator, and then converted to outlines to serve as a plan for extrusion later (9.53).

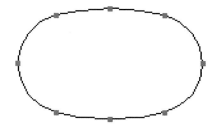

9.51

9.52

9.53

ADDING THE DIMENSION

In the three-dimensional environment, the link was created and duplicated to make the chain (9.54). The camera angle was also set for the perspective (9.55). Before the materials were assigned, the image was roughly rendered to check the geometry of the model (9.56). A PICT file of a rusted tin texture was chosen from a selection of stock images. Adjusting the contrast in Photoshop (9.57) enhanced the texture. The PICT image served as a bump map for the chain links. The color was created using a combination of RGB.

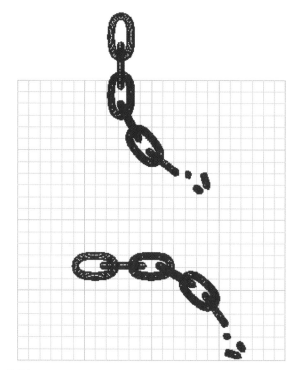

9.54

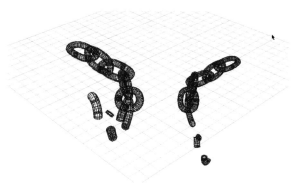

9.55

3D VERSUS PHOTOSHOP

Bergman feels that although it is possible to render a complete scene in any three-dimensional program, he finds much more flexibility if he renders the image as a series of layers. These layers he puts together in Photoshop so he can add further touches and effects. The model was broken into three layers. The first layer is the chain in front of the @ mark (9.58). The second layer is the chain in the back of the @ mark (9.59). The third layer is the @ mark itself.

CREATING THE @ MARK

The Illustrator artwork of the @ mark was imported into Alias Sketch!. In the three-dimensional program, it was then extruded and beveled (9.60). It was rendered roughly to check the geometry (9.61). When the

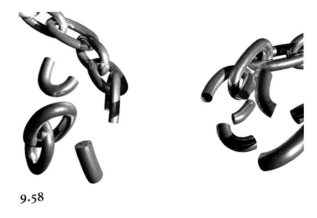

9.58

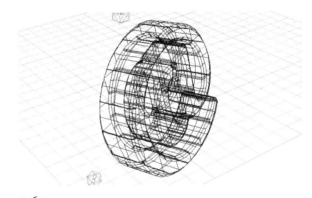

9.59

9.56

9.60

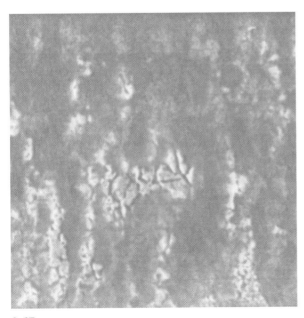

9.57

9.61

geometry looked correct, the lights were positioned, set, and then previewed (9.62). The final step in the three-dimensional program was to set the image size and resolution, queue, and then render the files.

9.62

9.63

9.64

9.65

BLENDING ALL PARTS TOGETHER IN PHOTOSHOP

"In Photoshop, I created a background using the Gradient tool (9.63). The back chain render was opened, and then copied and pasted into the main file as the second layer (9.64). The @ mark was pasted in as the third layer (9.65) and the front chain layer was pasted in as the final layer (9.66). The sense of depth was enhanced using a Gaussian Blur on the back chain layer (9.67)."

To enhance the weak shadows in the render of the @ mark, Bergman used a combination of the HSL dialog box and some airbrush effects (9.68). At first, he

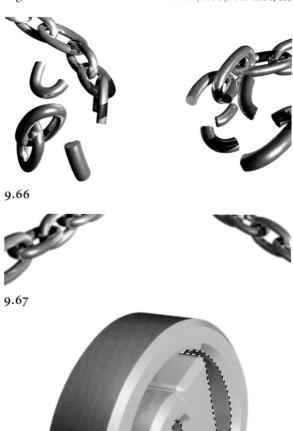

9.66

9.67

9.68

thought using a motion blur (9.69, 9.70) might add to the drama of the illustration, but later discarded it because it didn't seem to add to the plausibility of the image. He then duplicated the front chain layer and set the mode to Normal and the opacity to 80 percent. A motion blur was then added to the chain (9.71). He also considered giving the @ mark an outer glow (9.72), and, rather than using the limited Layer Effects dialog box, he duplicated the layer, scaled the mark, and blurred it using Gaussian Blur with the layer mode set to Lighten and the opacity set to 40 percent (9.73). Again, he omitted this from the final because it seemed too unreal (9.74). After the layers were finalized, the image was flattened and the Lighting Effects filters were tested and applied. Although this composition didn't use any real "tricks," without Photoshop, the final image could not have been made so quickly or successfully. To Bergman, Photoshop's strength lies in its capability to mix layers and quickly apply filters, and in how it helps the artist compare alternatives and arrive at a final image that represents what he or she intended without compromise.

9.71

9.72

9.69

9.73

9.70

9.74

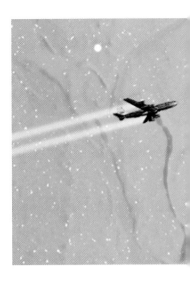

CHAPTER 10
THE TAO OF LAYERING

G reg Vander Houwen is easily one of the most cerebral Photoshop artists we know. To his credit, the guy spends as much time analyzing and reflecting on what he does as he spends doing it. In the eight years he's worked with Photoshop, he's discovered three broad and unifying principles of computer imaging:

"First — and I think everyone has discovered this — computers don't like us for the way we use them, and they pay us back by stealing our time. Probably one out of every ten times I walk up to my machine, there's some new problem that I have to mess with. It's no use fighting; the computer always has the upper hand. It literally owns your data. You have to coax the machine to share its data through attentiveness and patient problem solving.

"Second, Photoshop is a great program, but it's by no means perfect. It's not even intelligent in any conventional sense. So it's up to you to recognize its shortcomings and anticipate them. Photoshop is like a force of nature that you do well to understand and embrace.

"Third, simplicity is key to the way I work. I'm not keen on complex sequences. The bottom line is, even though I'm technically capable, I can't remember long procedures. The best techniques are the simple ones that I can mix and match like jazz licks. If I can quickly recall and 'play' the operation, only then does it become practical."

The net result is an artistic philosophy based on anticipating mistakes and working with as little fanfare as possible. Vander Houwen's primary ally in this quest is the common layer. "Layers have made my life

Photoshop is like a force of nature that you do well to understand and embrace.

GREG VANDER HOUWEN

substantially better. I have clients who perpetually come back to me and say, 'Gee, Greg, that's great, but you know, what we were thinking was *this*.' It always translates to me having to change something. But so long as I stick with virtual compositing — relying on blend modes, layer options, layer masks, and adjustment layers — then I can always go back and retrieve the original data." With layers, Vander Houwen makes it easy and keeps it safe.

BASE CAMPS AND SERIOUS ALTERATIONS

"Two concepts are central to the way I think — 'base camps' and 'serious alterations.' A base camp is just a saved version of a file at a certain stage in its development. Back in Photoshop 2.5, before layers came along, I was constantly saving versions so that I could revert back to previous stages of the artwork. Now that I have layers, I still use base camps as an added precaution. I tend to save a base camp whenever my gut says, 'You know, if you lost this, it could be very bad.'

"A serious alteration is a modification that you apply directly to a pixel. For example, applying the Levels command directly to an image is a serious alteration; using an adjustment layer is not. . . . I try not to commit a serious alteration when an alternative is available. But many serious alterations are unavoidable. The trick is, before I commit a serious alteration, I make sure to create a base camp. Then, I'm covered."

Vander Houwen even goes so far as to archive many base camps to CD-ROM on the off-chance he might need them in the future. "On CD, I can go back years and extract bits and pieces from files because I've been working this way. It doesn't happen very often, but I've had situations where the client calls up and says, 'Now, we know this is a big change and we know it was six months ago, but the thing is, we got this deadline. We realize you'll have to work through the night, and this is going to cost us a huge sum of money.' I'm tempted to say, 'Yeah, it is. That's going to hurt a lot. Boy, are you right.' But instead, I pop in the CD, grab the right base camp, and surprise the client with a miracle turnaround."

The figures (10.1, 10.2, and 10.3) demonstrate the lengths Vander Houwen goes to in his virtual compositing. "Don't get hung up on the numbers. These are just demonstration composites, but they should give you a good idea of how I work."

ROUGHING OUT A COMPOSITION

"I always start off by blocking out the basic composite. I throw things onto their own layers, so as not to damage them. Then, I add layer masks using gradients and brushes. I might play with the Opacity setting, too. The bottom line is, I'm trying to build the roughest, fastest composite I can, so I can make decisions and figure out if any problems exist with the composite. You might have a nice sketch put together, but until you get the

ARTIST:
Greg Vander Houwen

ORGANIZATION:
Interact
P.O. Box 498
Issaquah, WA 98027
206-999-2584
gregvh@netcandy.com

SYSTEM:
Power Mac 8100/110
6GB storage

RAM:
110MB total
90MB assigned to Photoshop

MONITOR:
Apple 17-inch

EXTRAS:
Wacom 12 × 12 electrostatic tablet

VERSION USED:
Photoshop 5.0

OTHER APPLICATIONS:
Adobe Illustrator, Fractal Design Painter, ElectricImage Broadcast

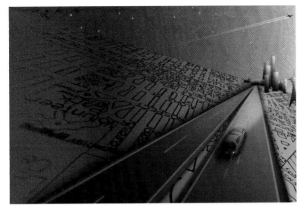

10.1

10.3

10.2

WORK HISTORY:

<u>1977</u> — Sold photographs for $200 to farming magazine at 14 years old.

<u>1983</u> — Searched around in vain for job in Los Angeles video industry, retreated to home-town computer store and began to pursue computer graphics.

<u>1989</u> — Acquired alpha version of Photoshop, created first published image for *Verbum* magazine.

<u>1991</u> — Started his own design firm, which now includes Apple, Adobe, and Microsoft as clients.

<u>1992</u> — Learned compositing and retouching techniques at Ivey Seright imaging lab.

<u>1997</u> — Helped Microsoft to develop new graphical interface.

FAVORITE CARTOON CHARACTER:

The Tick ("Aside from Buddha, he's the most enlightened intellect I've ever encountered.")

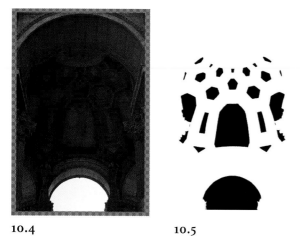

10.4

10.5

10.6

10.7

images nested, you can't see exactly where things work and where they might go wrong."

Photoshop 6 includes layer sets within the Layers palette. Also added to the adjustment layers is the Gradient Map that lets you map colors to your image. Because Version 6 enables you to use vectors, you can incorporate the vector art in a mask through the Layers palette. Photoshop 6 has added the option to let you save a certain creation as a layer style to access at any time.

CHAIN SAWING A LAYER MASK

As an example, Vander Houwen had an idea to create a dome with transparent windows looking up into a cloudy sky. Up front, there was one obvious problem: the dome didn't have any windows (10.4). But it did have indented panels that could be removed to serve as windows. Rather than deleting these panels, Vander Houwen converted the dome to a floating layer and added a layer mask (10.5).

"I clicked around with the polygon lasso tool until I selected the panels. It's like chain sawing—I just hacked through it in rough slashes. After I got a halfway decent selection, I Option-clicked the layer mask icon at the bottom of the Layers palette to mask away the selected areas. Then, with the layer mask on, I took out my brushes and tweaked it. I used the Shift key and clicked from point to point along the straight edges." The result is a windowed dome, without so much as a pixel in the original image harmed (10.6).

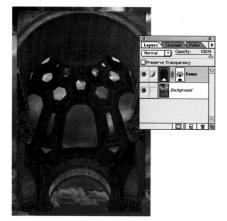

10.8

10.9

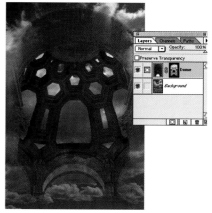

10.10

DROPPING THE DOME

Compositing the dome against the sky (10.7) was a simple matter of dragging the dome with the move tool (or ⌘/Ctrl-dragging with some other tool) and dropping it into the sky image. By pressing the Shift key during the drop, Vander Houwen center-registered the dome inside the sky (10.8).

The layered image wasn't quite the same size as the sky, so the dome had a harsh rectangular edge around it. Rather than resizing the dome or cropping the sky, Vander Houwen decided to simply brush around the layer mask some more. He applied a black fringe with the paintbrush tool (10.9), starting with a big fuzzy brush and working down to smaller ones. "Begin big and general, and then work toward precision," Vander Houwen advises. Although the fringe took just a minute or two to create, it rendered a very serviceable fade (10.10).

THE LIGHT FROM ON HIGH

Finally, the dome needed a bright, glorious light streaming in from the sky. Vander Houwen created a new layer and filled it with a very simple white-to-black radial gradation (10.11). Then, he applied the Screen blend mode from the Layers palette to drop out the black and highlight the layers below (10.12). "I always tell people, Screen and Multiply are 90 percent of what they need to know about blend modes. Screen stacks lightness; Multiply stacks darkness. So I use Screen to keep light stuff such as glows, and Multiply to keep dark stuff such as shadows."

No special filter, a very simple approach, and not a single serious alteration — it's the ideal composition. "My first goal is always to assemble the rough elements together so I can quickly adapt if needed, or call the art director and say, 'Mayday! This is never going to work!' A rough composite gives you a basis for negotiation and compromise."

USING LAYER OPTIONS

"For another composition, I was asked to layer some lightning (10.13) against some clouds (10.14). Obviously, I wanted to keep the light stuff and make the dark stuff go away. Blend modes and layer options

10.11

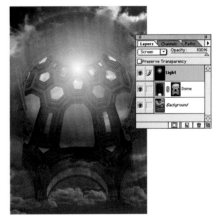

10.12

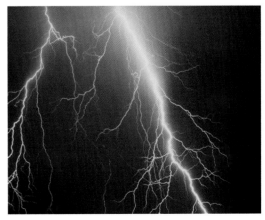

10.13

10.14

10.15

10.16

are great for that. You don't need to use the magic wand tool and get those jagged halos around the edges, and you don't need to resort to a complex mask. Let Photoshop do the work for you."

Vander Houwen started by layering the lightning in front of the clouds and applying the Screen blend mode from the Layers palette (10.15). But this method resulted in a universal lightening effect that washed out the clouds below. The trick is to keep only the lightest pixels in the lightning layer and make the others invisible. Sounds like a job for layer options.

DROPPING OUT AND FORCING THROUGH

Vander Houwen double-clicked the Lightning layer in the Layers palette to bring up the Layers Options dialog box. In Photoshop 6.0, when you double-click the layer, you activate the Layer Styles dialog box. The Layer Styles dialog box not only lets you change the blending mode of that layer, but you can also access any of the Layer Styles found under the Layer menu, such as drop shadow, glows, bevel, and embossing. Then, he adjusted the black triangle in the slider bar labeled This Layer. This dropped out the original background for the layer. To soften the transition between visible and invisible pixels, he Option/Alt-dragged the triangle to break it in half. The result is lightning that looks like it was photographed with the original image (10.16).

But that wasn't enough. Vander Houwen also wanted to force the lightest colors in the clouds in front of the lightning. So he dragged and then Option/Alt-dragged the white triangle in the Underlying slider bar. This created the effect of the lightning going through the clouds (10.17).

NEVER TRY TO MASK LIGHTNING

"I had a client who said, 'We know how hard it is to knock out lightning because it's got all those fingers. Maybe you could use an alpha channel or something.' And I thought, if I had to create a mask for lightning, it would take me a week and it probably wouldn't look right. The layer options effect takes a few seconds to pull off, it doesn't harm the original image, and it looks better than anything I could accomplish with a mask," as the magnified detail shows (10.18). "And it's not just lightning. It's stars, it's city lights, it's anything light. Or anything dark — for example, layer options are great for compositing scanned logos against different backgrounds. I just move the white slider, and the paper goes away.

"Along with blend modes, layer options are basically your way to control the overlay of light and dark stuff. If you can get your head around that, then you can even control how individual color channels land by editing red, green, and blue separately. For example, blue skies can be made to go away rather easily by tweaking the sliders in the blue component."

TONAL ADJUSTMENTS IN LAYER MASKS

"One of my favorite little techniques to show people that they should care about layer masks is just to put a couple of images together and run gradients across them. If you don't like the way the effect works, you don't need to undo. Just run gradient after gradient after gradient. Each new gradient will obliterate the last one. Or you can run a simple black-to-white gradient. And then use a tonal control such as Levels or Curves to manipulate the mask transitions."

GRADIENT LAYER MASKS

For this example, Vander Houwen took a photograph of a woman's face (10.19) and layered it against a sunset (10.20) so the woman's right eye aligned exactly on top of the sun. "I just dragged on the eye and dropped onto the sun. If you know a little about your composition ahead of time, alignment is easy."

Vander Houwen added a layer mask by clicking the layer mask icon (second from the left) at the bottom of the Layers palette. He selected the gradient tool and chose Foreground to Background in the Gradient Tool Options palette (with the foreground and background colors set to their defaults of black and white). Then, he dragged from the lower-right to the upper-left corner in the mask (10.21). The lower-right corner became transparent and faded into opacity (10.22), again without upsetting a pixel in the original images.

10.17

10.18

10.19

Using the Curves command, Vander Houwen created a spiky color map that resulted in an alternating series of blacks and whites inside the layer mask (10.23). "A simple black-to-white gradation can yield all kinds of effects with Curves." The upshot is a strobe effect that flashes the face on and off over the course of the image (10.24).

TONAL EDGE ADJUSTMENTS

"I also use this technique to refine selections. I make a hasty selection around an image element that's just roughly in the shape of the thing. Then, I convert the

10.20

10.22

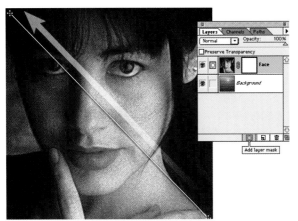

10.21

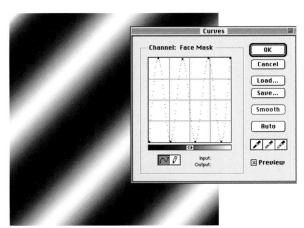

10.23

selection to a layer mask (10.25), blur the heck out of it (10.26), and go into Levels or Curves and manipulate the edge (10.27). This way, I can draw the layer into the background or draw it away from the background, without a lot of work. In most cases, I have to go back and edit the mask further (10.28), but this simple spreading and choking technique eliminates about 70 percent of the job."

The lasso isn't the only selection tool that can benefit from this technique. "One of the key things I've learned about Photoshop is that if I had to rely exclusively on the magic wand to make a selection, I'd be a sad puppy. So I use the magic wand to get me half the

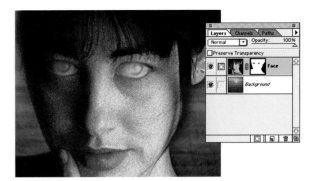

10.26

10.24

10.27

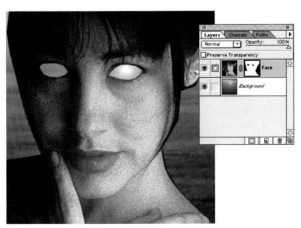

10.25

10.28

10.29

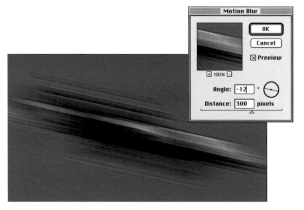

10.30

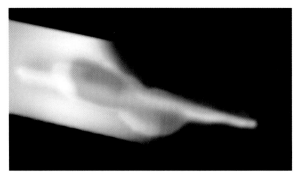

10.31

10.32

way, and then play with layer masking from there. Suddenly, it's a cool tool that quickly eliminates a large part of my work."

QUICK EFFECT MASKS

"A lot of special effects can be achieved with the help of layer masks. For example, Photoshop doesn't offer a unidirectional motion trail filter. That's okay, because you can easily whip one together yourself."

The jet fighter (10.29) is an image that's just begging for a motion trail. Vander Houwen duplicated the image to a new layer and applied a hefty dose of Motion Blur filter. "I matched the Angle value to the angle of the jet, and I changed the Distance to 300 pixels." That's a pretty huge value considering the modest resolution of this image. In fact, the jet is pretty well blown to bits (10.30).

Vander Houwen then added a layer mask and painted in the forward part of the blurred plane to reveal the original underneath. "I start painting with huge brushes — the bigger the brush, the better to start with. I just knock it out at first, and then I refine with smaller brushes. I hit the number and bracket keys like a madman to adjust the brush settings on the fly. I never touch the palettes if I can help it — it takes too long and interrupts the flow."

He Shift-clicked along the sides of the wings — with the grain of the motion blur — to get rid of any blurring Photoshop may have applied to the sky. And he filled in a few spots inside the jet with light grays to bring back some of the detail. The finished mask appears in grayscale (10.31) with the resulting motion trail effect shown below it (10.32).

"Sometimes the simplicity of these effects is a little painful. This one in particular makes me flinch a little because, in the past, I did it so badly. I would hand-draw the motion trail with the smudge tool or something equally difficult. But that's the way it is, right? The price of today's success is often yesterday's pain."

WALKING THE VIRTUAL MILE

"This last file includes a bunch of good examples of how you can easily layer image elements using the techniques I explained before, all working together in concert. I started by dragging and dropping all my elements into a single composition. I have to say that I've really embraced drag-and-drop lately because I finally figured out its advantage. Everyone tells you that drag and drop doesn't take up any clipboard memory. But you know what that means? You aren't leaving the picture of the 5MB duck or whatever up in the clipboard for two hours while you wait for it to cause an out-of-memory error. Besides, it's easier — you just grab the thing and haul it over."

10.33

BUILDING THE LAYERS

Vander Houwen started this particular image by filling a layer with black and adding stars to it (10.33). To make the stars, he applied the Add Noise filter and turned on both the Gaussian and Monochrome options. Then, he applied Gaussian Blur with a Radius of 1.0 and used the Levels command to exaggerate the brightness of the blurred dots.

He next dragged in a sky photo and set the blend mode to Screen so the stars would remain visible (10.34). Then, he introduced two more elements — the Golden Gate bridge and a statue in harsh light (10.35). Both elements consume relatively small chunks of the image window and require blending. Vander Houwen dropped away the sky pixels in the bridge layer using the Layer Options dialog box. He set the Blend If pop-up menu to Blue and adjusted the white This Layer triangle. (Try this on any bright sky image, and you'll quickly see how well it works.) Then, he added gradient layer masks to both layers to create even fades (10.36).

The last image to be tossed on the stack was the rolling fog (10.37). This image completely covered the stuff behind it, so Vander Houwen again relied on his friends, the layer options. By adjusting the black triangle in the This Layer slider bar, he was able to drop the black sky away and melt the fog gracefully into its background (10.38).

10.34

STRIKING BASE CAMP

"I often modify the position of the elements with the arrow keys and Shift keys. It's fast and accurate — whether you have a dirty mouse or what, the arrow

10.35

10.36

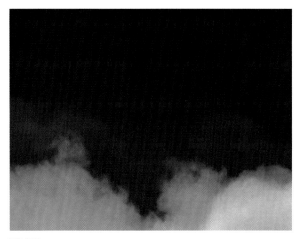

10.37

10.38

keys let you get the layer exactly where you want it. Also, up here in Seattle, my caffeine intake makes it impossible to nudge stuff by any other method.

"When I get it all together and everything's basically in place, I save my base camp. This is a separate file — dot 2 or whatever — so that the previous file remains fixed in time. Of course, I save the base camp in the Photoshop native format; and I can't think of any reason for using another format until my image is 100 percent finished. And even then, I always keep a Photoshop file as backup."

THE FINISHING TOUCHES

The text is Helvetica Compressed, further squished and skewed using the Free Transform command, and then filtered with Motion Blur. Vander Houwen also added a gradient layer mask to fade the text in the corners (10.39). Finally, he added a layer mask to the second-to-bottom sky layer. Then, he airbrushed in black with the airbrush to uncover an area of starry night behind the text (10.40).

"When I was doing 9-to-5 production work, I learned the hard way that you don't worry about the details until the end. You concentrate on the biggest problems — the major composite parts — and work your way down to increasing levels of refinement. Otherwise, you end up blowing away that detail work you did earlier, and you waste a lot of time."

10.39

Once again, we have an example of a composition in which no scanned image was directly modified. "I messed with the text, but I can redo that in a few seconds. After I get the image finessed to the point I'm more or less happy with it, I save another base camp. Then, I merge some layers or flatten the image and move on. It gives me piece of mind and sheer naked freedom to continue on to the next job without any worries of losing my work."

FOLLOWING THE PATH THAT IS ALWAYS IN MOTION

"Ideally, the goal for me is to play Photoshop like an instrument. Playing jazz Photoshop is where I'd like to be someday. But I figure I need about ten more years—if they'd just quit changing the program. Imagine if you were playing the sax, and they kept moving the buttons on you every couple of years. Not that I don't like the changes—sometimes they're great. But becoming a musician with an instrument that's in constant flux is a challenge.

"Even if the program stood still, I might never master it. Every week it seems like I figure out a better way to do something and realize how hard it was to do it the old way. In fact, I kind of hope I never get it down completely. I hope I always cringe at the way I used to do things because that means I'll be getting better."

GREG KEEPS THE SKETCH HANDY

Vander Houwen likes to scan his original sketch (10.41) and stick it in a mask channel. This way, he can refer to the sketch at any time by clicking the eyeball next to the mask name in the Channels palette. The sketch channel appears as a color overlay (10.42) without affecting his ability to edit the image file. "This lets me position, rotate, scale, and distort elements with extreme accuracy. But it can also help when explaining images to art directors. When there's an approved sketch, it's hard to argue. The sketch is like a visual contract."

10.40

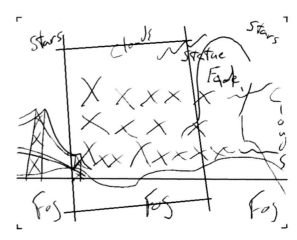

10.41

10.42

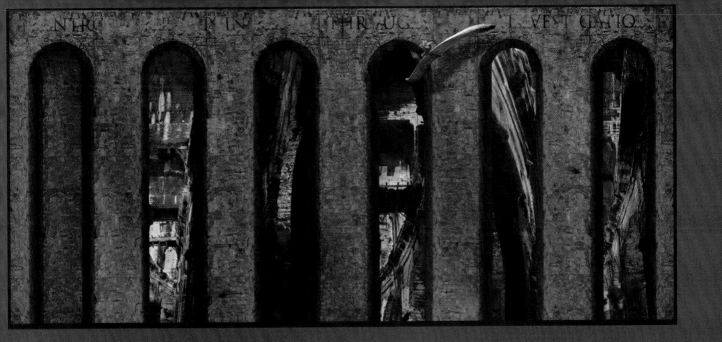

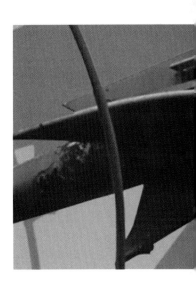

CHAPTER 11
HIGH-RESOLUTION IMAGING FOR ADVERTISING

The world of high-end advertising is a world of painstaking illusion and deliberate trickery. The companies who commission these ads are not simply trying to exaggerate the quality and performance of their products. If it were that simple, we would all own Vegematics and Ronco would be king. A good advertisement misleads with the intent to entertain. It lures you inside it; offers a brief thrill, a smile, or a moment of glamour; and invites you to leave with the promise that more can be had for a price. Purchasing the product pays admission into the illusion. The fact that you receive a physical good in return is often little more than a nostalgic formality paying homage to the old barter-based society.

As one of Manhattan's most respected and admired commercial artists, Robert Bowen understands the role of illusion in advertising. "I've spent a fair amount of time looking at the history of art. I'm particularly interested in an approach called trompe l'oeil (pronounced tromp-loy) — which is French for 'trick the eye.' Trompe l'oeil images want to look real, like they were arranged and photographed exactly as you see them. But they're actually impossible."

Hollywood is the most conspicuous purveyor of the craft. "The intention of a typical movie — particularly an effects-oriented film — is to convey the look of realism without suggesting that what you're seeing actually happened. Everyone who goes to see a movie such as *Twister* or *Volcano* knows that it's not real. But if it has the appearance of realism, then they can suspend their disbelief and give themselves over to what they see. It's all based on an aesthetic of photorealism, as opposed to a more illustrative look that's grounded in the graphic tradition."

> *Trompe l'oeil images want to look real, like they were arranged and photographed exactly as you see them. But they're actually impossible.*
>
> ROBERT BOWEN

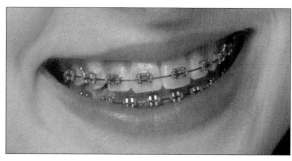

11.1

11.2   Photography by Dennis Gallante

BOB'S EXPLORATION INTO THE UNREAL

Bowen's art expresses roughly as much reverence for the laws of nature as a Lewis Carroll story. He grabs elements from the normal world, flings them down the rabbit's hole, and reassembles them on the other side. Curiously, the view from the bottom of the hole is often better than the one from above.

For example, we are all aware that young girls sometimes wear braces (11.1) and that cows as a rule do not (11.2). And yet, the appearance of a photo-realistic cow undergoing dental adjustment is somehow extremely attractive. It amazes because it's peculiar; it amuses because it's so incredibly absurd. Without its accompanying ad copy, we may never understand why AT&T commissioned this artwork to target college students. But chances are good that the image of a "Cheshire Cow" will stick in your head. It's a smiling, ungulate, radioactive aberration.

The same goes for the mouse-headed man Bowen created for the high-tech company SDRC (11.3). This time, inspiration was close at hand. "I find this image kind of haunting. It reminds me of how I feel after a really bad day." But while the image looks a little painful, Bowen claims it was relatively easy to create. "I just painted the colorized mouse layer in and out with the face layer. I also threw in a few adjustment layers to match the highlights and colors."

Not all of Bowen's images are so outrageous. Sometimes he bends reality to soothe it. Several years

ARTIST:
Robert Bowen

ORGANIZATION:
Robert Bowen Studio New York City, NY
www.bowenstudio.com
bowenbob@aol.com

SYSTEMS:
PowerWave 604/150 (Power Computing)
10GB storage
Silicon Graphics Indy 4400

RAM:
212MB total
190MB assigned to Photoshop

MONITOR:
Radius IntelliColor 20e

EXTRAS:
Adaptec Ultra-Wide controller with two-drive 8GB Barracuda array

VERSION USED:
Photoshop 5.0

OTHER APPLICATIONS:
On Mac: Live Picture, Adobe Illustrator, QuarkXPress
On SGI: Barco Creator, Alias Power Animator

ago, he worked with photographer Ryszard Horowitz on a series of images for Adobe that featured giant watery slabs hovering in space. "In this case, a slab of green universe pours water into the desert (11.4).

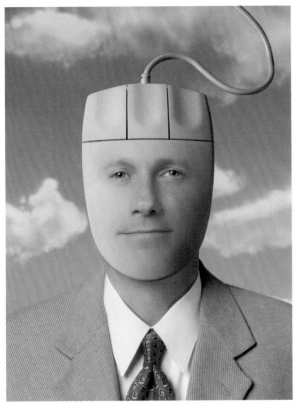

11.3   Photography by Howard Berman

11.4   Photography by Ryszard Horowitz

WORK HISTORY:

<u>1979</u> — Graduated from Pratt Institute with MFA, experimented with Polarized light projection.

<u>1984</u> — Studied computer science at Pratt and wrote simple 3D wireframe animation program.

<u>1986</u> — Designed 3D animation and TV commercials for Fantastic Animation Machine.

<u>1990</u> — Headed up print division at R/Greenberg Associates, worked on TV commercials and feature films (*Predator II* and *Last Action Hero*).

<u>1994–present</u> — Started his own company called Robert Bowen Studio, aimed at creating final art for high-end ad campaigns.

FAVORITE OLD MOVIE MAXIM:

"Time flies like an arrow; fruit flies like a banana." (Courtesy of Groucho Marx)

11.5 Photography by Howard Berman

It's kind of a pleasant idea — bringing life to a difficult world." Another image Bowen created for Adobe's introduction of Photoshop 5.0 is more fanciful (11.5). "I used lots of channel operations and adjustment layers to get the water ripples. The background was an invention created from chunks of photographic stuff that I shot during my teaching stint at CCI (the Center for Creative Imaging) in Maine."

In addition to his paid work for clients, Bowen devotes a modicum of time to creating stock images and purely personal art. Even then, he plays with what is real and what is not. "When I was in Italy, I took a lot of pictures of Roman ruins and came up with what amounts to a game of spaces (11.6). It's just something I did for myself, and this is the first time it's been printed. The whole foreground is tiled from a single arch that's about as tall as it is wide." Bowen cloned bits and pieces of the foreground texture to interrupt the repeating patterns. "If you look closely, you can still find a pattern, but I've worked it until it doesn't annoy me."

The most surprising elements in the image are found inside the archways. What initially appear to be rocky groves are actually distant views of the Roman Colosseum. "Everything about it is a contradiction. I repeated a small fragment to make it large and reduced the large elements to make them small. The overall image has a brooding interior quality, and yet

11.6

11.7   Photography by Ryszard Horowitz

it was all photographed outdoors." Last but not least, out of ruins, Bowen has created an inviolate structure.

"I'm trying to trick the eye without putting one over on anybody. I'm not seeking a photo-journalistic effect, but rather one that is obviously faked with all the hallmarks of realism. In a sense, I'm painting an impossible picture using stuff that you see every day." The most unlikely contradiction of all, however, may be Bowen himself. Soft-spoken and unassuming, widely regarded as one of the easiest people to work with east of the Mississippi, Bowen just so happens to occupy the exact point where reality hits the fan.

MANAGING POPULATIONS OF A FEW MILLION PIXELS

Unfortunately, churning out elaborate visual fantasies is not all fun and games. Bowen has to deal with the same grim facts of Photoshop that confront every other professional image editor. Extreme resolutions and color space conversions take their toll.

"Typically, I work at very high resolutions. And much of what I do is poster art, so the images get very large." A piece of art commissioned by The New School, a New York City art school, is a case in point (11.7). Originally measuring 6,561×4,200 pixels (about 78MB), the image was large enough to double as both front and back cover for the summer course catalog and a poster-sized subway advertisement.

11.8

"The clear blue Caribbean water against the backdrop of the Manhattan skyline made for a utopian view of New York harbor. Parsons also wanted me to push the concept of hats. Students have to try on different hats to decide what they want to be." In order to get the entire image — water, skyline, hats, and all — to fit on this page, we had to downsample the artwork to a paltry 30 percent of its original size. But never fear, we've also included a detail at full resolution (11.8). Regardless of size, the clarity is impeccable.

WORKING WITH SUPER-HUGE FILES

Things must get miserably slow when editing such incredibly large images, particularly when you start slapping on the layers. But Bowen knows from experience that today's slowdowns have nothing on the past. "In the old days, we were working with images this size on IIfx machines. That was pitiful. I don't know how I survived. But with a Power Mac, lots of RAM, and a fast disk array, Photoshop is actually pretty fast, even when I'm working in poster-sized images with 10 or 12 layers. I love Barco on the SGI and Live Picture on the Mac, but I still spend most of my time in Photoshop because of the blend modes and other compositing advantages."

Bowen argues that speed buys you more than lost time; it gives you greater freedom to experiment. "Something big happened to me when the Power Macs came out. Suddenly, I could work in real time. Before then, I had to spend a lot of time planning and imagining what it was going to look like. But with faster machines, I can just do stuff and see it happen on screen. You wouldn't believe what a difference that makes in the way I work. The experience is becoming more and more immediate—almost like working with traditional tools, except that these tools are hundreds of times more powerful."

11.9   Photography by Robert Bowen and Howard Berman

11.10

11.11

CMYK FILES AND RGB TRANSPARENCIES

Some service bureau technicians will tell you that a guy like Bowen never ventures outside CMYK in his life. But like most Photoshop artists, Bowen spends his creative time in RGB with periodic visits to Photoshop's CMYK preview mode (⌘Ctrl+Y). And for about half of his jobs, he never converts to CMYK at all. "When I deliver digital files, I always convert to CMYK. I never let anyone do an RGB to CMYK conversion of a Photoshop file on a different computer. That will always be bad. But lots of times, I give the client an RGB transparency. Then, they scan it with a Scitex or other high-end CMYK scanner. Different clients prefer one or the other."

But with transparencies, aren't you effectively printing a digital file, only to have it rescanned again? "Yes and no. When you record to film, you simply match its full resolution. Unlike printed separations, RGB film resolution is measured in pixels per millimeter, which is called 'rez.' Some film is rez-20, some is rez-40." That's 20 or 40 pixels per millimeter — or the equivalent of 500 to 1,000 pixels per inch — on film that measures 4×5 or 8×10 inches. "A rez-20 transparency is a little soft, a rez-40 transparency is sharper. I stick with rez-40 because I like to deliver a sharper product.

"After that, the transparency is treated like a resolution-independent source, just like photographic film. There's no attempt to scan one pixel in a CMYK file for each pixel in the RGB transparency. It can basically be projected to any size. It's sort of like the difference between 35mm and 70mm film. Both can be projected onto huge screens in a movie theater, but the 70mm film has less grain."

CASE STUDIES AND NONEXISTENT WORLDS

Now that we have all the exposition and technical stuff out of the way, it's time to peek over Bowen's shoulder and see how he creates his artwork. Throughout the remainder of the chapter, we'll pull apart four jobs that have appeared in major magazine ads in recent years. With clients as varied as Panasonic and Johnnie Walker Black, this small collection represents a few of Bowen's best.

STAGING AN ILLUSTRATION

In an ad for Adaptec (11.9), Bowen wanted to create the effect of sudden and dramatic color set against a drab background. "The Adaptec image is one of the best examples of my use of trompe l'oeil. I was inspired by a short story by Jorge Luis Borges called 'The Aleph.' The title refers to a place where you can literally see a whole universe from a single point of view. I turned this idea into a theatrical set. The stage is a loft roof somewhere in Brooklyn on a rainy, dismal day (11.10). But the roof scene is really just a backdrop. The color image of these buildings is leaning up against it, even casting a shadow (11.11). The result is a spatial play."

Bowen's construction is extremely simple. Each element — roof, shadow, color buildings, and vent (lower-right corner) — appears on its own layer. The shadow required some layer masking, but that's it. "Of course, for this particular ad, the client wanted a lot of color. I started by adding some depth inside the buildings (11.11), but then I substituted the green space instead."

This was an unusual ad in that Bowen actually appeared inside it. Photographer Howard Berman shot Bowen against a plain white backdrop, with the base of his coat elevated to indicate a small breeze (11.12). After scanning himself, Bowen created a rough mask around his body, dragged and dropped the selection into the Adaptec composition, and scaled the layer to match its new surroundings (11.13). He finessed the edges with a layer mask and added a shadow by applying Levels adjustments to the background layers. To make the tie-dye pattern in the shirt, he applied a rainbow gradient to a separate layer, subject to the Color blend mode. He also added small color highlights to the function strip along the top of the Wacom tablet clutched in his right arm (11.14).

"There are three levels here, with the gray city interrupted by the color city which is interrupted by the green country. But the thing that interests me most is that the most drab element in the image — the grunge background — is presented as a total fake.

Nothing about the entire image is real, except for me. Even my shirt is a forgery."

DRINKING WITH DOLPHINS

"This next ad is part of a campaign that Johnnie Walker's been running for a couple of years. Each ad shows an individual involved in a creative pursuit set against a natural landscape. There's been a sculptor, an architect, a painter, a filmmaker. One golfer. A jazz bass player. This one is about a computer artist (11.15), a topic that's particularly near and dear to my heart.

"We had lots of pictures for this ad. There were two background shots, both from the California coast." One photograph served as the main background (11.16), with additional waves brought in from the

11.12

11.13

11.14

11.15 Photography by Eric Meola

11.16

11.18

11.17

second image (11.17). "The deck and computer stand are both props that we shot inside the studio (11.18).

The sky in the Johnnie Walker ad is an all-digital creation. If you've ever tried to work with a flat gradient in Photoshop, you know there's always some degree of banding (11.19). The way to get around this is to put the gradient on a separate layer and then apply the Add Noise filter to each color channel independently. For this image, I think I applied an Amount of 8 in the Red channel and 4 in the other two (11.20). I also applied Gaussian Blur separately to each channel at very low values — 0.5 one time, 0.3 another (11.21). In the worst cases, I might create a couple of skies on different layers and then combine them at 50 percent Opacity or so." The inset boxes in the figures show magnified views.

"The dolphin came from two pieces of stock art, including a photograph and a piece of 3D clip art (11.22). Once we chose the stock image for the front part of the dolphin, I imported the image as a template layer into Alias Power Animator on the SGI machine. Then, I rotated and bent the model into the correct position until the wireframe matched the

photo. Then, I antialiased the wireframe and imported it into Photoshop." After aligning the wireframe and dolphin on separate layers (11.23), Bowen brushed in layer masks to erase away the left side of the wireframe layer and the right side of the dolphin (11.24). The result was a graceful transition between the physical and digital worlds. We also had several shots of the computer artist. He's the product of two or three different photos.

"The wireframe shown on the computer screen in the ad is the same 3D dolphin model. But it had to be big enough so you could see it easily and make out

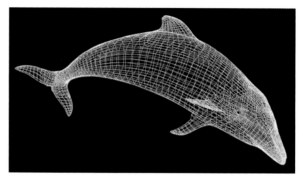

11.22

11.23

11.24

11.19

11.20

11.21

what it was. So I rotated the model into a different position and magnified it so we see just the tail." The relationship between the onscreen tail and the leaping dolphin in digital transition questions the nature of creativity. Is the artist sketching what he sees, or is the dolphin a product of computer-aided manufacturing? Bowen consciously sprinkles these ambiguities throughout his artwork. "I don't know about you, but I've never seen anyone work with a computer on a pedestal. Where's the keyboard? What's it plugged in to? Little puzzles and contradictions such as these invite the viewer to get involved in the artwork."

CRAFTING A SPONTANEOUS SNAPSHOT

"The circus image comes from an ad for a warehouse management product by Computer Associates. The

11.25

BOB URGES YOU TO GO ALL THE WAY

An off-center image is one thing, but a completely cockeyed composition is another. Isn't it? Bowen suggests that it rarely pays to work in small increments. "Let's say a client says to you, 'I want that elephant moved a little to the left.' If you're a little green, you'll do as you're told and move the elephant just the slightest amount. Then the client looks at it and decides that the elephant has nothing to do with it — some other piece of the artwork needs rethinking. All the while, the first impression was right. It was the elephant, you just didn't take it far enough. My advice is to take things too far. Then, evaluate and come back midway if you need to. But don't take baby steps. Take your risks up front and try to push it all the way out there.

"I decided to capture the appearance of an instantaneous photograph. The final artwork is off center to suggest that is was captured with a 35mm camera. For one brief moment, all these animals were just in the right place at the right time. That's what I love about working in Photoshop. You can create a scene that says, 'Here's something ridiculous that happended for a split second. We were forntunate enough to record it on film.' But it's really just another trick."

11.26   **11.27**

11.28

idea was, if your current warehouse management software is like this (11.25), then you need our product."

Although the main subject of the image is based on a living, breathing elephant, she wasn't actually caught in the act of dancing the hula. "A trained elephant can manage to sit up, but it sits on a stool with both legs on the ground (11.26). It can also raise its legs up, but at most two at a time. The final elephant is close to an actual pose, but it's an amalgam of two or three pictures (11.27). Not including the hula skirt or the hat, of course."

One of Bowen's early drafts includes a parrot on the monkey's head and a second little dog on the left side of the weight (11.28). What made Bowen cut these elements out and submit such a strangely balanced composition (11.25)? "When you create these complex composites, you start off with the intention of building the whole world. But very often, after working for a few days and zooming in on a few details, you find that a slice of the image is far more dynamic than the whole. It happens so often that I made a decision up front to experiment with the framing on this image."

THE PHYSICS OF CLONING SHEEP

One of Bowen's most complex images called for a wolf rising up from a sea of sheep. And just to keep things interesting, the client, Panasonic, wanted to see every animal wearing headphones (11.29). "If you're a farmer, then your eyes are probably pretty accustomed to picking out sheep. You might recognize that there are just three sheep repeated over and over a hundred or so times."

Photographer Howard Berman shot the sheep in his studio, complete with headphones (11.30). But Bowen wasn't satisfied with the results. "There's something I call 'cartoon physics.' It applies to anything nonsensical, like the way headphones look on a sheep. The camera doesn't lie, so it shows headphones on a sheep the way they really are. But if they don't look right, then they don't conform to the laws of cartoon physics. You have no choice but to edit them."

But the real fun came in duplicating the sheep into tidy and infinite rows. "For me, this was a fun perspective problem. Philosophically, we know that the sheep in front should be bigger than the ones in back. But what percentage do you scale down the sheep for each row? The solution of course is to apply some more cartoon physics. Maybe try reducing each row by 10 percent. That works for the first four rows, but then you have to try something different. It was a matter of experimenting row by row.

"After I got the sheep arranged in rows, I had to deal with the focal issues. As you can see, there's a depth of field going on here — a nice sharp foreground, getting blurry as we move toward the back. I spent a lot of time applying the Gaussian Blur filter in incremental steps and then painting in shadows."

To us, this job in particular seems like a recipe for aggravation. Photographing sheep, outfitting them with headphones, cloning three sheep into 300, experimenting with depth and perspective, and grappling with some of the more difficult applications of cartoon physics — it takes a while to say, let alone do. "After I put together the rough comp (11.31), I knew right away it was going to be a learning experience. If you compare the rough to the finished piece (11.29), you can see that I had a lot of depth and perspective

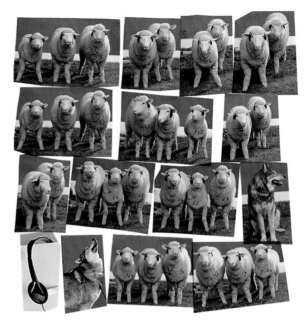

11.30

11.29 Photography by Howard Berman

11.31

11.32 Photography by Howard Berman

11.33

11.34

issues left to work out on the job. Still, I figured it would be interesting, so what the heck? Sure, I probably ended up spending a couple extra days on it, but it didn't kill me."

THE INFINITE DINER

Bowen used a combination of cartoon physics and straight perspective drawing to pull off an ad for IBM servers (11.32). "The idea was that one server could service an infinite number of people." The problem, of course, was rounding up an infinite number of people for a photo shoot. Even hiring 100 or so models — infinitely shy of infinite — is prohibitively expensive. So Bowen again turned to cloning.

"Howard Berman photographed a small group of people — about a dozen — in different locations in the diner (11.33, 11.34). We changed the colors of their clothing, experimented with different camera angles, changed the lighting.

"I finally committed to one camera angle, but we had to use a wide-angle lens, which really distorts space. The center seats had the least amount of distortion, so I built my perspective around them. I ended up repeating a series of seats over and over again, each time scaled to about 50 percent (11.35). I must confess, the finished effect still looks a little wonky, maybe impossible. But it has a consistent vanishing point, which is what you need to create a credible sense of depth.

"In the end, I spent a lot of time retouching the people and the ceiling. The hardest part was the checkered floor. Luckily, there was an overlay of black text in the final ad, which helped cover up some of the weirdness."

11.35

AND NOW FOR SOMETHING COMPLETELY DIFFERENT

Before we said our good-byes, Bowen had the uncommon courtesy to walk us through an image that has nothing whatsoever to do with advertising (11.36). "If you have a pair of 3D glasses lying around — the kind with the red and blue lenses — take a look at this image. It's called an anaglyph. You've probably seen this kind of effect printed in comic books, but I think you'll find that this might possibly be the best anaglyph you'll ever see. You can really feel the space of the great valley between the buildings. It stretches way, way back.

"As you probably know, a stereo picture is made from a left and right view, one for each eye. So I started by taking photos from the position of the left eye and the right eye — actually a little wider apart. In this case, I was shooting from the offices of Apple Computer here in New York.

"Then, I took the photos into Photoshop and converted them to grayscale. I copied the left-eye view, created a new RGB image, and pasted it into the Red channel. Then, I copied the right-eye view and pasted it into the Green and Blue channels of the new image. Switch back to the RGB view, and the two views converge.

"On top of all that, I've added a very simple warp inside Photoshop. I merely applied Filter, Distort, Shear, which is great for creating vertical waves. For me, it's the Shear filter that really makes the picture. You just don't see buildings roll back and forth like that in real life." Not in New York, anyway. Now, if this were San Francisco....

Bob can now create the vertical waves using Photoshop 6's Liquefy function. This new feature enables you to warp, twist, and mangle a selection or whole layer in a fluid form.

By the way, most 3D glasses work better for viewing RGB light than printed CMYK colors. If you want to see the image without any ghosting, you can load Bowen's full-resolution original off the CD-ROM included at the back of the book. "Open it up in Photoshop and zoom into it. Then, move it around. It'll blow your mind." Honestly, if you don't learn one thing from this book, playing around with this image will make it a worthwhile purchase.

11.36

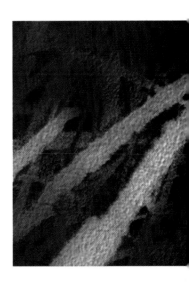

CHAPTER 12
PRINTING FINE ART

T he goal of a typical commercial artist working in print media is to create a piece of artwork that the client can reproduce hundreds, thousands, or even millions of times. Computers are perfect for this purpose because they help you create camera-ready files that include lots of different elements and layers, which eliminates the need for fragile mechanicals and expensive stat-camera composites. When the artist hands off the finished Photoshop file to an art director or client, the file includes all elements fully intact. All the production designer has to do is to convert the image to CMYK, slap it on a page, and send it to the printer.

But not all artists design for mass-market output. Consider the case of fine-artist Karin Schminke, cofounder of the loose-knit Unique Editions. ("We're really just five independent artists who have come together to form a support group.") As the name of the organization implies, Schminke and her colleagues create one-of-a-kind artwork, suitable for framing and hanging on the wall. For Schminke, the electronic files are just approximations of the effect she wants to achieve. The final physical, tangible paper output is the stuff that really counts.

In Schminke's world, a color inkjet printer is just another tool in her paint box, one that she can mix freely with other media. Obviously, she can't paint onto the paper while she's printing, nor can she attach a brush to the printer head, so she does the next best thing—she applies her elements in passes. She frequently starts with a layer of acrylics or other media, prints a lightened version of an image over the dried

It's mostly inaccessible — except to the eye!

KARIN SCHMINKE

acrylic, paints in a few areas, prints over a few other areas, and so on until the artwork looks finished.

"Before I started printing my own art, I looked at what I was getting on the monitor and made decisions based on that. The screen was the determining factor. But once I got involved in the output process, it started to reflect back on the decisions that I made while I was working in the image. There's no longer a break between when I'm done creating the artwork and when it's time to print. It all blends together. Now the printing reflects on everything I do — down to the way I shoot the original photo. And obviously, everything I do affects the print." For Schminke, the printer is a full-fledged element in the creative process, not just a machine that churns out the finished piece. The result is an interactive continuum that weaves Photoshop so tightly into the fabric of the fine-art tradition that it's often impossible to tell a computer was involved at all (12.1).

THE MESSY WORLD OF MIXED MEDIA

Schminke's current digital tools include an Epson Expression 836 scanner, an Olympus Camedia C-2500L camera, Photoshop, and a 44-inch-wide Epson Sylus Pro 9500 inkjet printer with pigmented inks. Her printing stock includes watercolor paper,

specially prepared inkjet canvas, and various cotton rag papers — all available commercially as inkjet products or precoated for use in the inkjet printer in her studio. She paints with just about any media she can get her hands on, including acrylics, pastels, diluted glue for sizing, and photo-sensitive pigments (12.2).

Schminke contends that by mixing digital and traditional media, she can expand her color gamut and achieve subtle variations in hue and saturation that simply can't be achieved with CMYK inks alone. She achieves her effects by printing on top of painted media, painting on top of printed ink, and even double-striking — that is, printing the same image twice in a row to burn in the inks and give them greater depth and range.

Obviously, it's a tricky and unscientific process, one that requires repeated inspection, testing, reflection, and a fair amount of old-fashioned creative brooding. Because she's working with traditional media, it's possible to reach a point of no return. Schminke freely admits that she failed — or at least dead-ended — at an effect that isn't altogether successful and had to start over. Failure is a risk you take when you work in the real world bereft of an Undo command, but it offers its share of unique rewards. And Schminke for one wouldn't have it any other way.

ARTIST:
Karin Schminke

ORGANIZATION:
Digital Atelier
425-402-8606
www.schminke.com
kschminke@schminke.com

SYSTEM:
Intergraph Extreme Z
13GB storage

RAM:
535MB total, 50 percent assigned to Photoshop

MONITOR:
Intergraph 21-inch

EXTRAS:
Wacom Intuos Graphics Tablet
Epson Expression 836 scanner
Epson Stylus Pro 9500

VERSION USED:
Photoshop 6.0

12.1

OTHER APPLICATIONS:
Genuine Fractals PrintPro, Adobe Illustrator

WORK HISTORY:

<u>1979</u> — Learned BASIC computer language in University of Iowa graduate MFA program.

<u>1985</u> — Developed and taught first computer graphics course at University of Wisconsin, Eau Claire.

<u>1987</u> — First exhibition of digital artwork at Wisconsin ArtsWest, a juried fine-art exhibition.

<u>1994</u> — Switched emphasis to fine art and cofounded Unique Editions.

<u>2000</u> — Digital Atelier exhibited large-scale lenticular fine art.

FAVORITE U.S. NATIONAL PARK:
Olympic National Forest, west of Seattle. ("It's got everything.")

PAINTING AND PRINTING, PRINTING AND PAINTING

The best way to get a feel for what Schminke is up to is to watch her work. Through electronic files, process snapshots, and finished artwork, we'll observe Schminke in her studio creating a piece from beginning to end.

CREATING THE SUBIMAGE

For starters, Schminke created the subimage, which is the underlying photographic composition that serves as a backdrop and foundation for her piece "Mountain Meadow." After scanning two of her photographic images to Photo CD — mountains (12.3) and sea foam (12.4) — she layered the second image on top of the first. Then she inverted the sea foam layer and applied the Overlay blend mode from the Layers palette. Finally, she duplicated the sea foam layer and reduced the Opacity to exaggerate the color and bring out additional details (12.5). As you can see, the mountains and trees from the bottom layer are clearer in the composite than they are in the original.

PRINTING THE SUBIMAGE

Schminke decided to create her artwork on rag paper with deckled edges. "It's a rough, natural edge that

12.2

12.3

comes from pulling the paper off the screen during the paper-making process," Schminke says. To bleed all the way beyond the last fibers in the deckled edges, Schminke taped an acetate strip to either side. "I used double-stick tape to paste the acetate to the bottom of the paper. The printer can only print so close to the edges of the media. So the acetate exaggerates the width of the page and enables me to print over the edges."

Schminke ran the 30×42 inch paper through the CalComp printer (12.6) to output the completed subimage (12.7). It's interesting to notice the difference in color between the Photoshop file (12.5) and the printed image (12.7). Likely the result of calibration issues, the inherent gamut of the printer, and the off-white color of the paper, these are conditions to which every artist has to adapt and work around. "Unexpected color shifts in the prints are just a part of the process. I calibrate enough to control them within an acceptable range, and then I make the most of the results," says Schminke.

After stripping the acetate away from the deckled edges (12.8), Schminke applied a layer of protective fixative. "I usually go ahead and apply some kind of spray-on fixative, although I'm not entirely convinced that it works. I apply several coats hoping they'll retard the bleeding of the inks into other media. It helps a little, but it doesn't altogether stop the problem," Schminke says.

12.4

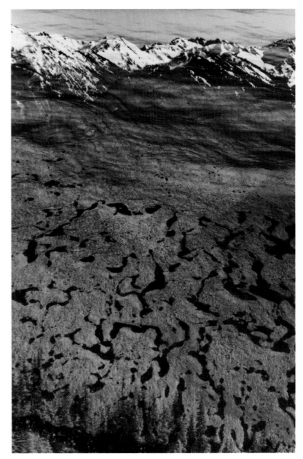

12.5

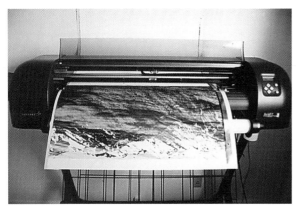

12.6

12.7

CREATING THE INSET IMAGE

Now for the next layer in the traditional media stack—the inset superimage. Schminke created a square composition in Photoshop that features two elks (12.9) layered on top of a leafless tree (12.10). To make the branches work as a framing device, she swapped the left and right halves of the tree. When viewed on its own (12.11), the composition is rather crude, with an obvious seam down the middle. But the seam will disappear when printed onto the final artwork. "With enough experience, you learn what will output and what won't," says Schminke.

A GOLD BACKGROUND FOR THE INSET IMAGE

Schminke wanted the inset image to occupy a square area in the center of the artwork. After laying down masking tape to block out a square in the artwork,

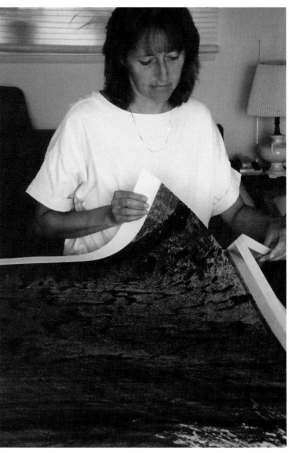

12.8

Schminke applied a coat of gold acrylic paint (12.12). If she had simply overprinted the image, it would have blotted out the artwork below it and turned it into a muddy mess. Instead, Schminke applied an underpainting to distinguish the inset image from its background. "The paint isn't entirely even or opaque. It's kind of a shimmering gold—just enough to set off the inset image from the subimage, so the two mix together while remaining independently identifiable," said Schminke.

TESTING THE OVERPRINT WITH ACETATE

For Schminke, testing the overprint with acetate helps her determine the scale, positioning, and color before printing directly onto the artwork. Schminke

says, "By the time I invest all this effort in the background, I get a little paranoid about printing directly onto the artwork and messing it up. So I'll print onto acetate and use that to mock up the image (12.13). Even though the colors are a lot different than they'll appear in the final artwork, the acetate helps me to determine scale, positioning, and get at least a feel for the color."

The acetate also helped Schminke determine the amount of ink to apply to the final overprinting: "I wanted the elk to appear somewhat 'illusionistic.' You have to look just right to see them—look away and

12.11

12.9

12.10

12.12

they're gone, just like real wildlife." Schminke lightened the image a few notches with the Curves command to get the desired effect.

OVERPRINTING THE INSET IMAGE

When overprinting one image onto another—particularly when a shimmering gold acrylic square is involved—registration has to be right on. "In the case of 'Mountain Meadow,'" Schminke says, "I had to make sure the inset image filled the gold square. In Photoshop, I sized the inset image so it was about a half-inch taller and wider than the square. And I left the masking tape in place as I printed the image. When I stripped off the masking tape, the registration was perfect (12.14)."

Does Schminke run the risk of peeling off paint and ink as she removes the tape? "I'm pretty careful, so it's usually not a problem. But if I do get a little crack or something, I'm mixing so much media that it's easy to go in and touch up the mistakes," she says. Having traditional tools lying around has clear advantages.

Naturally, Schminke uses Photoshop's Canvas Size command to make sure that the images are the same physical size and resolution. But she also has to be careful that the paper is registered properly as it feeds through the printer: "Every printer has something that you can use as an alignment marker. On my CalComp, it's the clamps that hold the paper in place. When I put the paper in for the first time, I make sure to draw little pencil marks on the sides of the artwork by the edges of the clamps. Then when I reinsert the paper for a second or third pass, I can make sure that the paper is properly aligned."

Now, in Photoshop 6, Schminke can choose Print Options from the File menu. This feature enables her

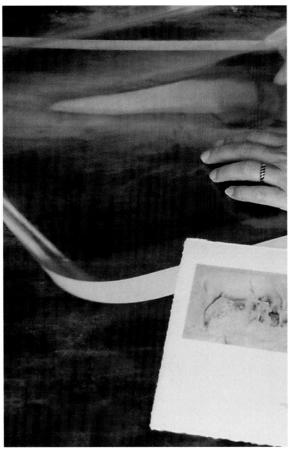

12.13

12.14

to check the Print to Fit Media box, which makes an image fit the paper being printed on and ensures a better overall registration.

PRINTING ON BLACK

The vast majority of commercial art is printed on white paper. Every once in a while, you might come across a flier output on some fluorescent parchment, but most designers regard colored stock with about as much enthusiasm as a school teacher grading a writing assignment on purple notebook paper.

Again, fine artists buck the trend. Recently, Schminke said she got the idea to print on black paper. Offhand, this sounds like a formula for disappointment, particularly given that inkjet printers apply translucent colors. In other words, the printer can darken the paper, but it can never lighten it. The solution, then, is to create an opaque underpainting and print on top of that.

PAINTING ONTO A PRINTED TEMPLATE

Schminke did just that: "I started with a photograph of some lily pads that I brushed and combined with two other photos inside Macromedia xRes (12.15). Then I increased the contrast of the image using Photoshop and printed it onto black rag paper (12.16). The printout wasn't super colorful, of course, but I could see it well enough to use it as a template. Then I painted over the image with acrylics to create the color underpainting (12.17)."

PRINTING ONTO ACRYLIC

Schminke has a suggestion at this point: "If you're going to print on top of acrylic, you need to put some sort of coating over it. A company called Stella Color makes a precoat that you can paint onto anything, and that provides a surface to accept the inkjet dot. Without the precoat, the ink would simply smear across the acrylic."

12.15

12.16

12.17

After applying the coating, Schminke ran the paper through the printer again, overprinting the same image she had applied before (12.18). "Painting an image over itself and then printing on top of that — it's obviously a lot of work. But I was able to come up with a much different image, while at the same time maintaining a consistent theme. It's a good demonstration of how you can take an image and greatly alter it by experimenting with the output. Better still, I sold the piece immediately, and I was asked to submit another version of the lilies to that same gallery."

12.18

PRINTING ONTO LIQUID PHOTO EMULSION

Another media that Schminke uses a lot these days is KwikPrint. KwikPrint is a special brand of photosensitive emulsion that you can apply with a paintbrush. Where the emulsion is exposed to light, KwikPrint adheres to the paper. Where the emulsion isn't exposed, the KwikPrint washes away.

What good is KwikPrint? Schminke says, "I use it for backgrounds. For example, 'Night Vortex' (12.19) is a piece that I created in Photoshop a while back. I really liked the image, but I had never managed to get an exciting print from it. But when I printed it against the KwikPrint background, it just came together (12.20)." It's easiest to see the light-blue KwikPrint in the border around the artwork.

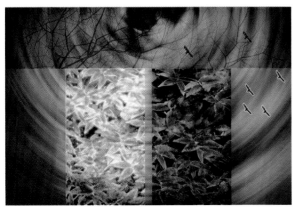

12.19

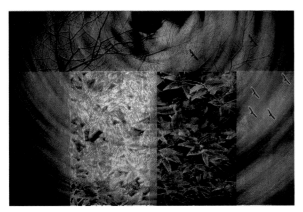

12.20

Schminke started by creating the wavy grass-like texture for the KwikPrint layer as a grayscale image inside Photoshop. Then she inverted the texture to create a negative (12.21) and printed the negative onto acetate. "Actually, I double-struck the negative. Before I took the acetate out of the printer, I had the printer reload it (a special function of the CalComp). The acetate automatically went right back to where it started, and then ran through again. This made the inks denser, so they would completely block out the light."

Next, Schminke pretreated a sheet of paper with iridescent gold acrylic, and then applied the light-blue KwikPrint. She laid the acetate on top of the KwikPrint-coated paper, exposed it for a few minutes to photographic flood lights, removed the acetate, and rinsed off the unexposed emulsion.

"When you apply paint with a brush, the brushstrokes have an inherent texture. But digital output is generally pretty flat, so sometimes it helps to build up a texture with different kinds of paints. The wavy KwikPrint substrate gave this image exactly the kind of texture I had been looking for. It also helped to enhance the color gamut. In 'Night Vortex,' I got colors that were brand new to the digital print world."

PROTECTING YOUR INKJET ARTWORK

High-end color output is notoriously fragile. The ultraviolet (UV) radiation in regular sunlight can cause visible bleaching of color output in a matter of months. Schminke recommends, "You should always

12.21

varnish your inkjet artwork to protect it. The best product that I know of right now is called MSA Varnish from Golden Artist Colors. It's a mineral spirit-based acrylic varnish with high UV protection that comes in three finishes — gloss, satin, and matte. You have to thin it with mineral spirits, not the odorless variety, and you have to apply four coats. The first two coats have to be the gloss because gloss absorbs into the paper the best. The next two coats can be anything, depending on what kind of finish you want. If you apply the matte varnish on top of the gloss, for example, the artwork will have a flat finish that's virtually clear."

According to Schminke, MSA Varnish is designed to last: "A guy from Golden varnished pieces we gave him from several different printers. Then he took some untreated watercolors and acrylics, and put them all under the lights. He kept them there for two weeks, long enough to simulate 30 years of museum conditions. The treated inkjet prints held up as well as the untreated conventional watercolor. It also protects your prints from water — without the varnish, the ink is water soluble.

"Now, this was a company rep, so you have to take his results with a grain of salt. But it goes to show that you should definitely apply some kind of coating. Or hire it out. I've found a local company that applies the varnish for me, because you need good ventilation to use this stuff."

What about UV-protective glass? "When you're shipping art around the country," Schminke says, "you can't use glass at all. It breaks too easily and it adds to your shipping costs. But if somebody wants to put UV glass on top of the artwork after they buy it, that's great. They're just adding another layer of protection."

SHOPPING FOR A FINE-ART PRINTER

For the fine artist on a tight budget, is owning a high-quality inkjet printer a realistic option? According to Schminke, "The industry is just now at the point where an independent artist can afford to purchase a high-end color printer. Right now, I have a wide-format CalComp printer that costs about $10,000. But the prices are falling rapidly. The next generation of that printer will cost more like $8,000, making it accessible for schools and groups of artists. The

smaller 1,440-dpi Epson StylusColor 3000 is less than $1,500. It's looking very close in quality to an Iris," the $40,000 color proofing device from Scitex.

If you happen to be in the market for a high-resolution color printer, one of the most important things to look at is the paper path. "You want the most straight-through paper path you can get, so the paper doesn't have to curl around a lot of rollers. You should be able to feed a stiff paper stock — such as an off-the-shelf watercolor paper — without it hitting up against the head or getting bent or mangled. You might even be able to build a collage and feed it through the printer," Schminke says.

As an ex-service bureau hack, Deke thought the idea of printing on a collage was a recipe for disaster. But Schminke isn't so worried: "I've cut up paper and put it through several times," she says. "Of course, I make sure I don't pile on too many layers. But something like rice paper against a thicker background — that works fine." While technically not making a collage, Schminke has also experimented with printing on coarse and inconsistent surface textures. "I've painted on pumice mixed in with acrylic and then printed on top of that (12.22)." The straighter the paper path, the less likely the paint and pumice will flake off.

"The second issue is the head clearance," Schminke says. "How much room is there between the print head and the surface that you're printing on? All printer manufacturers have approved substrates — papers they've tested that they know will work. But artists are going to immediately start putting their own paper in." Too little clearance causes paper jams and can damage the print head; too much clearance lowers the clarity. "The ideal solution would be an adjustable clearance. But these printers are just starting to come out.

"Finally, you also want to be able to adjust the position of the paper after you've loaded it into the printer. This facilitates overprinting and other alignment tasks."

When making any major purchase, it's a good idea to test the printer firsthand. Schminke recommends that you experiment with different paper stocks as well as different artist materials: "In one test, I laid down a layer of oil pastels and then ran it through a Hewlett-Packard 560c (12.23). The girl, the shadow, and the triangle come from a Photoshop file; the background strokes I applied traditionally."

WHY MIX DIGITAL WITH TRADITIONAL

Some digital purists might venture to suggest that Schminke spends so much time outside Photoshop that she might as well not use the program at all. After all, one of the main reasons that artists turn to computers is to get away from the limitations and sheer messiness of conventional tools. What's to be gained by mixing the digital and traditional worlds?

12.22

As Schminke emphasizes, "Photoshop is an extremely enabling tool. It enables you to try out a lot of different ideas and put artwork together in ways that were very difficult before. Superimposing a photograph on top of a painting — there's an example of something that I simply could not have accomplished without a computer. With Photoshop, you can bring together elements of printmaking, painting, and photography in ways that you couldn't have before.

"It's such a natural mix that one of the artists in my group, Judith Moncrieff, came up with a name for it. We tell people we create 'tradigital' artwork. It fits, don't you think?"

12.23

CHAPTER 13
DIGITAL CAMERAS COME OF AGE

Whether you're a photographer, a commercial artist, or a weekend Photoshop enthusiast, you've probably heard the siren call of digital photography. The very idea that you snap an RGB photograph and download it to a hard disk in less time than it takes to drive to your local film developer and ask, "Are my prints ready?" has a certain universal appeal.

In fact, according to electronic photographer and industry consultant Katrin Eismann, those photographers who haven't yet gone digital can look forward to a complete transformation of their craft. "In the next five years, 80 percent of professional photographers will be involved in some form of digital imaging. That's up from about 30 percent now. Conventional photography as we know it will be a thing of the past very, very soon. The long-term forecast for digital photography is very sunny; digital cameras are now available for practically every use and every budget."

In this chapter, Eismann walks us through the three prevalent issues of digital photography: when to buy and what to look for in a digital camera, and how to edit images in Photoshop once you start snapping pictures. Much as we would like to think that if you've seen one Photoshop image you've seen them all, digital photography presents its own share of special concerns.

My advice is always: Get the image right in front of the lens and fix as little as possible in Photoshop.

KATRIN EISMANN

IS A DIGITAL CAMERA RIGHT FOR YOU?

Naturally, no photographer wants to trade in a tried-and-true film camera for something that isn't capable of producing at least the same level of quality. So it's important that the new technology measure up to the old. Eismann insists that it does. "If you just want a quick yes or no, then rest assured—the quality is there. Numerous professional-level digital cameras are every bit as good as film, in some cases better. More interestingly, if you only need 5×7-inch or 8×10-inch prints, a lot of $1,000 digital cameras put a film camera to shame in terms of quality, convienence, and sheer fun."

Eismann photographed this cat (13.1) with a (at the time when it was released) $10,000 Kodak DCS420, one of the earlier professional 35mm-like digital camera models. In the magnified view (13.2), you can clearly see individual hairs around the eye and capillaries in the iris. You can even make out a reflection of a house with a silhouette of Eismann shooting the picture.

The salt shaker (13.3) is the work of a $30,000 Leaf Digital Camera Back II affixed to a Hasselblad ELX

13.1

13.2

ARTIST:
Katrin Eismann

COMPANY:
photoshopdiva.com
600 Harbor Blvd. #940
Weehawken, NJ 07087
201-223-5410
katrin@photoshopdiva.com

SYSTEM:
Apple G4 450/MP
20GB storage

RAM:
512MB total
400MB assigned to Photoshop

MONITOR:
SGI 1600 Flat Panel display 17-inch

OTHER STUFF:
Ergonomic MacTable ("You have to consider your working environment. I've seen people with $15,000 systems using tables from Wal-Mart."), 12×12-inch Wacom tablet, and Kodak 8600 Thermal Dye-Sublimation printer

13.3

camera body. Even when printed at 300 pixels per inch, the image manages to fill the page — and this is just a detail from the full 12MB file. "If I take a 12MB drum scan off a professional piece of film and compare it to a 12MB image shot with the Leaf DCB II, I'll be able to blow up the Leaf image more because there's no grain in the digital file. The grain is actually nonimage information, and when blowing up a film scan, it is the grain that sets the limit as to how large you can go (13.4)."

But while the quality is dreamy, the costs are enough to shock you wide awake. "Granted, you no longer have to pay for film or developing. But a digital camera costs anywhere from a few hundred bucks for a consumer model to $28,000 at the very high end. And that's not including the $10,000 or more for a desktop system required to process these 5MB to 150MB files. I mean, you're not borrowing your kid's iMac. We're talking about enough money to make a down payment on a home or very nice car."

So the real question is not whether digital measures up to film, but whether it warrants your personal investment. "For every kind of photography, you're going to get a different answer. First you have to determine what photographic niche you fit in, and then you can decide if a digital camera will work for you."

Eismann has identified three major niche criteria — time, quality, and budget. The amount of emphasis you place on each criterion determines what kind of digital camera — if any — will best satisfy your needs.

TIME WAITS FOR NO ONE

"As soon as time is an important factor, digital cameras win hands down," Eismann explains. This includes folks who work in news, medicine, government, or any other arena where pictures need to travel quickly. "At the major news services and *USA Today*, the typical picture deadline for digital files is an hour and a half later than for the guy who's shooting to film. And in the news business, an hour and a half is a major chunk of time."

13.4

Just out of curiosity, how do these roving digital journalists transfer their images? "If you're lucky, you have a land line and you use DSL or a T1 line. But most of these guys work with cell phones, which enable them to transmit from buses and even airplanes, as high as 6,000 feet. And in really remote situations, you might find a guy schlepping around a 20-pound satellite dish to transfer files back to the newspaper picture desk."

A MATTER OF QUALITY

The three primary digital camera technologies in use today are the one-shot, three-shot, and scanning-back cameras. The one-shot cameras work just like your film camera — you push the button the camera takes the pictures and you're done. The three-shot cameras take three black-and-white pictures — one with a red filter, one with a green filter, and one with a blue filter. The camera software then merges the three black-and-white images into one RGB full-color file. A scanning camera does exactly what its name implies — it scans the image. The one-shot cameras are the most similar to film and are perfect if you're taking pictures of people, moving subjects, or need the speed and convenience of a "push the button" system. The three-shot cameras are used for catalog work, and the scanning cameras beat film hands down and are used where the highest image quality is essential — museums, car photography, and art reproductions.

"Digital cameras are really taking over the catalog business. Sharper Image, Harry and David, LL Bean, Bon Marché — they're all digital. Ninety percent of catalog images are printed smaller than 8×10 inches. So, with an approximately $22,000 MegaVision S2 or T3 or Kodak DCS520 (13.5 and 13.6), you've got it made. The catalogs are produced electronically anyway, so there's just no reason to shoot, process, edit, and scan film."

Another quality-related issue to keep in mind is the difference between competing three-shot and one-shot technologies. Both permit you to shoot flash pictures (something the scanning backs don't permit).

13.5

13.6

But where a three-shot camera back captures an image using multiple exposures with red, green, and blue filters, the one-shot camera embeds the filters onto the individual CCD cells. (Incidentally, a CCD is basically the electronic equivalent of film in a digital camera. A huge array of CCD cells—one for each pixel—makes up the imaging surface.) As a result, three-shots are studio cameras ill-suited to moving objects, while the more prevalent one-shots are portable and work like conventional 35mm devices.

But one-shots are not without their failings. "Because you have the RGB filter right on the CCD, you'll often encounter little rainbow patterns in reflective areas and in finely patterned areas such as cloth or hair (13.7). One filtered cell is seeing something that its immediate neighbor does not. With a three-shot, you don't get the rainbows because you're taking full advantage of the resolution of the monochrome array (13.8)." Eismann tells us how to eliminate the one-shot rainbows in Photoshop in the section "Fixing Rainbows" later in this chapter.

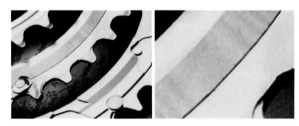

13.7

13.8

If quality isn't important, then you can get by for considerably less money. "For folks who work in documentation, real estate, or insurance (13.9), color and clarity aren't big concerns. If you intend to print the photo on inexpensive paper or post it on the Web, then why even bother with the quality film can offer you?" For these folks, the midrange "megapixel" cameras are ideal. Virtually every major imaging company—Kodak, Olympus, Nikon, Fuji—sells a digital camera that takes pictures with 1,024×768 pixels or more for well under $1,000.

THE COST OF DOING BUSINESS

Assessing your financial niche helps you decide if a digital camera fits in your budget. "At the professional level, this is a major business decision. You have to ask yourself, 'What am I saving by investing in this camera?' The obvious answers are film, Polaroid, processing. But more importantly, you're creating a more efficient environment. You're eliminating that delay between shooting the picture and confirming that the job is done so you can move on to another shoot."

So a digital camera may help you squeeze a few additional shoots into your schedule, or it may prevent another business from encroaching on your territory. "You know who's buying the $10,000 cameras right now? The service bureaus, the prepress houses, the professional color labs. They're offering digital photography as an added value." Therefore, the ambitious photographer will need to pay to play. "You ultimately want to get into the digital workflow and start offering retouching and compositing services. The longer you can stay with your image—shoot it, retouch it, composite it, and submit the final image file in CMYK—the longer you will literally be in business."

FILM STILL HAS ITS MERITS

But surely, even a photographer who fits perfectly into a digital niche is going to experience some separation pangs from film. "Oh, there's no doubt. Give me a conventional camera—be it a Nikon or a Hasselblad—and ten rolls of film, and I can shoot landscapes, portraits, still life, underwater photography—I've got the whole breadth. No digital camera can beat the versatility of conventional film. That's why finding your niche is so important. If you can identify a specific range of photographic requirements, you're more likely to find a digital camera that suits your needs." If a photographer buys a digital camera, it is not about replacing film. Rather, he or she is expanding business—and that's a good reason to add digital photography to your services. By developing a digital workflow, you can offer more services to your client in retouching, design, Web services, and so on, and, of course, you can charge for these new services.

SELECTING THE BEST CAMERA

Digital cameras are in a rapid state of flux. In several cases a vendor has introduced and discontinued a specific model within the same year. So there's no way to create a buyer's guide within the context of this chapter. Computer magazines such as *Macworld*, *Publish*, and *Popular Photography* routinely print camera roundups and are better suited to releasing timely recommendations.

That said, Eismann can offer a few general guidelines for evaluating cameras on your own. "Whenever people look at digital cameras, they always ask, 'How big is the file?' The problem is, that's just one of the issues. The other issues—what does the image look like and how does the camera handle—are ultimately more important. If you have to spend too much time editing the images and you don't like working with a camera, then I don't care how big the images are, you're not going to use it. Your investment is just going to sit around and molder on a shelf."

13.9

So how do you make sure you'll enjoy using a camera? You have to look at what you are going to do with it as well as how much control you want over the camera. Do you just want to point and shoot images? Then go with an automatic camera. If you are a more advanced photographer, then go with a camera that enables you to use manual settings.

"When buying a point-and-shoot device, you want to look at the viewfinder." Eismann shot some pictures comparing one of the least expensive cameras ever produced, the Kodak DC20 (13.10), with a more expensive rangefinder model, the Polaroid PDC-2000 (13.11). She framed both pictures identically, and yet the DC20 shot is mostly hay. "Its viewfinder is just a hole—it's not accurate at all. Here's an example of a camera that's cheap, but what good is it if you can't frame a picture? This is parallax at its worst."

Most rangefinder devices now have color LCD screens (13.12), which can serve as excellent framing aids. But refresh rates vary anywhere from a few frames per second (terrible) to 30 fps (TV quality) or better. And if you're going to use an LCD for live preview, you need lots of juice. "The batteries have to be rechargeable. Some people think this is nit-picking, but wait till you go out in the field and run out of power after half an hour. It can be devastating."

Another consideration is reaction speed. "If you're working with children or animals, having a delay—even one or two seconds—just isn't acceptable." The Polaroid PDC-2000 is an offender here. The camera spends so much time charging its flash that the shutter release may be temporarily inoperable.

"Removable storage is a definite must. This one fellow told me that his camera got digitally constipated. I was like, 'Excuse me, have we met?' But he was right. You have to be able to switch out media when the memory gets full." You have to look at what kind of removable storage you want. You can choose from low-end to high-end, with floppies, smart media, compact flash, Sony Memory Sticks, IBM Microdrive, or mini CDs.

13.10

13.11

13.12

For those of you in the market for a professional level camera, there's no substitute for a hands-on inspection. "Before you sink $5,000 or more into a device, make sure to give it the full digital test drive. Most reputable resellers will be happy to visit you in your studio so you can see how the camera performs on your home turf."

SHOOTING AND EDITING YOUR PHOTOS

Much as Eismann appreciates Photoshop, she doesn't recommend it as a panacea for framing and compositional errors. "What I've seen happen when some people get digital cameras is that they'll get lazy. I was out shooting with this one guy and he takes a picture of a model so she looks like she has a telephone pole coming out of her head. He told me, 'Oh, I'll fix that with the rubber stamp.' I was like, 'Wouldn't it be easier to just move over three feet?' My advice is always: Get the image right in front of the lens and fix as little as possible in Photoshop.

"Another thing: When using the low-end cameras, you should make an effort to shoot really graphic subjects. And get in close — no, I mean closer, no I mean really close." The chickens bear out Eismann's advice. The top group of hens were shot (13.13) with an Olympus D200L, a very good low-end camera in its time. The photographer made a total mess of the subject by standing what might as well be five miles away. The two close-up hens (13.14) are much more successful.

13.13

13.14

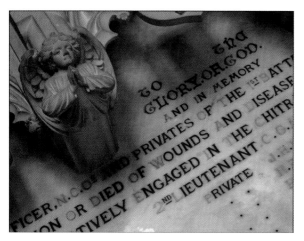

13.15

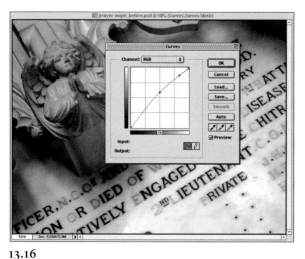

13.16

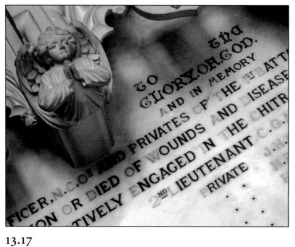

13.17

ADJUSTING LIGHTING IRREGULARITIES

But even with the best of precautions, pictures will go awry. Eismann shot her prayer angel (13.15) at dusk with a Polaroid PDC-2000—which despite its shutter release problem, produces excellent midrange images. The subject is close, the detail is smooth, and the lighting is soft. But when Eismann opened the image in Photoshop, she knew she could add clarity and definition to the image.

She added a Curves adjustment layer (by ⌘/Ctrl+ clicking the page icon at the bottom of the Layers palette). But in adjusting the prayer angel, she managed to bring out the golden color and clarify the edges of the text using Curves (13.16). Luckily, every adjustment layer permits a layer mask that you can use to paint away portions of the color correction. The final image shows the prayer angel and text with the clarity and color of the original (13.17).

FIXING RAINBOWS

Earlier, we explained how one-shot cameras can capture unwanted rainbows along the edge of reflective surfaces. The rainbows appear in full bloom in the chrome Marina logo (13.18), which Eismann shot with a Kodak DCS420. Luckily, you can remedy this problem with little effort inside Photoshop.

The rainbow is caused by disparity between neighboring pixels. So the solution is to blur the colors slightly and then sharpen the detail, both of which you can accomplish in the Lab mode.

First choose Image ➤ Mode ➤ Lab Color to convert the RGB image to Lab. Then go to the Channels palette and click a channel. (If you want to preview the effect in color, click in the eyeball column at the left of the Lab composite.) Apply the Gaussian Blur filter with a Radius of about 1 pixel for every 1MB of image data. In the case of the 4.5MB Marina logo, Eismann applied a Radius of 3. Then switch to the b channel and press ⌘/Ctrl+F to reapply the filter.

So far, all you've affected is the color; the detail is still saved in the luminosity (L) channel. Press ⌘/Ctrl+1 to go to the L channel and choose the Unsharp Mask filter. "I tend to raise the Amount value to 175 percent. And I play with my Radius. Usually it's between 0.75 and 1.5.

"The blurring gets rid of the color artifacting; the sharpening brings out the detail (13.19). Nowadays, I apply this technique to just about every picture I shoot; often there's artifacting that's much more subtle than the rainbows but equally harmful to the appearance of the image. And you can even script this operation from the Actions palette to apply it with a single keystroke in the future."

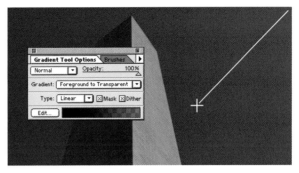

13.20

SIMPLE BUT SPECIAL EFFECTS

"Every photographer occasionally wants to darken edges or burn down corners, where the edges fade in from black, to help frame the image. To do this, I go into the Layers palette and make an empty layer. I select the gradient tool and set it to Foreground to Transparent. The foreground color is black. Then I drag from a corner about a fifth of the way into the image and let go (13.20). I do that in all four corners. Now, it looks like the image has just gotten ruined. But if I set the blend mode in the Layers palette to Soft Light, I can really control how much I want to burn down those edges. Then I experiment with the Opacity until I get the effect I want (13.21).

13.18

13.19

13.21

Low-end cameras suffer from pixel shortages, and they spoil what few pixels they have with an excessive dose of compression. So you have to make the best of what little you have to work with when taking the picture. Eismann recommends:

■   Get in close so your subject fills the frame (13.23). Change your perspective (13.24) and shoot a lot (13.25).

■   Beware of parallax when shooting closer than three feet. (If you anticipate doing a lot of close-up work, get a camera with an LCD preview.)

■   Avoid high-contrast light. "Don't shoot someone at noon, or he'll have dark shadows on his face like a raccoon."

■   If the sunlight does create shadows on your subject (13.26), there's an easy way to fix it. "Just turn on the flash. A daylight flash is called a 'fill flash' because it opens up the dark shadows (13.27)."

■   Because you can see the image immediately, you can improve it immediately. Use the digital camera to shoot a lot, learn, and experiment as you go (13.28).

■   Carry a camera with you wherever you go — you never know when you are going to see something interesting, beautiful, or unique that you can use as a note or foundation for a design project or creative image (13.29).

"Another way to focus the viewer's attention on the foreground image is to blur the background. In the case of the forks (13.22), the background is a light box with gumdrops on it. I used the pen tool to select the forks and the big gumdrops, and then I inverted the selection and applied the Motion Blur filter — not much, maybe 7 or 8 pixels — to give the background a little more dynamic appeal. This also enhances the depth of field, forcing the forks more into the foreground."

13.23

13.22

13.24

13.25

13.27

13.26

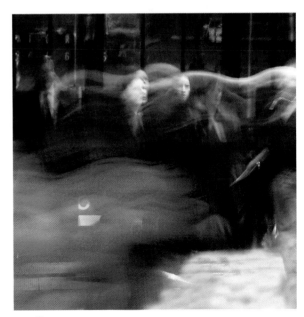

13.28

13.29

KEEPING YOUR PHOTOS SAFE

Eismann offers one last word of advice to photographers making the transition from film. "Archiving may be the most important issue of all for digital photographers. Once again, look at film — it's your capture device, and it's your storage device." There's a good chance that film lasts longer than magnetic media, too. The only electronic media that come close are CDs, which may endure several decades of use. "I even archive my film shots to PhotoCD, because that way, I know I'll use them." What about Zip, or Jaz? "I just use that stuff to transfer files."

What exactly should you save? "Media is too cheap to cut corners. So save everything. For example, a lot of the high-end cameras will automatically shoot into an archived format, with compressed files arranged neatly in folders. You then acquire the images for editing in Photoshop one picture at a time. I always save back the entire archive. As Leaf, Kodak, and other manufacturers improve their software, I can go back and reacquire the images. It's like reprocessing the images with fresh chemicals."

DIGITAL PHOTOGRAPHING FOR THE EVERYDAY USER

It seems that everyone today is looking to shoot digital photographs. Whether it be the new mom and dad sending pictures via the Internet, or distant relatives wanting you to see their new house. Anyone today can afford a digital camera and print his or her images for little cost. Incorporate using Photoshop to fix or improve any images, and your possibilites are endless. Holiday cards, calendars, business cards, and more can be done on your computer at home. Even businesses such as Walgreens have a photo box that you plug your digital camera's card into so you can adjust and make your own prints.

CHAPTER 14
PHOTOGRAPHING FOR PHOTOSHOP

Prior to the advent of computer imaging, photographers' choices were relatively limited. Compositing was by no means impossible, but the costs were high and the results were frequently crude. More often than not, the ideal solution was to set up a shot as commissioned and steer clear of special effects.

For example, if a client asked you to come up with a picture of a pig wearing a baseball cap and tennis shoes, your most efficient approach may have involved calling a few local animal trainers and asking if by chance they handle porkers who enjoy playing dress-up. If such a ham could be hired, the real fun would begin. The fact that clothes are generally designed to fit humans presents a few costuming challenges. How do you keep tapering hooves inside shoes? How do you attach a hat to an animal whose neck is higher than its forehead? And if by chance the beast is not as enthusiastic about fashion as advertised, how much time is wasted as the trainer pulls the battling bacon off the photographer's flattened form?

Chicago-based photographer Jeff Schewe has little doubt that the new ways for creating such images are an improvement over the old ways. Having graduated from the prestigious Rochester Institute of Technology more than a decade before anyone had even heard of Photoshop, Schewe is steeped in the traditional studio experience. He continues to use traditional tools, and his conventional training is every bit as applicable now as it was 20 years ago. The difference is that these days, he sets up his shots with an eye toward editing them in Photoshop.

Each time I start a job, I establish one strategy that encompasses both the photography and the imaging. I can shoot exactly what I need and put it together exactly the way I want.

JEFF SCHEWE

So, if the need arises for Schewe to put clothes on a pig — as indeed it did — he photographs animal and clothing separately and combines them digitally. Schewe explains, "Each time I start a job, I establish one strategy that encompasses both the photography and the imaging. I can shoot exactly what I need and put it together exactly the way I want." Together, camera and computer give you absolute control over the creative process.

HOW EXACTLY DO YOU DRESS UP A PIG?

"The Chicago Board of Trade commissioned me to do a piece that promoted trading in pork bellies. The headline was, 'Hogs are hipper than you think.' So we

got this hog in the studio. He was someone's 4-H pet — his name was Pork Chop — and he came in a large dog carrier. I shot him on a white background (14.1). At first, it freaked him out because he couldn't see anything to stand on. Then, shortly after we got that problem resolved, he got this really relaxed look on his face; then he peed.

"Any time you photograph animals, you have to operate inside the framework of what they'll do. The art director wanted the pig's head up, but pigs are made to keep their noses in the dirt. We went through half a dozen types of food to see which one would get him to lift his head. The one he liked best was whole wheat bread. After a lot of messing around, we got fifty or so shots off. And out of those fifty, the art

14.1

14.2

ARTIST:
Jeff Schewe

ORGANIZATION:
Schewe Photography
624 West Willow
Chicago, IL 60614
312/951-6334
schewe@aol.com

SYSTEM:
Genesis 720 (DayStar, four 180 MHz 604e CPUs)
16GB storage (two 8GB Seagate arrays with JackHammers SCSI accelerators)

RAM:
1GB total
925MB assigned to Photoshop

MONITOR:
Radius 17- and 21-inch PrecisionViews

EXTRAS:
Wacom 12×12 tablet, Light Source Colortron color sampler, Leaf 45 slider scanner, Shinko ColorStream II

VERSION USED:
Photoshop 5.5

director and I got it down to three or four where he looked like he was smiling.

"After we selected the pig picture we wanted, I bought two pairs of kid's sneakers and positioned them very carefully to match the location and angle of the pig's feet. Then, I flew in a scrim to cast a pig-like shadow (14.2). And I put the hat up on a balloon."

We've gone ahead and composited the pig against his clothes to show how well they line up (14.3). The alignment isn't exact, but it's close enough to make the lighting consistent and keep the compositing time in Photoshop to an absolute minimum. How does Schewe line up his shots? "Back in the early days, I used to do complicated tracings. Now, I just hold up the transparency and eyeball it."

The final composition (14.4) involved more than nudging the shoes and hats into place and slapping them onto the pig. "It's very unusual to find an old pig with a curly tail. Their tails are typically docked, and this guy was no exception. So I had to curl the tail by cloning it inside Photoshop. I used the Spherize filter to distort his body and give him an extra 50 pounds. I think pigs look a little happier when they're fattened up." Then, there's that bizarre concern that never fails to pop up in commercial mammal photography. "The art director wasn't terribly comfortable with the exact state of the genitalia, so I more or less unsexed him."

14.3

14.4

OTHER APPLICATIONS:

Adobe Illustrator, QuarkXPress, Valis MetaFlow, Live Picture, Corel Painter, Specular Collage

WORK HISTORY:

1978 — Received B.S. in Commercial Photography from Rochester Institute of Technology, graduated with highest honors.

1981 — present — Opened commercial advertising studio, specializing in large negative compositing and multiple-exposure work.

1984 — Bought first Mac out of back of semi, created first computer imaging job on proprietary system.

1991 — Created first job in Photoshop, structured Photoshop course at Center for Creative Imaging.

1993 — Bought into early adopter program for Live Picture, later brought in as alpha tester for the likes of xRes and Photoshop.

FAVORITE MOTORCYCLE:

BMW R1100GS ("After sitting in a darkened room for hours on end, I like to sit outside for a few hours on end.")

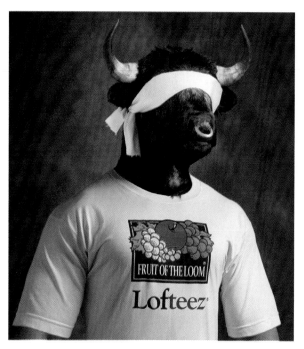

14.5

14.6

MATCHING BACKGROUNDS

When photographing his raw images, Schewe is always careful to match the position of his elements and the lighting conditions. But he's equally careful to match backgrounds. "According to the old wisdom — prior to computer imaging — you used a white background whenever you wanted to composite something, so the printer could make a knock-out litho. In this day and age, unless you want white as your final background, it's the worst color to shoot against. Your edges become overly hot, making compositing very difficult.

"So, I try to make sure that I photograph all elements against a background that matches or is at least appropriate to the final background. For example, the Fruit of the Loom ad shows a bull's head coming out of a muscular guy's body (14.5). I shot the live human element first (14.6) because the live element requires the most care. The art director and I had to figure out the pose, adjust the appearance of the lighting on the T-shirt, play with the body language, and make all the little decisions that come into play when setting up a shot.

"After we picked out a shot we were both happy with, I photographed the bull's head under the same

14.7

light and against the same background (14.7). I positioned it so that the angle of the head and neck pretty much matched the body." With several days between the shots, Schewe must occasionally strike and repitch his backdrops. Doesn't that make it difficult to get everything exactly right? "I don't spend any time trying to register the background for one element to the background of another. I care about the density and the hue, so that the darkness is similar and the colors are approximately the same.

"Finally, I almost always shoot the background by itself. This gives me the option of working with the background as a separate element. So in this case, I masked the body, masked the head, put the head and the body together, and then put them both against the empty background. Because the backgrounds are consistent, I don't have any problems with haloing or weird edge artifacts. I have a little bit of latitude with my masks, and yet my edges appear completely natural, as if I had shot everything exactly as you see it."

Just out of curiosity, where in the world did Schewe come across such a photogenic bull's head? "One of the advantages of working in a big city is that there's no end to the weird stuff a photo-stylist can find. You wouldn't believe the junk you can find if you search long enough. As I recall, we rented two bull's heads for this job, one black and one brown. I think it cost me around $100." Decapitated bulls at $50 a head — there's an offer you can't refuse.

MIXING MULTIPLE LIVE ELEMENTS

When Schewe combines living and inanimate elements, he always starts off by shooting the less predictable living item. Then, he sets up the more obedient inanimate objects based on the position and lighting of the live ones. By starting with the most chaotic element in a composition, he can achieve higher levels of control and order as he works through the job.

But how does it work when he has to shoot two or more live elements? "One job I did called for a centaur — in this case, half woman, half Shetland pony (14.8). Even in Chicago, you can't rent one of those, so I had to merge a woman and a pony together. Any time I work with two live elements, I start with the less intelligent and less versatile of the two. So I had to shoot the pony first and work within the limitations of what he could do.

14.8

"After taking a lot of shots, we managed to get an attentive pose with the head high up (14.9). I'm imagining the woman taking the place of the pony's head, so I need the neck nice and vertical. Once I got the transparency back from the lab, I was able to position the woman so she stood at the same three-quarter angle as the animal's head (14.10). We also outfitted her in a wig that was more or less the same color as the pony's mane."

METICULOUS PATHS FOR INTRICATE EDGES

Obviously, Schewe's compositions involve some complex masking. But he works a little bit differently from other artists. "I use paths to create about 80 percent of my selections (14.11). I usually draw the paths at 200 percent view size so that I can clearly see the line of demarcation between the subject and the background (14.12). I can literally decide while I'm creating the path exactly where I'm going to clip something. If I see a piece of material that looks goofy, no problem; I just clip it away."

Schewe acknowledges that paths can be exasperating and time-consuming, particularly when taken to these extremes. "But I've found that if you spend the time up front making a really excellent selection, you spend far less time fixing problems in your final composition."

14.9

14.10

After Schewe completes his paths, he converts them to a selection, saves the selection as a mask, and adds soft edges where needed using filters such as Median and Gaussian Blur (14.13). "One of my strategies is to mimic the photographic resolution of an image as accurately as possible. If something is critically sharp in the photograph, I'll make sure it's critically sharp in the selection. If it's slightly soft in the photo, it'll be slightly soft in the selection. Again, it takes a while to get it just right, but it's worth it in the end."

14.11   14.12   14.13

14.14

14.15   **14.16**

ALL AGAINST A GRADIENT BACKGROUND

Here again, Schewe layered his elements against an empty version of the background. "But this time I lit the background more dramatically, so that it was dark at the top and lighter at the bottom. Then, I played with the gradation and lighting inside Photoshop to get the final effect I was looking for (14.14)."

Merging the elements together was mostly a matter of blending the horse's neck into the woman's torso. "I selected the horse from the neck down and the woman from the waist up, and then I layered them against my empty background with the woman in front (14.15). I added a layer mask to the front layer to fade out the woman's torso (14.16). I also had to distort the pony's mane to send it flowing into her hair, and I lightened her hair to match the mane. There's always a lot of back and forth work in an image such as this, even when the original elements are so painstakingly matched."

PLAYING WITH SCALE

If a shot involves strictly inanimate objects, you might expect Schewe to set up the scene exactly as he wants it and steer clear of Photoshop. But that's rarely the case. "You have all kinds of reasons to shoot inanimate

14.17

elements in groups and composite them in Photoshop." A good example is the spud family portrait that Schewe created for a potato fungicide ad (14.17), which toys with the notion of relative scale. "I've got three different levels of scale going on here. A potato isn't really big enough to wear a hat or jewelry. And both the potatoes and their accessories would have been dwarfed by the TV if they were really seated as close as they're pictured in the ad. So I had to shoot each of the three groups of items separately.

"The main background shot is the TV against a plain wall with this kind of skylight lighting (14.18). That's relatively a straight shot — I may have gone in there and experimented a little bit with the gradations. Then, I propped the potatoes against a little model of a sofa (14.19). The pattern on the sofa is even miniaturized so that the flowers look the same relative size as they would on a real sofa.

"I had to play with the light so that the potatoes cast the same shadows as the TV, despite their smaller size. This was largely a matter of bringing the lights in closer and adjusting the intensity. I also included a little blue light down in front so it looked like a glow was coming from the TV. You can see that the blue glow doesn't exactly match the blue from the TV screen — it's a little more purple — but I was able to correct that

when I composited the images in Photoshop (14.20). The light was really just a color cue so I could see how a cool glow would reflect off the potato bodies.

"Then, I needed the beanie for the baby spud, the pearls for Mom, and the glasses and pipe for Dad (14.21). I shot two pipes because the art director

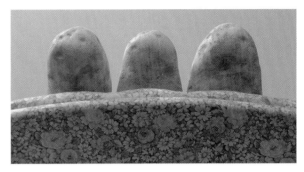

14.19

14.20

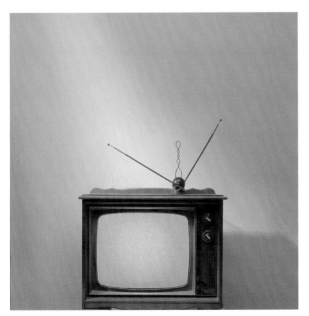

14.18

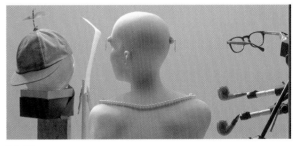

14.21

couldn't decide which one he wanted to use. There was also a discussion about whether we should add earrings to the side of Mom, so the mannequin actually has a couple of earrings stuck to her head. As usual, I had to adjust the lighting, including bringing the blue glow in from the left side. That sheet next to the mannequin is there to reflect the glow onto the beanie. Then, I shot it all to a single piece of film to keep the scanning to a minimum.

"The one element that's strictly digital is the smoke coming off the pipe (14.22). I added the smoke inside Photoshop by airbrushing with a small brush and light Exposure settings. I believe I split the pipe and glasses onto separate layers and then added the smoke on another layer in between the two. That way, I could erase the smoke and adjust the Opacity without harming any of my original elements.

"My one big conceptual contribution was to put a bowl of potato chips on top of the TV (14.23). The

art director loved that. But then, somebody actually wrote the company to complain about the suggestion of cannibalism." Either it's a tuber-based homage to Soylent Green, or these are some very sick taters.

REFLECTIONS AND REFRACTIONS

According to Schewe, glass and water are some of the hardest substances to photograph. "Because of the way they reflect and refract the elements around them, you have to be very careful with your lighting." Things become even more complicated in the compositing phase. Any time you position an element near glass or water, you duplicate and distort the element to account for reflecting and refracting.

Schewe's snowglobe artwork is an example of just how difficult the process can get. "The concept was to take a snowglobe filled with a little snowy golf scene and then composite it against a stock photo of a golf course (14.24). Again, we have an issue of scale — an enlarged globe against a reduced background — but the more complex task is the globe itself. I guess I

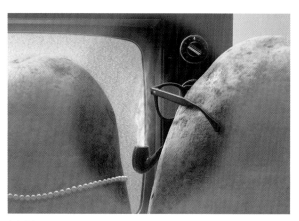

14.22

14.23

14.24

could have built a little golf scene inside the globe, kind of like a ship in a bottle. But I doubt that would have given me enough control over the lighting and refraction. For me, it was easier to photograph the pieces and glue them together inside Photoshop."

WITH AND WITHOUT FLAKES

"I started by shooting a snowglobe on a stand, under what appeared to be hard outdoor light (14.25). I set the globe against a green background with a blue overhead to simulate the general appearance of grass and sky. The globe had a rubber stopper at the bottom of it so I could empty the water and fill it up again. After shooting it empty, I took several shots of the globe with the snow floating around inside it (14.26). Interestingly enough, to get the amount of snow I wanted, I had to break open three small Jesus snow-globes and steal the snowflakes from them."

Schewe modeled the contents of the globe from scratch (14.27). "I contoured the base out of foam

and coated it with fake snow. The miniature trees came from a model train set. I painted a long thin dowel to make the flagpole, and then I added a piece of red tape for the flag."

14.26

14.25

14.27

14.28

INNER AND OUTER REFRACTIONS

Having photographed his raw materials, Schewe began to assemble them in a layered Photoshop file. "I started by masking away the background behind my snowy golf scene. Then, I used Filter Distort ➢ Spherize to warp the scene around the globe (14.28)." Schewe spent some time examining the way a globe refracts light to get his layers just right. "A glass ball is a curious thing. It bulges elements inside it, but it flips and pinches the stuff behind it. If you look at the original globe shot (14.25), you'll notice a layer of blue along the bottom of the glass. That blue is actually hovering a few feet above the frame." Peering through two surfaces of curved glass — one concave, the other convex — turns the world upside-down.

"To get this effect, I selected a portion of the stock photo background, rotated it 180 degrees, and then applied Filter ➢ Distort ➢ Pinch two or three times in a row (14.29). I think I also used Spherize with a negative setting a couple of times to give it some roundness. After that, I added my spherized golf scene (14.30). Because it's just behind one layer of glass, it appears right-side up."

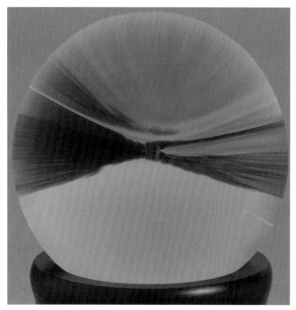

14.29

14.30

REINSTATING THE REFLECTIONS

By this point, Schewe had covered up the reflections from the original globe, which diminished much of the realism of the image. To restore the reflections, he selected some of the highlights from the base globe layer and duplicated them onto a new layer.

"The best selection tool for this purpose is Select ➢ Color Range. The Color Range command has a great inclusion/exclusion capability, but it's global — that is, it selects colors from all over the image that fall inside the range. So, when I use Color Range, I make three passes. With the same colors selected, I'll run high, medium, and low Fuzziness values. I'll save each selection to a separate channel. Then, I'll combine elements from each of those channels to create the final mask."

After arriving at a satisfactory mask, Schewe selected the highlights — which we've set against black to make them easier to see (14.31) — and copied them to a new layer, which he dragged to the top of the stack. Then, he selected Lighten from the blend mode pop-up menu in the Layers palette, which instructed Photoshop to hide any pixels in the reflection layer that were darker than the pixels below. The result was a universally lightening effect (14.32).

SPRINKLING THE SNOWFLAKES

The last step was to add the floating snowflakes. "The snowflakes needed to be in front of the trees and pinched background, so I had to select them from the snowflake shot and composite them on top." Again, Schewe selected the flakes with the Color Range command (14.33). Then, he pasted the flakes on top of

14.32

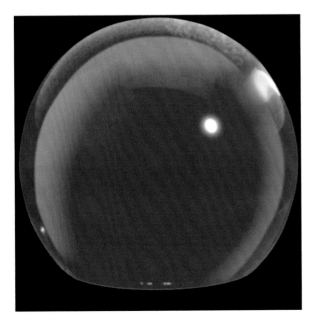

14.31

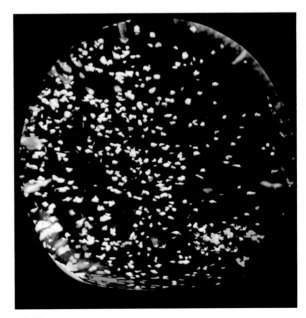

14.33

the composition (14.34). "The interesting thing here is that the flakes already had reflections built into them, because I photographed them inside the globe. So it didn't matter if I stacked them on top of the reflection layer or underneath; either way, it looked the same."

MERGING PASSION AND PROFIT

In the periodic skirmishes between photographers and digital artists, Schewe manages to occupy both fronts. It's a lucky thing, too, because his photography gives him a clear advantage over artists who

14.34

depend on stock images. "One of the things I try to emphasize is that you just can't take disparate images, jam them together in Photoshop, and expect them to be convincing. You can be really skilled and create an interesting montage, but you'll never achieve realism. It's the difference between a photographic marriage and a digital relationship."

Schewe manages to marry image capture and image manipulation so seamlessly (14.35 and 14.36) that you would swear there was never any doubt in his mind that he wanted to be a digital artist. But in truth, his transition to computers had as much to do with maintaining his livelihood as following his creative passions. At the risk of sounding crass, Photoshop is where the money is.

"Right about the time Photoshop came out, I had a couple of jobs where the computer imaging paid twice as much as I made for the photography. It was immediately clear to me that these computer people were taking a big chunk of the overall production pie."

Schewe did what any enterprising photographer would do. After quickly assessing that there was no beating 'em, he joined 'em. "I rented a Macintosh IIci (roughly equivalent to a 386 PC) and spent the weekend doing a job and learning Photoshop at the same time. I picked up the computer Friday night, and I had the job done Monday morning. My wife came in and found me asleep at the keyboard.

"The final piece was output to 4×5 film, and the client was tickled to death. At that time, I charged just about what it cost me to rent the computer for the imaging. It was definitely a valuable way to start out." Schewe has been evolving his craft on the job ever since.

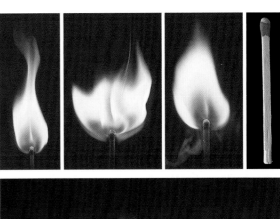

14.35

14.36

CHAPTER 15
CREATIVE QUICKTIME VIRTUAL REALITY

The physics of photography use optics and light-sensitive materials to fix the three-dimensional world onto a two-dimensional surface that reflects a fixed point of view at a specific moment in time. But wait, photography is more than a physical reaction of light hitting silver. The art of photography includes the photographer's interpretation and the craftsmanship that polishes the initial exposure into a final piece. How does a photographer decide when to take a picture that reflects the mood of a scene? Is one picture enough to convey the atmosphere or to tell the whole story? Many times it isn't, and if you have ever looked at a photograph and wanted to see more or wondered what was just outside of the frame, then QuickTime Virtual Reality (QTVR) photography will intrigue you, as you view a scene with a 360-degree point of view, zooming in on details or moving back to see the bigger picture.

Developed by Apple Computer and released in 1995, QuickTime VR enables photographers, artists, Web designers, museum directors, real estate professionals, forensic experts, and others to take pictures with standard 35mm cameras or digital cameras and then stitch the images to create panoramic scenes that place the viewer in the middle of a 360-degree image. But isn't this book about Photoshop and not about dry definitions of photography and the history of Apple Computer software development? Yes, and this is exactly where Janie Fitzgerald enters the scene. Fitzgerald is a photographer and digital imaging artist who has been working with QTVR since before Apple launched it to the public in May of 1995.

> *QTVR is interesting and unique; it may be around for a while.*
>
> JANIE FITZGERALD

As Fitzgerald explains, "When I saw QTVR for the first time, I was intrigued. I went to several presentations that Apple gave, to understand how QTVR was photographed. When Apple finally gave me specifications for how to shoot QTVR, I went to New Orleans and shot some VR scenes without knowing what the next step was. When I came back, I went to another Apple seminar on QTVR and showed them my prints, which I had Scotch-taped together from 360 scenes. Apple then asked if I'd be interested in shooting QTVR of the Salk Institute in La Jolla, an architectural study they wanted for the Apple Web site for the launch of QTVR. It was actually my first job in QuickTime VR."

QTVR AND THE PHOTOGRAPHER

"I have always loved making pictures. QTVR is a blend of still imagery and motion pictures. QTVR is unique and it's nonlinear, meaning there is no timeline in the same way there is in a movie track. Viewers have the choice to look not only *where* they want but *when* they want." An excellent example of how working with and viewing QTVR adds to the art of photography is one of Fitzgerald's early pieces. The opening scene of a New Orleans dress shop window (15.1) is reminiscent of Jean Atget's (1857–1927) body of work, which documents the empty streets, shop windows, and parks of Paris at the turn of the

15.1

15.2

ARTIST:
Janie Fitzgerald

ORGANIZATION:
Axis Images
P.O. Box 381195
Los Angeles, CA 90038
www.axisimages.com
janie@axisimages.com

SYSTEM:
Macintosh G4-Dual Processor 500
Macintosh 8500/180 (for audio)
G3 PowerBook
Mac OS 9
60GB Storage

RAM:
256MB total
150MB assigned to Photoshop

MONITOR:
Apple 21-inch and an Apple 17-inch

EXTRAS:
Wacom Tablet
CD-ROM and DVD Burner
Flatbed Scanner
QS-8 Audio Synthesizer
Epson Stylus Photo EX printer

VERSION USED:
Photoshop 6

century. Fitzgerald's store window reminds viewers of earlier, idealized times. As you pan to the right, you see more information (15.2), and the meaning and interpretation of the image change dramatically as you zoom in on the art that is for sale (15.3 and 15.4).

FITZGERALD'S COMMERCIAL WORK

Fitzgerald specializes in panoramic and interactive panoramic QTVR. Her commercial clients include Apple Computer, Eastman Kodak, Dodger Stadium (15.5), and the *Los Angeles Times,* for whom she recently shot the QTVR to accompany an article about

15.4

15.3

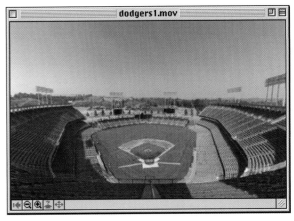

15.5

PHOTOGRAPHY EQUIPMENT FOR QTVR:

Nikon 35mm with 15mm, 18mm, 20mm, 24mm, and 28mm lenses
Nikon CoolPix Digital Camera
PanoScan Digital Camera
PeaceRiver 360 Panhead
Kaidan Multi-Row Pan Head
Kaidan Magellan 2000 Object Rig

OTHER APPLICATIONS:

Apple QTVR Authoring Studio, VR HotWires, LiveStage Pro, ConVRter Studio Vision Pro, SoundsaVR, MapsaVR, Premiere, Adobe GoLive 5.0.

WORK HISTORY:

1980s — Worked in a 3D animation studio in Hollywood; learned photography.

1992 — Opened studio in Los Angeles. Photographer for Christo's Umbrellas Project and concerts for Peter Gabriel's W.O.M.A.D.

1994 — Went to a party at the American Film Institute for the launch of Apple QuickTime 2.0; saw first demonstrations of QTVR movies.

1995 — QTVR 1.0 released. Shot QTVR in Louisiana, Yosemite National Park; Bath, England; and for Warner Brothers.

1997 — Photographed *Batman & Robin* movie sets for Warner Brothers and Apple Computer. Produced *www.vrview.com*, a gallery dedicated to the noncommercial QTVR, sponsored by Apple Computer and the Eastman Kodak Co.

1998 — Special Projects Director for the International QTVR Association. Produced the Sacred Worlds Project (*www.vrview. com/sacredworlds*).

2000 —Worked in Switzerland on a large scale VR project, designing a magazine of virtual environments. Worked in Italy and Germany for Active-Film, a German company. Photographed cubic QTVR movies in Paris and London for her company, Axis Images.

2001 — Shot QTVR of the N.A.S.A. space centers.

15.6

15.9

the Spanish missions in California. Notice that you have the choice to view a high-resolution (400K) or a low-resolution (100K) version, depending on your connection, patience, and need for quality (15.6). With a 28.8 modem, the high-resolution QTVR files take approximately 2.5 minutes to fully download into browser cache and the low-resolution version comes in well under a minute. Interestingly enough, the entire

15.7

15.8

15.10

file doesn't need to download before the you can begin to pan around the image. You can choose to see the inside (15.7 and 15.8) or the outside of the Mission (15.9 and 15.10). For the Hard Rock Café, Fitzgerald shot dozens of scenes and created a multinode QTVR movie. By clicking hot spots linked to additional QTVR movies, the viewer can move from scene to scene (15.11–15.14).

15.11

15.13

15.12

15.14

FITZGERALD'S PERSONAL WORK

Fitzgerald's personal work reflects a sharp sense of humor and interpretation that takes the viewer by surprise as huge bugs come into the scene. In the QTVR movie *Island*, a collaborative project with artists (and 3D specialist) Robert West, the artists hot-glued plastic bugs to flowers that Fitzgerald photographed with a blue screen to assist in the masking and selection process. The background image is the "bug's eye" view of a gas station. Fitzgerald used Photoshop (15.15) to lay out the images against one

another and Apple QTVR Authoring Studio to make the final movie (15.16 and 15.17).

In some of Fitzgerald's other personal work, the image becomes so abstract that you feel as if you are seeing into her mind's eye (15.18 and 15.19). "Most people think that you have to shoot original photography to make a QTVR movie, but I love to rework my older photographs with Photoshop to create new images for QTVR." In this example, Fitzgerald reworked an original collage (15.20) into a QTVR movie to create an image that is more effective with motion than the still image was alone (15.21 and 15.22).

15.15

15.16

15.18

15.17

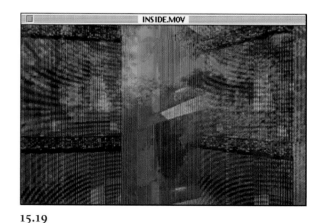

15.19

THE VRVIEW WEB SITE

In addition to doing commercial work and developing a large body of personal work, Fitzgerald also produced and maintains *www.vrview.com,* a Web site dedicated to the artistic exploration of QTVR, featuring the work of numerous international artists (15.23–15.25). VrView was designed by West, whose own site can be found at *www.vrview.com/robertwest.*

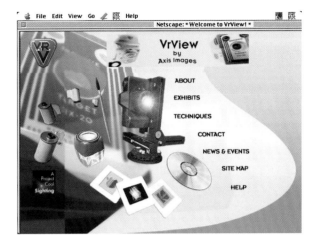

15.23

15.20

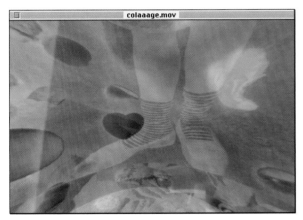

15.21

15.24

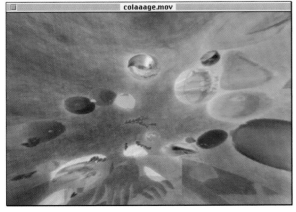

15.22

15.25

15.26

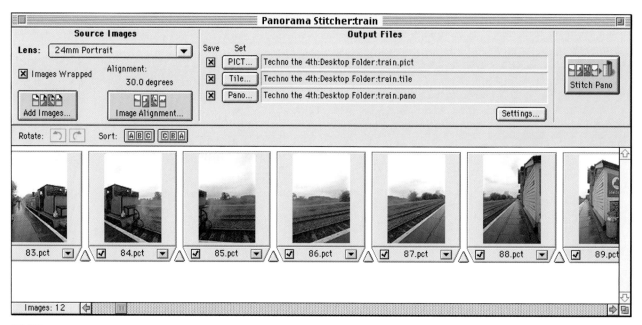

15.27

QTVR IN A NUTSHELL

A QTVR panoramic movie begins with the photographer in the center of the environment taking a full set of photos in a 360-degree circle. "Depending on how wide your lens is, you take 12–18 pictures that overlap by 25–40 percent to complete the 360-degree circle of view. After the film is processed, scanned, and prepped in Photoshop, the individual PICT files (15.26) are brought into Apple QTVR Authoring Studio (15.27) and stitched together to create a single 360-degree image (15.28)." The resulting QTVR movie (15.29, 15.30) makes you feel as if you are standing on the train platform waiting for the train to pull out of the station.

PHOTOGRAPHY FOR QTVR

Shooting photographs for QTVR on location takes a lot of concentration. Fitzgerald takes the following approaches to ensure that she captures the best images:

■ Find the best image composition and check that the camera placement, height, and orientation are optimal for the scene. "Shooting in a portrait orientation will give the image better visual height."

■ Examine the entire 360-degree scene through the viewfinder and with the lens that will be used for the shoot, concentrating on the foreground to background relationships. QTVR images that have something in the foreground are more interesting and give the viewer a feeling of being in the scene.

■ Study the light in the scene. "When working on location with a 15mm lens, it is practically impossible to use flash to light a scene because the lens is so wide. If a scene has existing lights, I may exchange the light bulbs for stronger ones. If the situation requires strobes or full lighting, there needs to be plenty of time dedicated to lighting the scene."

15.28

15.29

15.30

■ "I use a light meter and work with the camera on manual exposure with the lens stopped down to ensure greater depth of field." If the light range varies a lot, Fitzgerald shoots the entire scene once and then with the camera still on the tripod, she pans back and brackets the exposures to take a set of images for the light parts of the image and a set for the dark parts of the image. "I work with color negative film because of its greater exposure latitude in regard to lighting and exposure." After the shoot, the bracketed images are merged in Photoshop to create one set of images that are well exposed for both the highlights and shadows.

■ "It is so easy to forget where you started or if you missed an exposure or not, so concentrating on the task is essential. I can't just go back to a location and reshoot a frame or two if I missed it the first time."

■ Fitzgerald tends to overshoot. It is better to shoot an extra set of exposures or redo a set if you have any doubt that you missed a frame. Using an extra roll of film is much more efficient (read cheaper) than having to go back to a location and redo an entire shoot because you missed an exposure.

Here are some additional considerations for capturing the best images for stitching:

■ "I work with a panoramic tripod head that can be moved in exact increments, which ensures that each exposure will have the same amount of overlap."

■ Allow for 25–40 percent overlap between images. This enables the stitching software to create seamless images.

■ Rotate the camera on the nodal point of the lens. The nodal point of the lens is the specific point where light rays intersect on the image plane and the image flips. Aligning the camera on the nodal point will minimize parallax errors that make elements look as if they are sliding in the image when the viewer pans.

■ Photographing the correct number of frames will simplify the stitching process. Tables 15-1 and 15-2 list the most common lens formats for 35mm cameras and digital cameras and how many images to take.

TABLE 15-1   NUMBER OF PHOTOGRAPHS FOR 35MM LENSES

LENS FOCAL LENGTH	PORTRAIT	LANDSCAPE
14mm	12	6
15mm	12	6
16mm	12	6
16mm fisheye	12	4
18mm	12	8
20mm	12	8
24mm	12	8
28mm	18	10
35mm	18	12

TABLE 15-2   NUMBER OF PHOTOGRAPHS FOR CONSUMER DIGITAL CAMERAS

CAMERA	PORTRAIT	LANDSCAPE
Apple QuickTake 200	18	12
Canon PowerShot 600N	12	8
Epson PhotoPC 500	18	14
Fuji DC 300	16	10
Kodak DC-50	18	12
Kodak DC-120	18	12
Kodak DC-210	14	8
Olympus D-200L or D-300L	16	12
Polaroid PCD-2000	18	12

PHOTOSHOP PRODUCTION FOR QTVR

As mentioned earlier, Fitzgerald works with 35mm color negative film. When she has the film processed she does not have prints made and, most importantly, she doesn't have the film cut into strips. "It is much easier to evaluate and find the beginning and end of a panoramic shoot if the film is left intact." After the film is processed, she has the required files scanned onto a Kodak PhotoCD Master disk. A PhotoCD scan comes in five different resolutions. Fitzgerald uses the 768×512 or 1,536×1,024 files for her QTVR work. "I like working with the larger files, because they have more image information and I can do finer retouching and correction with them." The wider your lens, the fewer pictures you have to take and the fewer images you will be stitching together, which will be reflected in a smaller stitched file, as shown in Table 15-3.

After acquiring the individual files in Photoshop, Fitzgerald retouches the files and matches the exposures using image adjustment layers. "The stitching software can balance out slight differences of exposure, but prepping the files in Photoshop before stitching helps the stitching software to build scenes that don't have obvious seams."

After bringing the individual files into Apple QTVR Authoring Studio, Fitzgerald stitches the files to produce a movie and a PICT file (15.31). She opens the PICT file in Photoshop and fine-tunes the color balance with an image adjustment layer (15.32) and masking (15.33). She then imports the improved PICT file back into Apple QTVR Authoring Studio's Panorama Maker and stitches a new panoramic QTVR movie. Fitzgerald also reworks straightforward PICT files, as shown in this example of the Salk Institute (15.34 and 15.35) and the resulting movie (15.36 and 15.37).

TABLE 15-3   PHOTOCD RESOLUTION CHOICES

RESOLUTION	INDIVIDUAL FILE SIZE	STITCHED FILE	MOVIE SIZE
768×512 (medium resolution)	1.1MB	5–7MB	500–600K
1,536×1,024 (high resolution)	4.5MB	20–25MB	1–2MB

15.31

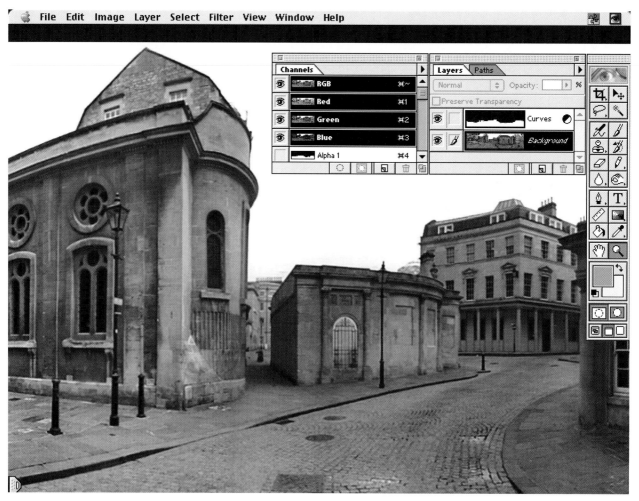

15.32

15.33

15.34

15.35

15.36

15.37

15.38

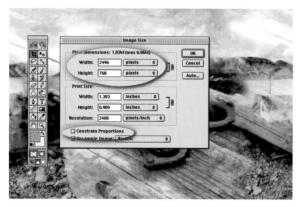

15.39

PROPORTION AND COLOR

In some of her work, Fitzgerald uses Photoshop to build QTVR spaces that seem familiar yet have an unsettling perspective. "I have a lot of photographs that I shot before QTVR and I use Photoshop to rework them to build QTVR movies." In *Chained Home*, Fitzgerald started with a double-exposure (15.38) and used Photoshop to stretch and tone the image before stitching it.

The most important thing to remember when creating original files for QTVR or when resizing existing files is to make sure the file's pixel width is divisible by 24 and the pixel height dimension is divisible by 96 (15.39 and 15.40). "The stitching process actually slices the image into 12 or 24 tiles, so making sure that the file's width and height follows the 24/96 rule will prevent any problems in the final part of the process.

"When experimenting with the KPT filters, I work on an empty new layer until I find a combination that I like. By keeping the effects on a separate layer, I can experiment without affecting the original background layer (15.41)." The curvature of the final movie adds to the sense of space and distance in the scene (15.42).

15.40

15.41

15.42

To add color to black and white and/or infrared photography (15.43), Fitzgerald also uses the duotone feature in Photoshop. In Photoshop 5 and above, duotones can be previewed. Fitzgerald experiments with tritones and quadtones to give her infrared images subtle color palettes that look like finely toned black-and-white gallery prints (15.44).

To add the finishing touches to the scenes, Fitzgerald uses QTVR Authoring Studio to determine where a viewer will start when he or she opens the QTVR file for the first time. When working with an individual PICT file, she imports the image into the Panorama Maker in QTVR Authoring Studio (15.45). After clicking Make Pano, a preview window appears that enables her to visually determine where the movie will open to in the image (15.46). By having the opening scene zoomed in on the cross, the viewer is taken by surprise and needs to take a moment to zoom out of the image to become oriented and see that they are "standing" in a graveyard (15.47–15.49).

15.43

15.44

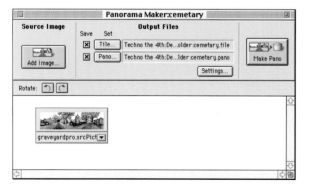

15.45

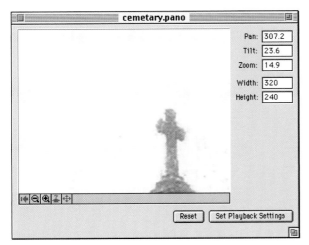

15.46

15.48

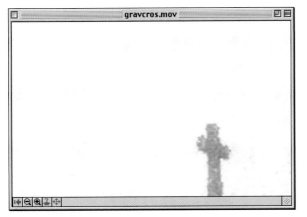

15.47

15.49

Fitzgerald explains, "QTVR is a fascinating way to look at an environment or to tell a story, and I hope that my images inspire a sense of wonder." In these desert scenes, the use of infrared film and heavy toning add to the oppressive yet seductive atmosphere in the image (15.50). The fact that the movie opens right on top of a cactus adds to the dramatic style of the scene (15.51).

IMAGINARY SPACES

QTVR is often used to document the real world, but Fitzgerald likes to create unusual worlds that don't exist anywhere in reality. In one example, she took beautiful macro shots of roses and used Photoshop to combine them into a long PICT file (15.52) that, when stitched, gives the viewer a decadent bug's eye view of a lush rose garden (15.53 and 15.54). "Everyone thinks that you have to start with a set number of photographs to do QTVR, but I often experiment with images that are not shot in standard QTVR format, depending on the look I want to get."

15.50

15.51

15.52

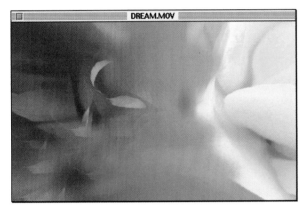

15.53

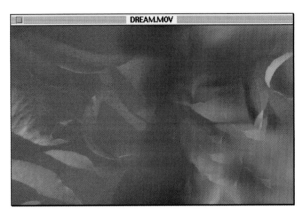

15.54

15.55

15.56

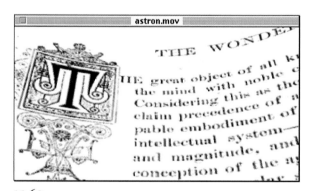

15.59

15.57

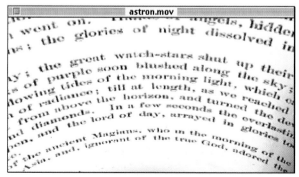

15.60

15.58

15.61

In the *Malibu* piece (15.55), Fitzgerald combined dozens of images together to create a final PICT file that is 384×11,136 pixels. When you pan through the image, there's no discernable beginning or end. "I wanted that effect because this piece is a combination of my early memories of Malibu going in and out of focus, how memories differ yet fit together as they fade in and out (15.56–15.58)."

NOT JUST PHOTOGRAPHS

Fitzgerald creates QTVR from photographs, sketches, direct scans, and even corrupted files. For the Ingrid project, she scanned in an antique book about astronomy (15.59) and then output the file into a QTVR movie. "In the authoring software, I can determine where the viewer will start the movie. And by zooming all the way into the text, it seems as if the viewer is very small, like Alice in Wonderland, and the book is huge (15.60 and 15.61)."

Another great example of experimenting and learning from what went wrong is the QTVR movie *The Maze.* As Janie explains, "I was batch-processing a number of VR files, and when I came back, they were all corrupted. I backtracked and found that I had allocated ten times more memory to the stitching software than was physically in the machine. Instead of throwing the files away, I used them to build images that have a distorted look of depth (15.62–15.64)."

15.62

15.63

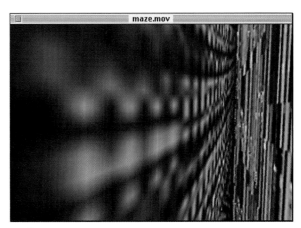

15.64

VIRTUAL GALLERIES

To create an imaginary gallery for her work, Fitzgerald began with an existing VR movie and used it as a template to create the abstract gallery. "I shot a VR (15.65) of my studio and traced the lines of the walls and placement of the window to create a space that is architecturally correct, yet abstract." By using the Offset filter (15.66), she can position the window and see whether the stitching process is going to leave an unseemly seam (15.67). "By using the Offset filter to check how an image is going to wrap, I can prevent any problems with some cloning before stitching the file."

Fitzgerald built a gallery for the photo-journalistic work that she did after the Los Angeles riots in 1992. "I created a blank white PICT file that was 3,936×768 pixels in size and pasted the individual files into it (15.68–15.70)."

FULL CIRCLE

What inspires Fitzgerald's work? "Music inspires my work. Music and life. Since working with QTVR, I find myself experiencing environments differently. I, too am inspired by people, details, or interesting landscapes. But in each case, photographs were looking in one direction, which was forward. Now this is different and I am more aware of what is all around, not just what is in front of my view. Because QTVR is cross-platform and the files are small enough, it works well for the Web, the main limitations being the ones that we give ourselves."

Note

Several of the QTVR movies in this chapter are included on the CD-ROM at the back of this book.

15.65

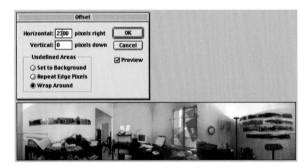

15.66

15.67

15.68

15.70

15.69

CHAPTER 16
HIGH-END TEXTURE MAPPING FOR 3D IMAGES

Illustration? Definitely, but as any practicing psychologist or analyst would concur, this type of work is indulgent and clearly a form of escapism. The fact of the matter is that out of all the graphic design and illustrations Joe Jones creates at his Art Works Studio, this type of work (photorealistic illustration) is the most interesting to him. "I can only explain it by saying that, from the moment I begin a project such as this, something just incredible happens as I am quickly carried off to another space and time until the illustration is completed. It's as if you can actually feel the early morning sun beating on your face, the humidity still hanging in the air and the smell of burnt oil and rocket fuel. I know, I know—sounds like I've been working just a little bit too long on the computer. Perhaps, but seriously, though, this illustration holds a tremendous amount of meaning to me and, coupled with the huge amount of research and the opportunity to fly in the nose of a B17 Flying Fortress and actually sit in the cockpit of a B25 Mitchell (16.1), this project quickly became a very real adventure for me as well. Very cool stuff!"

GETTING THIS BIRD OFF THE GROUND

In this photorealistic type of 3D illustration, many key steps occur between concept and actually holding a framed print in your hand. These steps include conceptual development, research, the modeling process, the mapping process, construction, lighting, sky and atmosphere, final camera angle, rendering, touch-up, and finally, prepress and output.

At the heart of great illustration is the story; at the heart of great 3D illustration is the modeling and texture mapping.

JOE JONES

16.1

STORYTELLER

Let's start with the concept. As we all know, an illustrator's job is one of a storyteller, no matter how simple that story may be. However, we have all seen way too many spheres and quick landscapes created in Bryce illustrations with little meaning or concept; this is not the thing to do, especially when so much is actually possible with a little help of some good modeling and texture mapping.

Jones states, "In honor of, and with respect to valiant aviators and their steadfast flight and ground crews, I pay tribute to their determination and personal sacrifice through such a difficult era, something that must not be forgotten. In my illustration, entitled 'West Field Yardbird'(16.2), I wanted the viewer to instantly be transported to the early hours at a distant airfield not so long ago. Sounds like a simple but good story to me. However, actually pulling it off wasn't quite so simple. As most artists who have worked a great deal in Bryce can tell you, creating something that actually looks real is not an easy thing to do. I knew that this piece had to be accurate down to the last rivet. Hey, I love a good challenge! After careful research through a vast archive, every element that was going to be seen in this illustration was carefully planned out. I worked from hundreds of photographs, many technical drawings, and an extremely accurate $\frac{1}{48}$-scale model of this North American B25 Mitchell to create all the artwork necessary for both the modeling and texture mapping in this illustration. Boy, I sure have a whole lotta books on airplanes now!"

THE 3D PROCESS

Most of you are familiar with the 3D process, but some may not be. 3D modeling is the process of "extruding" or "lathing" one or more drawn paths into a three-dimensional object, a finished wireframe model. It's kind of like drawing your own outline shape for a balloon, and then blowing it up as big as you want.

In this particular illustration, there were more than 4,500 individual objects or models made. A simple metaphor to describe texture mapping is spreading a set of designer sheets on your bed, no matter what shape of bed you may have. However, precisely wrapping an image around a 3D model, or texture mapping, is usually not quite as easy as making a bed — unfortunately. If it doesn't look right at this point, believe me, you'll see every mistake in the final render.

In this piece, there were close to 50 extremely accurate texture maps and many others that had to be created through both Adobe Illustrator and Photoshop. Again, over 4,500 objects had to be texture mapped or surfaced in the end.

Are we having fun yet?

ARTIST:
Joe Jones

ORGANIZATION:
Art Works Studio
802 Poplar Street
Denver, CO 80220
303-377-7745
www.artworksstudio.com
joejones@artworksstudio.com

SYSTEM:
PowerMac G4 500 MHz
2 RAGE 128 cards for dual monitor
support

RAM:
640MB total
400MB assigned to Photoshop

MONITORS:
Radius PressView 21-inch and Apple
Multiple Scan 20-inch

EXTRAS:
Hewlett-Packard ScanJet 3C

VERSION USED:
Photoshop 5.5

OTHER APPLICATIONS:
Adobe Illustrator 8.0 and 9.0, RayDream
Studio 5, Poser 4, and Bryce 4

16.2

WORK HISTORY:

1983–86 — Meier and Frank Merchandise; in-house artist/art director.

1980–93 — Cotton Grafix; vice president/ art director. I started my own small screen printing company that, over a course of almost nine years, became a large production plant and nationally recognized for its preprint line.

1993–95 — Alan Silverman and Associates; in-house artist/assistant manager.

1995 — A.O.S. Associates Degree in applied graphic design with highest honors. Platt College.

1996–99 — Instructing courses in advanced computer illustration at Platt College.

1995–present — Art Works Studio; owner/ art director.

1999–present — Instructor at the Rocky Mountain College of Art and Design where I teach both Adobe Illustrator and advanced computer illustration classes.

FAVORITE SPACECRAFT:

Although *Star Trek*'s U.S.S. *Reliant* and U.S.S. *Defiant* are both very cool ships, I would still have to say, hands down, Han Solo's–Ralph McQuarrie's *Millennium Falcon* takes it! Yeah, I know you're saying, "What a piece of junk," but we all know there's nothing like a good ol' Corellian freighter!

PARTS, PARTS, AND MORE PARTS: THE MODELING PROCESS

In Jones' words, "Creating a detailed model of a B25 from scratch was a huge undertaking and, after building virtually every part of this plane, I could probably qualify as an aviation mechanic. Not having the luxury of working with high-dollar modeling and rendering tools, an artist works with what he or she has to work with. Personally, I construct and assemble all of my modeling in RayDream Designer, and then build and render the entire scene in Bryce.

"Typically, starting in Illustrator, and using technical drawings as a template, I carefully drew to scale both a profile outline and cross-section path for almost every part of this airplane. Next, importing those paths one by one into RayDream Designer, I began to build this B25 piece by piece, constructing and refining until the final model was complete and ready to be imported into Bryce as an OBJ file.

"To give just a glimpse of what goes into this process, I have picked four key components to demonstrate: the wing, fuselage, propeller, and front landing gear.

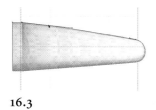

16.3

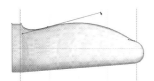

16.4

16.5

To help visualize how this works, I'll start with the wing. Shown here accurately (16.3), and then exaggerated (16.4), you can imagine how an illustrator path is imported and adjusted on all sides to create an accurate wing shape. Because most parts are not simple symmetrical shapes, it is necessary that, along with the top-view profile path as shown here, a side-view profile path, known as a 'cross section' must be created and then merged to create this finished wing. In the next example, the fuselage, this process was quite a bit more difficult as additional cross sections are needed to accurately describe the shape (16.5, 16.6). As more parts are built, the plane is assembled to scale (16.7)."

In many cases, it is only necessary to draw half of an object's profile to later be merged with the corresponding cross section, as in the case of the propeller (16.8). Three separate cross sections were drawn in Illustrator to accurately describe the shape of the propeller blades (16.9). The model of the propeller blade is then twisted to a 22-degree angle between its quarter point and tip to get a correct blade pitch. Each component of the propeller assembly is constructed to scale and precisely assembled (16.10). The final modeled propeller assembly is prepared and

16.6

16.7

16.8

saved as an OBJ file later to be imported into Bryce for final assembly and texture mapping.

After constructing the front landing gear (16.11, 16.12), Jones was still a long way from home as the list of components still needing construction grew long. Still needing to be constructed were the canopies, tires, wheels, turrets, vertical and horizontal stabilizers, guns, motor assemblies and housings, not to mention a whole array of other elements that were commonly seen at airfields during that period, all completely to scale. Whew—and that's just the modeling.

GIVING THIS BIRD ITS FEATHERS: THE TEXTURE MAPPING PROCESS

To make anything look convincingly real in a 3D environment can be difficult at best. As any top-drawer ILM 3D artist could tell you, your texture mapping is everything! The appearance of decay and weathering is a critical element to pull off the illusion of reality. Even a newly erected building shows signs of grime and wear in a very short period of time, and in the case of a plane that has been in service for any length of time, you can bet it's gonna look pretty beat-up!

To produce the grittiness of reality, Jones begins his work in Adobe Illustrator. Working from the same scaled line work he had created for the modeling of the plane, he began to accurately produce on separate layers each surface element of the map, its shape and

base color, panel edges, insignias, bolts, screws, markings, rivets, and nose art. Jones also created a special layer for all elements that would appear to be transparent areas in the map, such as the windows of the fuselage and canopies, landing lights, and also the hinged areas between the motor housing flange, tail fins, stabilizer, and ailerons. This layer is used later specifically as an alpha channel mask in Bryce. After completing the base art in Illustrator, He then exported each map as a 300 dpi RGB Photoshop file, maintaining each layer so he could produce effects on each element separately.

As far as resolution goes, the general rule, as an illustrator for print, is that if a mapped object is seen in printed form at 8 inches at full resolution, ideally that's precisely how big the map should be. Plus there's only so much detail you can hold at 72 dpi, and with this illustration, Jones wanted the viewer to see every single detail of this airplane accurately, down to the rivets. It's not perfect, but very close! Here's a peek at some of the work done in Illustrator to be rendered in Photoshop (16.13–16.19).

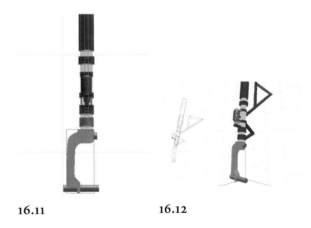

16.11   16.12

16.9

16.10

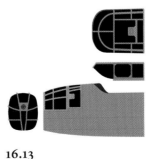

16.13

16.14

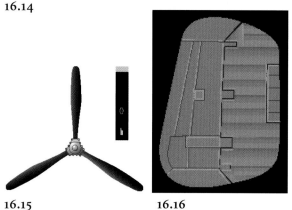

16.15   **16.16**

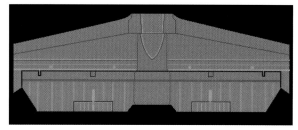

16.17

16.18

GETTING INTO PHOTOSHOP

Jones explains how he uses Photoshop: "Here's where I really get to work in Photoshop. I started by creating a series of test maps and render studies to determine how much detail I could actually hold in my texture maps, starting with no maps (16.20). I did quite a bit of experimenting and refining (16.21–16.25) to accurately and convincingly create the various surfaces of the plane. This proved to be one of the most critical stages of development. To the guys that still fly these birds, an illustration depicting one of these vintage planes is either right or wrong. I am very happy to say that I did get the thumbs-up from the Confederate Air Force of Texas who actually own and operate one of the few remaining B25 Mitchells still in existence. After determining the level of detail I hoped to achieve, final base color, stroke weight of every line, and size of every rivet and bolt, I completed each vector map and exported all Illustrator art as .psd files."

USING IMPORTED ILLUSTRATOR FILES

Jones began by opening the map in Photoshop, where he applied separate edge treatments and effects to the rivets and panel edge layers, hand-painted the camouflage scheme using Adjustment Layers, and created various custom brushes. With digital pen in hand, Jones began to paint the appearance of weathering on multiple grime and streak layers. He does this by using many different techniques, typically painting in steps and, with light brush opacity settings, using Multiply or Darken modes on oil and grime, and using Screen, Overlay, and Lighten modes on certain highlight and lighter distressed areas while on separate layers with different layer opacities.

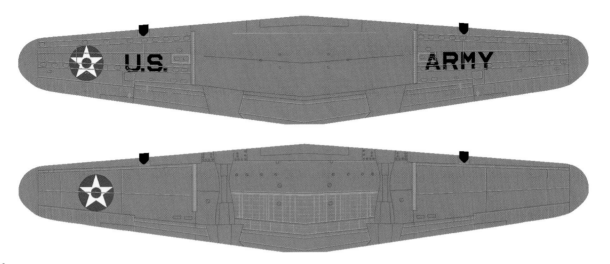

16.19

16.20

16.21

16.22

16.23

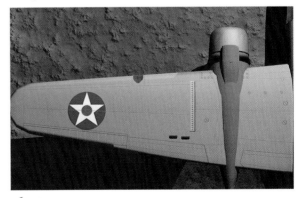

16.24

16.25

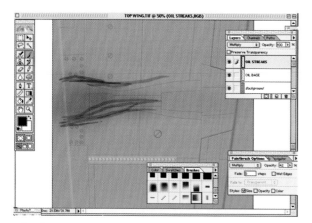

16.26

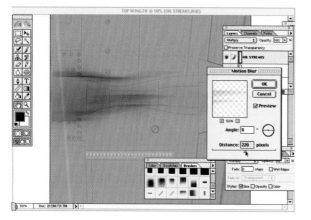

16.27

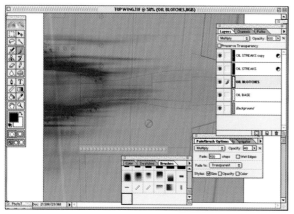

16.28

16.29

Another great trick Jones uses is demonstrated in 16.26, 16.27, and 16.28, and in the final texture map, 16.29.

To help create the appearance of burnt oil blasted on the leading edges around the engines and exhaust, Jones uses this simple technique where he quickly paints rough oil streaks and blotches, and then applies the Motion Blur filter. When carefully done, this can be very convincing. He then creates an alpha channel for masking out not only the windows and other transparent areas of the map, but also areas where he wants the appearance of chipped paint, a very cool trick he had to come up with! For some elements such as insignias, Jones created a layer mask where he will give the appearance of wear and distress, because the base paint will show through in such areas (16.30) and in the final map (16.31).

CLEARLY SEEING TRANSPARENCY

Jones explains about alpha channel masking:

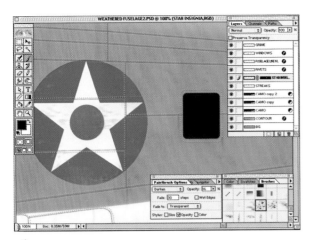

16.30

"As I had mentioned earlier, for every visibly transparent slot in each wheel, window, hinged assembly, and areas of chipped paint, there had to be an alpha channel mask that needed to either be created in Illustrator or Photoshop or both. Using the hangar as a basic example of how this is done, the alpha channel mask knocks out all pixel information from the black portion of the channel (16.32, 16.33), and in the final view (16.34). In the case of the canopies, this process got much more difficult as I went on to create the main canopy. In this example of the front canopy map, not only did I have to create the original art and

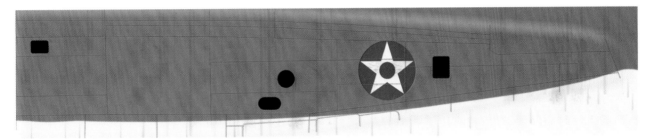

16.31

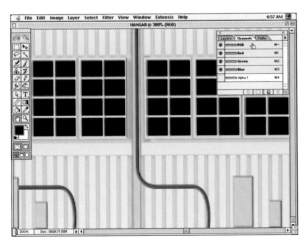

16.32

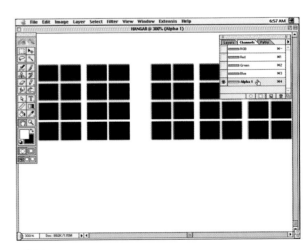

16.33

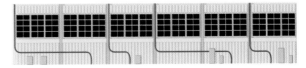

16.34

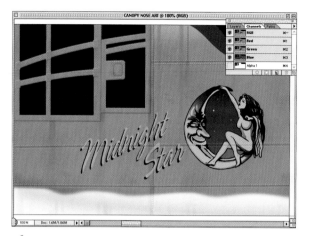

16.35

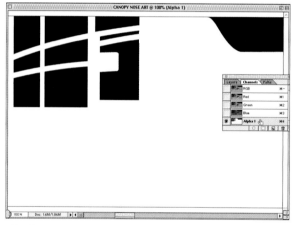

16.36

16.37

16.38

16.39

16.40

the mask for the windows to scale (16.35, 16.36), but much like in Flexograghy printing, the artwork had to be modified by slightly stretching it to match the contour of the front canopy model — a little tough, to say the least, as these two canopies proved to be the most difficult to texture map in the whole project."

After producing a series of test canopy maps and rendering their results (16.37–16.39), Jones carefully worked to refine one of the most critical maps on the plane (16.40): "Thinking to myself, 'That didn't ruffle my feathers too much,' I began to work on what was by far the most difficult element in this entire illustration to texture map — the main canopy. Hey, if it were easy,

everyone would do it! Although I tried many different techniques to accurately map what I had not thought would be such a difficult area, I ended up having to break up the main canopy into three separate components (16.41–16.43). Only by creating and then carefully stretching and combining these three separate canopy maps did I gain the control necessary to accurately create this most difficult and critical airplane element."

Still, a long way from home, even by plane: After the main canopy, everything else seemed like a breeze to Jones (16.44–16.47). Many other great texture maps needed to be produced (16.48–16.53). Of course, these

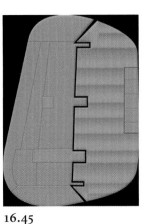

16.45

16.46

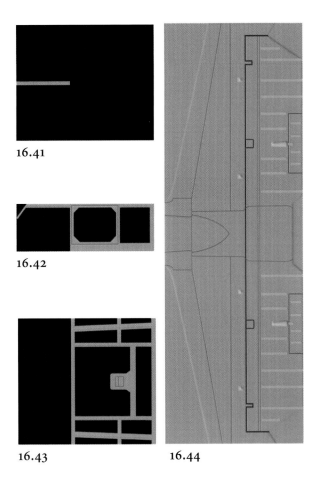

16.41

16.42

16.43

16.44

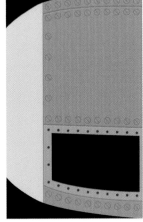

16.47

are only the maps for the airplane itself. A slew of other objects depicted in this illustration needed to be created, modeled, and mapped as well (16.54–16.58). All in all, close to 100 individual maps were generated and used in this illustration.

Why create a 2D illustration in a 3D world? Good question. My answer? Total control! After 3D objects are created and assembled, and the environment is constructed, you can often refine even the best of ideas. You have the ability to try out new ideas that you hadn't even conceived of just moments earlier, quickly changing camera angle, lighting, and atmosphere. What's more, if you ever have the notion of animating the scene, you're good to go! Amazing stuff! Here are just three of the various skies Jones tried on for size

16.48

16.50

16.51

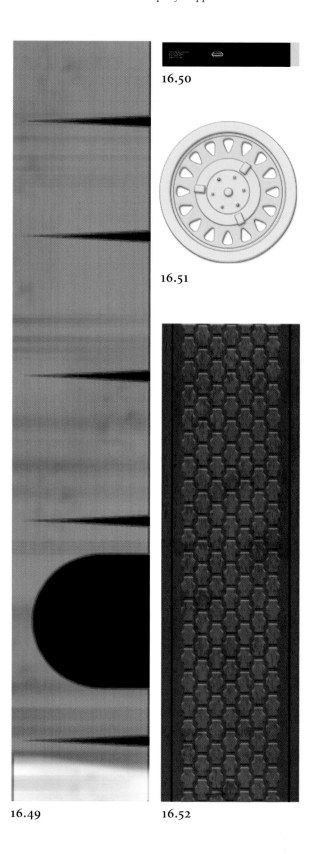

16.49   16.52

(16.59–16.61). Doing this on canvas took Jones an hour or less — you might not think he is so crazy after all.

MISSION ALMOST COMPLETE

After this scene was meticulously constructed and refined to a high standard in Bryce, the image is rendered. This process of rendering a high-resolution Photoshop file can take anywhere from one hour to five days, depending on the total number of objects, lights, and transparent and reflective materials, the atmosphere, and the final pixel count of the rendered illustration. Just as a photographer tries to do everything in-camera as much as possible, so it is for Jones and his work. Touch-up in Photoshop is a great thing to be able to pull off; however, if you don't go to some length in the mapping process, an animation quickly falls apart in the first three frames. He tries very hard to keep the touch-up to a minimum in Photoshop, mainly cleaning up object edges, color correction, a little bit of touch-up brushing, and, of course, prepress.

16.53

16.55

16.54

16.56

16.57

16.58

16.59

At this stage most of his time is spent painting the folds and creases in each figure's clothing, which is actually a considerable amount of work in itself. After the illustration is flattened, Jones always converts the images to Lab Color mode and does final sharpening in small steps only on the Lightness channel using the Unsharp Mask filter. From there, depending on the type of paper stock and type of press the image will be printed on, he sets the dot gain, and in this case he set this image up as a UCR "light" separation and dropped the black ink limit amount to about 95 percent to help control the subtle detail in the shadow areas. Jones says, "Nothing worse than an illustrator messing up his or her own work with a bad separation. From press to frameshop this baby's ready to fly! Mission complete."

PORT MERILLIA

Jones explains, "Though I would never claim to be as gifted as some of the texture mappers, 3D modelers, or science-fiction illustrators in the industry, which I certainly aspire to be, these techniques do give me the incredible opportunity to visit distant worlds that I

16.60

could only dream of, much like Port Merillia. I wonder if Steve Jobs ever has this kind of fun on his computer? Thanks, Steve."

In this project, Joe Jones worked with Adobe Illustrator, Adobe Photoshop, RayDream Studio, Poser and Bryce.

FORGING STRANGE NEW WORLDS

Early on while experimenting in a 3D environment, Jones quickly realized the key was to map as much detail as possible. "Creating a wireframe for hundreds of windows, lights, and surface molding in my architecture would create just incredibly huge files, and take a week or more to render—just a little crazier than even I cared to be! I had to come up with a system to compose the level of detail in my illustrations that I needed to get. After working at this process for quite some time now, when it all comes together it's nothing less than incredible to me."

This illustration was yet another simple story, but a large-scale project. Jones was inspired by the brilliant work of Ralph McQuarrie (who he had the honor of actually meeting in person—one of the most genuine

16.61

16.62

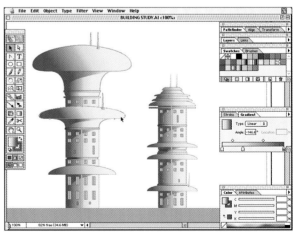

16.63

and humble artists he says he's ever met). From this original conceptual sketch (16.62), he created a series of small thumbnail drawings through much more developed vector art studies (16.63, 16.64). With blueprints in hand, he began to design all profile and cross-section outlines for each element of each building as paths in Illustrator, later to be used in the modeling process. Each path was then imported in RayDream Studio where each model is built and quickly surfaced to judge optimal smoothness of each structural element (16.65, 16.66). Jones says, "I can't tell you how inspiring it is to transform lifeless inanimate objects into incredibly rich futuristic superstructures (16.67)." Very cool stuff!

16.66

16.67

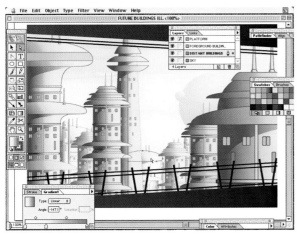

16.64

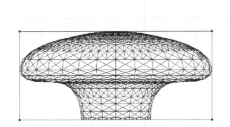

16.65

REFLECTIONS OF DISTANT EMPIRES: THE MAPPING PROCESS

Although creating texture maps for his science-fiction illustrations may be much more forgiving than, say, a B25, creating worlds to come from scratch can be quite the challenge as well. After developing a series of conceptual sketches and refining the look of his architecture, Jones began his work in Adobe Illustrator creating each element, base color and shape, multiple window frames, panels, molding, and art for the lights and windows mask, all on separate layers (16.68, 16.69).

This artwork was then exported in RGB as a 300 dpi Photoshop document maintaining all layers. He then begins to color-correct, create all edge effects, and hand-paint the weathered appearance using various custom brushes. Jones then painted in steps, building up layers of grime and streaking, typically using Multiply and Darken modes. You can see this process in 16.70, 16.71, and 16.72. Usually, he works with both warm and cool grays and uses various fade settings on his brush to get different effects. It's amazing what an old coat of paint will do!

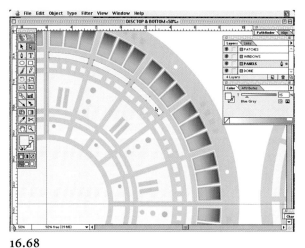

16.68

16.69

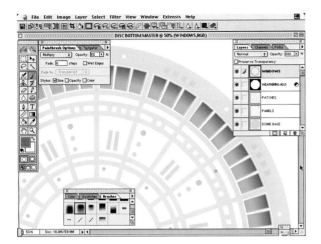

16.70

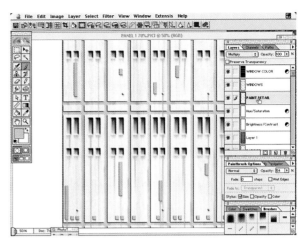

16.72

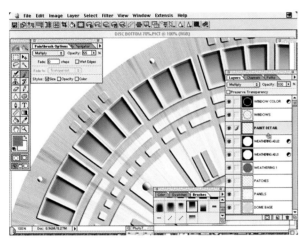

16.71

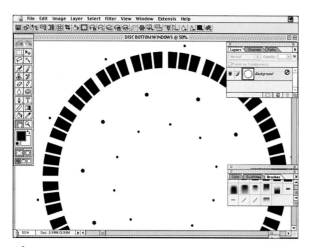

16.73

16.74

As with Jones' previously described technique of creating transparency in his maps, at this point he created an alpha channel mask for the window and lights, enabling him to illuminate those areas later in Bryce (16.73). Although Jones tries to do all of his Photoshop work before he renders the piece (16.74), inherently he has a moderate amount of clean-up work on edges and needs to perform final color correction using Adjustment Layers.

Jones' final comments: "With Wacom brush in hand, I also spend a considerable amount of time carefully painting hair and clothing. Last, but certainly not least, I do a little prepress. You sure don't want to blow it here! I carefully prepare the final TIFF file for film output as a UCR light separation in order to maintain my soft pastel, and set my Black Ink Limit to 93 percent to dramatically help control the three-quarter tones and shadows (16.75). Another world conquered!"

16.75

CHAPTER 17
INVENTING PHOTOREALISTIC WORLDS

Eric Chauvin has a dream job. From his home on the coast of northern Washington, about 45 minutes south of the Canadian border, he creates digital matte paintings for major studio movies and television shows. "I've created the mattes for every episode of *Babylon 5* that has a matte shot in it, with the exception of the original pilot." How did Chauvin land such a cushy client? "While I was working at Industrial Light & Magic (ILM), I was hired to do a single painting for the first regular episode of the show. I created this little 1MB painting entirely in Photoshop on my home computer and then e-mailed it down to the production in Los Angeles. Two weeks later a check arrived in the mail. It couldn't have gone any easier."

While at ILM, Chauvin worked on several feature film projects including *The Mask*, *Forrest Gump*, *Jumanji*, and *The American President*. After three years at ILM, he left to pursue his burgeoning freelance career. "By the end of the first season [of *Babylon 5*], I was averaging one painting for every episode. By the end of the second season, I was up to three or four shots per episode. It exponentially increased as the seasons progressed. They've also given me a great deal of creative latitude; very rarely will I turn something in and have them send it back and ask me to make some changes. As far as clients go, they're wonderful people to work with."

For the studio, hiring a talented artist with low overhead has its rewards as well. "Warner Brothers owns and distributes *Babylon 5*, but a team of independent producers really runs the show. They took

I use Photoshop to paint in elements, add shadows and haze, adjust the lighting, and fill in textures. I can take an entirely fabricated 3D rendering and turn it into something that looks like a real set.

ERIC CHAUVIN

over a warehouse in Sun Valley, retrofitted it to shoot sound, and built their own sets. Because of that, they can do an episode—including all these effects shots—for under a million bucks. For an hour-long sci-fi show, that's a bargain."

From his house, Chauvin has also worked on all three recent *Star Trek* television series, as well as such films as *Sleepers* and the 20th anniversary *Star Wars: Special Edition* trilogy. When we first spoke with Chauvin, he was working on the Robert Zemeckis film *Contact*, less than a month away from its scheduled debut. Having already seen three or four previews ourselves, we figured *Contact* would already be in the can. "Oh no, they'll be working on it until the absolute last minute. The shot that's going to kill me is due in seven days.

"I'm really fortunate. I knew at some point I'd be able to break away and work freelance. But I had no idea I'd be able to do it this soon. Almost all my peers have been doing matte painting longer than I have, and they're all very talented. My advantage is really the computer. Programs such as Photoshop have permitted me to be competitively priced, turn out a good product, and do it much quicker than I could if I were using older techniques and materials."

THE BASIC MATTE PROCESS

Up until five years ago, a matte painting was a still background image painted onto glass. But with the help of digital technology, modern mattes are actually

short animated sequences that feature tiny people milling about, birds flying through the air, and water cascading over falls. Chauvin creates his digital scenes by constructing a 3D wireframe model in Form•Z (17.1), rendering and sometimes animating elements from ElectricImage (17.2), editing and compositing the still portion of the backdrop in Photoshop (17.3), and putting the whole thing together in After Effects.

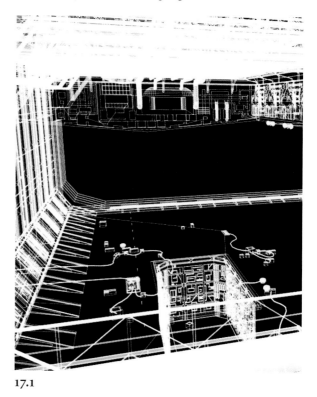

17.1

ARTIST:
Eric Chauvin

ORGANIZATION:
BlackPool Studios
P.O. Box 175
Bow, WA 98232
360-766-6140
www.blackpoolstudios.com
echauvin@sos.net

SYSTEM:
Mac G4 450
80GB storage

RAM:
1 GB total
500MB assigned to Photoshop

MONITOR:
ViewSonic Pro Series 21-inch PT810 and 15-inch 15ES

EXTRAS:
VST Portable firewire drive, AIT backup tape drive, CD burner, USB Wacom tablet, Epson flatbed scanner, Nikon LS-2000 slide scanner, and Nikon D! camera

VERSION USED:
Photoshop 5.5

"I spend most of my time in Form·Z simply because the modeling is such an intricate process. The rest of my time is pretty evenly split between ElectricImage, Photoshop, and After Effects. The Photoshop work is probably the most subtle, but it's also some of the most important. Without Photoshop, the 3D images would have a synthetic appearance that would immediately brand them as fake. I use Photoshop to paint in elements, add shadows and haze, adjust the lighting, and fill in textures. I can take an entirely fabricated 3D rendering and turn it into something that looks like a real set."

17.2

17.3

OTHER APPLICATIONS:
Adobe After Effects, ElectricImage Animation System, AutoDesSys Form·Z, Commotion

WORK HISTORY:
1987 — Hired at mortgage company — got so bored he spent most time writing golf statistic program in Lotus 1-2-3.
1989 — Entered graduate school, introduced to ILM matte painter who critiqued his paintings.

1991 — Got job as "glorified brush cleaner" for Steven Spielberg movie *Hook*; painted mattes for *Star Trek 5* and *Memoirs of an Invisible Man*.
1993 — Landed full-time job at ILM; used Photoshop for the first time to paint digital mattes for *Young Indiana Jones*; won Emmy for visual effects.
1995–present — After moonlighting as matte artist for *Babylon 5*, eventually left ILM to freelance full time.

FAVORITE RIDING MOWER:
John Deere ("With 2.5 acres of lawn, I really need it.")

ELIMINATING FILM GRAIN

Film grain on a still image is death at the box office. Normally, film grain is in constant motion because it changes from one frame to the next. But grain on a matte image just sits there. Even a hint of grain can make a still painting look like a cheesy backdrop. To kill the grain in his "Cloud City" sky, Chauvin took several pictures in a row and averaged them. He mounted a 35mm camera on a tripod and shot a dozen or more pictures to standard print film. Then he scanned them and layered the 10 best images inside a single Photoshop document.

After aligning the images as best he could — "the registration wasn't exact, I just eyeballed them" — he adjusted the Opacity of each layer according to a secret formula hitherto known only at ILM. "The background layer is always opaque. You set the Opacity of the next layer up to 50 percent, then the layer above that to 33 percent, then 25, 20, 17, 14, 12, 11, and finally 10. In each case, you're taking the layer's number and dividing it into 100. So Layer 2 into 100 is 50 percent; Layer 3 into 100 is 33. You keep going until you get to Layer 10, which goes into 100 10 times."

Are 35mm pictures common elements in big-budget Hollywood movies? "Normally, I like to work from better source material than a handful of marginally registered snapshots. But clouds are pretty amorphous objects so a little softness didn't hurt them."

CAN'T AFFORD THE HIGH-END?

Together, the full versions of Form•Z and Electric-Image cost somewhere in the neighborhood of $4,500, as much as a highly sophisticated computer system. Chauvin saved a little money by splitting the cost of ElectricImage with the producers of *Babylon 5*, but what's a mere mortal with limited means to do?

You could do the same thing Chauvin did when he was first starting out. Not so long ago, Chauvin did all his 3D work in Specular International's Infini-D, an all-in-one 3D program for the Mac that runs about $450. "A lot of the early episodes of *Babylon 5* feature mattes that I created in Infini-D. I haven't used Infini-D in about three years now, but I still look back on it fondly. It served my needs at the time, and it

gave me the rudimentary knowledge I needed to create images using 3D tools."

LITTLE IMAGES FOR BIG MOVIES

When you see a spectacular other-worldly landscape projected onto a massive two-story screen, you naturally assume that the resolution of the image must be fantastic. If a magazine cover equates to a 20MB file, a film image must be 10 or 20 times that large. But in fact, Chauvin's images are relatively modest in size. "Different studios have different pixel dimensions that they want you to work in, and they're all very secretive about it. But in general, we're talking in the neighborhood of 2,000 pixels wide $\times$ 1,000 pixels or less tall, depending on the aspect ratio of the movie." And because it's film, Chauvin spends all his time in RGB. This means the largest digital frame for a major film such as *Star Wars* weighs in at less than 10MB.

"That doesn't sound like many pixels when you think how big the image appears on screen. But the best you can do is to resolve at the resolution of the film. Even 70mm film stock is relatively small — each frame is less than three inches wide. The resolution we use makes the digital images look every bit as smooth as the live-action stuff." Sometimes too smooth. Occasionally, Chauvin has to add a little bit of noise so that his matte painting matches the graininess of the film.

THE EMPIRE SHUTTLE BAY

A good example of the very least that Chauvin does in Photoshop is the shuttle bay matte he created for the rerelease of *The Empire Strikes Back* (17.4). "This shot is supposed to take place inside one of the big star destroyers. In the original movie, there was no shuttle bay shot of any kind, but George Lucas decided it was necessary to show Darth Vader moving from one scene to another. So they lifted a sequence of Vader walking down a gangplank that was originally shot for *Return of the Jedi*. They had me create this establishing scene to edit in front of it."

If the scene is new, why does it look so familiar? "The art director reasoned that the Empire liked to use a generic docking bay plan, so I modeled this scene after the old Death Star bays in *Star Wars* and *Return of the Jedi*. But they gave me total freedom to enhance the design and set the camera angle. I created the ceiling and gantry from scratch. I also added some cables and other elements to give the painting some depth. But the walls and floors are almost identical to the sets they built back in the '70s and '80s."

Although Chauvin modeled every cable, box, and crevice in Form•Z and rendered the surface textures from ElectricImage, he assembled the bits and pieces into a complex layered file in Photoshop (17.5). Why render groups of elements in a 3D program and composite them in Photoshop when you can simply render the whole scene out of ElectricImage in one fell swoop? "It takes a little effort to break up the scene into pieces, but it doesn't take any more time for ElectricImage to do the rendering. Another plus is that Photoshop gives me a lot more flexibility by enabling me to isolate elements and apply different lighting effects. For example, in the case of the shuttle bay, I was able to quickly use the Levels command to make the walls a little lighter than the floor. I can also filter individual elements and make other minor tweaks that would involve a lot of work in ElectricImage."

PAINTING THE VOID OF SPACE

One of the few elements that Chauvin created entirely in Photoshop was the layer of stars at the bottom of the stack. Although his basic approach is similar to the one used by Greg Vander Houwen (Chapter 10), Chauvin's medium compels him to employ more subtlety. Chauvin's stars are projected onto huge movie screens, where a single pixel may grow to a half inch tall. If the stars are too numerous or too bright, the effect looks garish and fake. By contrast, Vander Houwen has to exaggerate his stars slightly so they survive dot gain and other darkening factors unique to the printing process.

That said, here's how Chauvin made his stars: He started by filling his background layer with black. Then he duplicated that layer and applied the Add Noise filter with a value of 68 set to Uniform. After pressing ⌘/Ctrl+F to reapply the filter and disperse the noise more evenly, he applied Image ➢ Adjust ➢ Threshold set to about 100 (17.6). He applied the Screen blend mode to the layer and set the Opacity to 50 percent to complete the dim background stars.

17.4   *THE EMPIRE STRIKES BACK™ & ©Lucasfilm Ltd. (LFL) 1980. All Rights Reserved.*

Next, he returned to the background layer and applied the Add Noise filter twice more with two whacks at ⌘/Ctrl+F. He again chose the Threshold command, but this time he set the value to 115 to create the effect of fewer bright stars. With Screen applied to the layer above, the work of combining bright and dim stars was already done (17.7), so he merged the two layers into one.

"If I were to send this directly to TV or film, these white and gray pixels would pop out like pinholes in the film. To fix this, I applied a little Gaussian Blur." Chauvin used a Radius value of 0.5. Then he chose the Levels command (⌘/Ctrl+L) and lowered the third Input Levels value to 70. This restored the brightness of the blurred stars (17.8).

Chauvin cautions that not all the starfields in *Star Wars* were created in this way. But in every star scene created by Chauvin, these are the stars you see. Who

would have guessed that Luke Skywalker battles the Dark Force in a tumult of Add Noise?

PLAYING WITH THE LIGHT

Chauvin spends a good half of his time in Photoshop adjusting lights and shadows. "It's very rare that I can set up my lights in ElectricImage exactly the way I want them. Also, ElectricImage doesn't do ray tracing, so it can't accurately match the way reflections look in real life. Sometimes I'll render an image with

17.6

17.7

17.8

17.5

several different lighting variations and combine them inside Photoshop. I'll put the two renderings on different layers and just erase through one to reveal the other. I also spend a lot of time with the dodge and burn tools, which are great for creating highlights and shadows based on the original colors in the image. There's just no sense knocking yourself out over lighting in ElectricImage when you can create more realistic effects inside Photoshop."

The floor of the bay is an example of an area that required lots of image-editing attention (17.9). "First, I rendered the reflected light and floor onto separate layers. Then I created a separate file with noise in it. I used Layer ➢ Transform ➢ Perspective to splay the noise so it was larger at the bottom and smaller at the top. Then I applied it to the light layer as a displacement map (using Filter ➢ Distort ➢ Displace) to give the light a modeled look (17.10). I also created a gradient mask that went from white at the bottom to black at the top and then blurred the light within that mask. This way, the light grows less focused, and it moves farther away from the floor's surface."

Chauvin tells ElectricImage to automatically generate an alpha channel along with each rendered image. These alpha channels prove useful not only for compositing the rendered elements in Photoshop, but also for adding lighting effects. "The lights around the air lock and bay walls looked a little flat right after I rendered them (17.11). So I generated alpha channels for the lights from ElectricImage.

"In Photoshop, I blurred the alpha channels to soften them a little (17.12). Then I loaded the side lights from the alpha channel as a selection and lightened these areas with the Levels command. This created the reflections along the wall (17.13). To get that blue glow around the air lock, I created a new layer and loaded the middle lights as a new selection. Then I filled the selection with light blue and applied the Screen mode."

17.10

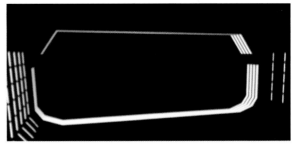

17.11

17.12

17.9

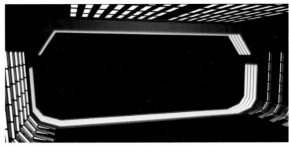

17.13

THE TINY BAY ACROSS THE WAY

If you look closely at the final painting (17.14), you may spy a tiny bay on the far side of the shuttle entrance (highlighted orange in 17.14). "That's really just a distant shot of this same bay. In ElectricImage, I moved my camera so it was really far away from the model and looking in the opposite direction. Then I rendered it independently and added it to the Photoshop composition."

THE ARCHITECTURE OF "CLOUD CITY"

Chauvin also provided a couple of new matte paintings for the "Cloud City" sequence, home of Lando Calrissian and demise of Han Solo. "The 'Cloud City'

17.14

sequence features these humongous cylindrical buildings set against an orange sunset sky. Rather than trying to render the sky, I just went out and shot a few rolls of film with a 35mm camera (17.15)."

ADDING BUILDINGS IN THE SKY

Chauvin designed the models for his "Cloud City" (17.16) from concept art provided by Lucasfilms. As with the shuttle bay art, Chauvin rendered his buildings in groups and assembled the pieces in Photoshop, starting with the background buildings (17.17) and working forward (17.18). "This gave me the freedom to change the relative locations of the foreground and background buildings. In the final version of the painting (17.19), you'll notice that I've moved the background buildings around and I have a lot more of them. In some cases, I copied and pasted parts of buildings to make the town look more crowded. I worked very carefully, of course; I don't think any two buildings are absolutely identical. I may have spent close to an hour cloning elements in Photoshop, but it was a heck of a lot easier than rerendering the scene in ElectricImage."

TURNING DOWN THE LIGHTS

The issue of light raises its head in this painting just as it did in the shuttle bay scene. Most of the buildings had rings of office lights ringing their perimeters.

17.15

Chauvin rendered the lights out of ElectricImage, but later decided he had gone a little overboard. "The original windows were too bright (17.20). It was like every office was filled to capacity with fluorescent bulbs. In print, the effect probably looks kind of cool.

But you have to remember, the scale of these buildings on screen was gigantic. Sizzling windows would have really distracted from the foreground activity."

Naturally, Chauvin turned down the lights in Photoshop. "In ElectricImage, I turned off all my light sources and made the windows totally luminous. This made the windows white and everything else black. Then I rendered that view (17.21), brought it into Photoshop as an alpha channel, and loaded it as a selection."

The next step was to stroke black around the outline of the selection. Chauvin could have used Edit➤Stroke or he could have gone with Select➤Modify➤Border. But he had something slightly more elaborate in mind. "In my experience, Border does a

17.16

17.17

17.18

17.19   *THE EMPIRE STRIKES BACK™ & ©Lucasfilm Ltd. (LFL) 1980. All Rights Reserved.*

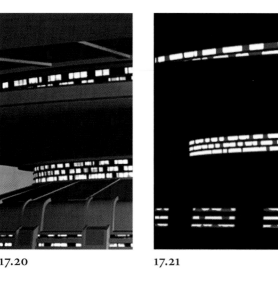

17.20   **17.21**

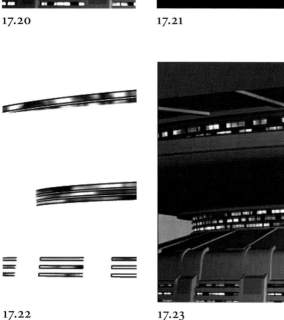

17.22   **17.23**

terrible job of making an even antialiased edge. I used Select➤Modify➤Contract to make the selection slightly smaller, I think I feathered it to soften the edges, and then I saved it to a separate channel." In the Channels palette, Chauvin ⌘/Ctrl+clicked the first channel to load it and ⌘/Ctrl+Option/Alt+ clicked the second channel to subtract it from the first. Then he made a new layer and filled the selection with black (17.22). When composited at full opacity against the buildings, these window outlines had the magical effect of dimming the lights (17.23).

THE TEAMING MASSES

Every thriving metropolis swarms with activity, and "Cloud City" is no exception. "If you look closely at the finished painting, you'll notice that the floor of the balcony (lower-right corner, 17.19) isn't very polished. That's because in the movie, this area is totally filled with people. This particular iteration of the scene appeared at the end of *Return of the Jedi*, where people across the galaxy are celebrating the Empire's defeat. You can't even see the railing through the crowds."

A hundred or so extras on the balcony wasn't deemed sufficient, so Chauvin was instructed to paint tiny crowds into the background. "Originally, I had painted a handful of tiny people in the lower courtyard off in the distance (17.24). But someone decided it didn't make sense for the background to be so sparse, so I added a ton of little specks to indicate the cheering crowds (17.25). I just scaled some noise and then painted on top of it."

17.24

17.25

If you compare Chauvin's early rendered models (17.18) to the finished city (17.19), you'll see that he's also added tiny spotlights, shadows, rust drools, spindly roof paraphernalia, and literally hundreds of other subtle elements, all inside Photoshop. "I keep massaging the image until it looks real. Most of the time, real means uneven and scuffed up. I guess I could return to ElectricImage and render this kind of stuff, but it's almost always easier to add the finishing touches in Photoshop."

THE DINOSAUR MOVIE THAT NEVER GOT MADE

Not being acquainted with every one of Chauvin's matte paintings, it's terribly presumptuous of us to say this. But from what we've seen, Chauvin's masterpiece never made it to the big screen. "I created this painting (17.26) a couple of years ago for a movie version of *Dinotopia*, based on the children's book series by Jim Gurney. He's a very talented artist, so the illustrations in his book worked great as concept art. Unfortunately, the studio abandoned the project pretty early on so it

was never finished. This is the first time I've ever displayed these images outside my demo tapes."

MODELING DINOTOPIA

"When I model something in Form•Z, I almost always work in the wireframe mode. After using the program more or less every day of my life, I'm pretty familiar with what I'm doing, so the pieces usually come out the way I expect them to. But this model was an exception. The *Dinotopia* city had become sufficiently complex that I found it helpful to take the model into ElectricImage and do a quick render while I was modeling. I even assigned a few parts different colors—such as green and blue—so I could discern them from the purple walls and buildings around them (17.27).

"After importing the model into ElectricImage, I applied the basic texture maps (17.28). The nice thing about having assigned garish colors up front is that I can see right off the bat where I've applied textures and where I haven't. After adding 20 or so textures, it's very easy to get mixed up and accidentally leave

17.26

something unmapped. This way, if I see something that's electric purple, I can say, 'Oh, there's something I forgot to map.' It makes for fewer surprises when I start playing with the image in Photoshop."

INTEGRATING THE NATURAL WORLD

"That's about as far as I took this in Form•Z and ElectricImage. I generally make my textures fairly generic, just enough to approximate the effect that I want. Then I go into Photoshop and age the walls, add the stains, paint the little statues, and generally add the realism. In this case, I also surrounded the city with a bunch of photographic elements such as buildings, mountains, rocks, trees, and lots and lots of water. I suppose I could have tried to model this stuff, but it takes less time and ends up looking better if I do it in Photoshop.

"The first thing I did in Photoshop was fill in the central area of the city (17.29). I actually lifted these little buildings out of a book, which raises an interesting point. I prefer to use my own photo reference or work from royalty-free CDs. But it's sometimes necessary to reference copyrighted material.

"When I was at ILM, the company attorney spoke with us on the topic of sampling photographs. He explained that it was a gray area, but that it was kind of like sampling music, which he said is legal as long as the sample isn't too long and the song isn't dependent on the sample for its success. So on the rare occasions that I scan copyrighted material, I make sure I work the images until you can't find any specific similarities between the original photo and my edited version. In this case, I've cloned the buildings into different locations, scaled the buildings independently, combined two half buildings from different photos, painted in extra details, changed the lighting, and made absolutely every other modification I could think of." In effect, the original photograph serves as a template; Chauvin's finished piece is something altogether different.

"If the foothills in back of the city (17.30) look suspiciously like the Headlands in Marin County, California, it's because that's exactly what they are. This was back in the ILM days, so I just went out with my camera and took pictures of nearby hills that looked like they might go with the *Dinotopia* illustrations. The distant mountains are stock photos of the Swiss Alps."

17.27

17.29

17.28

17.30

THE CASCADING FALLS

"I spent a lot of time looking at the waterfalls in Gurney's paintings to try and determine which falls I needed to shoot and from which angles. I finally came to the conclusion that if I was going to get the right kind of water, I would have to go to Niagara Falls. So I called a cameraman friend of mine, and we were on a plane for Buffalo, New York, three days later. We scouted the whole thing out that afternoon, spent the night at the Holiday Inn near the Falls, shot the water elements I needed the next day, and were back on a plane that night. I had the film transferred to videotape so I could see which sections I wanted to digitize. Then I had to go back and scale them, paint on them, and make the masks so they all fit into place (17.31). The payoff is that it's all real water so it moves exactly like you'd expect it to."

Naturally, Chauvin can't add full-motion video inside Photoshop. "The water you see here is just for reference. I replaced it with the moving footage inside After Effects. Because After Effects retains Photoshop's layering scheme, I can just sandwich the various falls in between the layers of building and rock." To see the completed scene in motion, play the QuickTime movie included on the CD-ROM at the back of this book.

ERIC'S INTERMITTENT FLASHES OF FAME

You might envy Chauvin for the visibility of his work. After all, how many of us can name a piece we've done and hold out even a remote hope that someone has actually seen it? Yet here's a guy who can site a few examples and be relatively sure that no one in earshot has missed his paintings.

But Chauvin's work doesn't necessarily have the bang for the buck you might think. "If I had to create a complex matte painting from beginning to end without doing anything else, it would probably take me three weeks. Full time." And what are we talking about? Maybe a minute of film time? "No way. My work is usually measured in under 10 seconds. I've worked on shots that have been on screen for 2 seconds."

So just because we've all seen Chauvin's paintings doesn't mean we saw them for long. Good thing Mother Technology in Her infinite wisdom has equipped us with the Pause button.

17.31

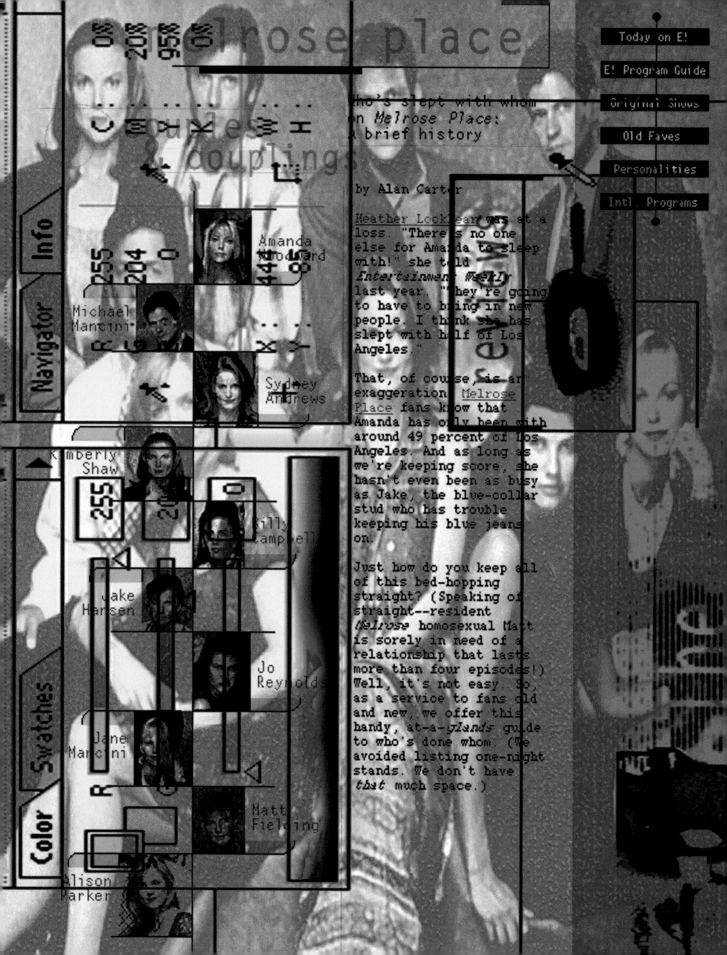

melrose place

comedies & couplings

Today on E!

E! Program Guide

Original Shows

Old Faves

Personalities

Intl. Programs

Who's slept with whom on *Melrose Place*: A brief history

by Alan Carter

Heather Locklear was at a loss. "There's no one else for Amanda to sleep with!" she told *Entertainment Weekly* last year. "They're going to have to bring in new people. I think she has slept with half of Los Angeles."

That, of course, is an exaggeration. Melrose Place fans know that Amanda has only been with around 49 percent of Los Angeles. And as long as we're keeping score, she hasn't even been as busy as Jake, the blue-collar stud who has trouble keeping his blue jeans on.

Just how do you keep all of this bed-hopping straight? (Speaking of straight--resident *Melrose* homosexual Matt is sorely in need of a relationship that lasts more than four episodes!) Well, it's not easy. So, as a service to fans old and new, we offer this handy, at-a-*glance* guide to who's done whom. (We avoided listing one-night stands. We don't have *that* much space.)

Amanda Woodward

Michael Mancini

Sydney Andrews

Kimberly Shaw

Billy Campbell

Jake Hansen

Jo Reynolds

Jane Mancini

Matt Fielding

Alison Parker

Navigator

Info

Color

Swatches

CHAPTER 18

CREATING IMAGES FOR THE WORLD WIDE WEB

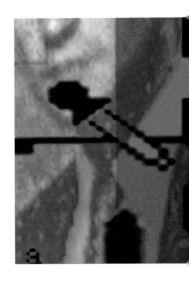

The World Wide Web is a truly wonderful, truly horrible medium. Its primary wonder is its ceaseless bounty. The Web is already so vast as to defy comprehension, and yet it continues to grow at an incomprehensible rate. The Web also rates high marks for anarchy. Just plain folks can post sites for little money, and they won't encounter any of the space limitations inherent in, say, print media.

The horror is the speed. It doesn't matter what kind of modem or direct wiring you use, this is one agonizingly slow delivery vehicle. Consider this comparison: When you pick up a traditional magazine, you can take in the entire full-color, high-resolution, uncompressed cover in the time it takes your brain to interpret reflected light. We're not physicists, but we're guessing that we're talking about a few nanoseconds, max. Now, imagine viewing that same full-color, high-resolution, uncompressed image posted on someone's Web site. We're not telecommunications experts, but if there was a race between that image and a snail crawling from Bangor to Tijuana, we would put our money on the snail.

BEN WOULD KILL FOR A KILOBYTE

Having served on the launch teams for such prominent online magazines as CNET (18.1) and E! Online (18.2), full-time Web artist Ben Benjamin is all too familiar with the benefits and handicaps of packaging content for the Internet. On one hand, you can post pages until you're blue in the face and make them as long as you like. On the other hand, Benjamin wages a perpetual battle to make his images small.

Compress till it hurts.

BEN BENJAMIN

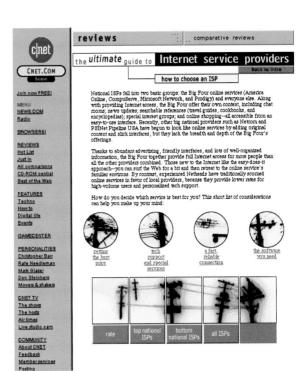

18.1

Reprinted with permission from CNET, Inc., © 1995-97

"File size is absolutely the biggest constraint that I work under," Benjamin says. "I use Photoshop and Equilibrium's DeBabelizer to automate some of the chores — like deciding the optimal bit depth of a GIF palette or the amount of compression to apply to a JPEG file. But I often revisit the image inside Photoshop and do some tedious cleanup work. With GIF files in particular, I might zoom in to the image and examine which colors I can eliminate on a pixel-by-pixel basis. Like, say a block of pixels is mostly one shade of green with a red pixel in the middle. I'll probably use the pencil tool to change the red pixel to green, as well. That not only gets rid of a color, but it makes GIF's run-length-encoding compression more efficient."

Pixel-level editing is a pretty extreme measure. Why go to that effort to shave a few bytes off the file size? "Commercial sites enforce per-page maximums — file sizes that you can't go over. It varies from site to site, usually between 20K and 50K." When you consider that each character of text and HTML code takes up a byte, and a single icon-sized button weighs in at 1K, these maximums are rather prohibitive. In print, four 50K images could fit inside one square inch.

So, how do you make the cut? "Small size is generally considered more important than appearance. So you keep the pixel dimensions of the graphics as small as possible. And you compress till it hurts. You keep nudging the bit depth or compression until the image looks awful. Then, you nudge it back one and leave it there." Good enough and speedy is better than beautiful and slow.

THE MELROSE MYSTERY

"*The Melrose Place* story went up when we launched E! Online (18.3). Basically, it chronicled who slept with whom (18.4).

18.2

ARTIST:
Ben Benjamin

ADDRESS:
812a Hampshire Street
San Francisco, CA 94110
415-920-9576
ben@superbad.com

SYSTEM:
Macintosh G4
27GB storage

RAM:
384MB total
70MB assigned to Photoshop

MONITOR:
Apple 21-inch

EXTRAS:
Global Village 56K modem

VERSION USED:
Photoshop 5.5

OTHER APPLICATIONS:
Adobe Illustrator, Equilibrium DeBabelizer, Netscape Navigator, Internet Explorer, Adobe ImageReady, Bare Bones Software BBEdit, GifBuilder (shareware)

"This page went up before we had a photo editor or anything like that. So, all I had to work with was a badly digitized cast photo (18.5). It's pretty high-res, but it's a blurry, grainy, messed-up scan. But because we were posting the images online, it didn't really matter. I made it work by downsampling the heck out of it. Then, I indexed the image to the 216-color Web palette, without dithering (18.6)."

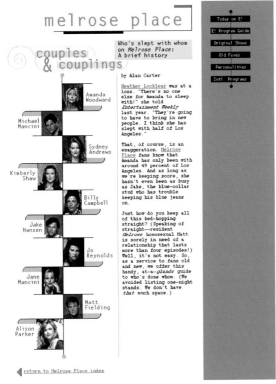

18.3

18.4

WORK HISTORY:

1990 — Hand-painted T-shirts and sold them to students at Indiana University.

1992 — Accepted one-day temp job shoveling dog food; created comic strip "Clod" for student newspaper.

1994 — Landed a job at Yo! Design; worked on Peachpit Press Web site back in the days of Netscape 1.0.

1995 — Joined CNET: The Computer Network as part of original launch team.

1996–present — Hired as art director for E! Online, the Internet Entertainment magazine.

1999 — Worked in Japan on a research project for NTT.

FAVORITE AMERICAN FOLKLORE HERO:

John Henry ("You have to admire the man's hatred of machines.")

DESIGNING PAGES IN ILLUSTRATOR

Benjamin composed his basic page design in Illustrator (18.7). "I selected each of the faces in Photoshop and then dragged and dropped them over into the Illustrator document. Then, I added the body copy and designed the headlines and other text treatments."

18.5

18.6

Why use Illustrator for this purpose? Why not use PageMill or one of the other HTML editors? "I'm not in charge of generating the HTML files. I'm just making a design that the coders will work from. I export the design as a big GIF file and post it for the editorial folks to look at in L.A. After it's approved, I save all the graphics and send them down the assembly line."

In that case, why not use a page layout program such as QuarkXPress? "Illustrator handles single-page designs really well, but it also permits me to add graphic elements and create special headline treatments. When I get the effect I want, I can export the graphics as GIF files, or drag and drop elements over to Photoshop. It's way more flexible than using a page layout program."

EXPORTING THE GIF IMAGE MAP

Benjamin exported a modified version of the "cast toolbar"—the column of characters' faces and names—as a GIF89a file (18.8). This toolbar was then tagged as an image map by the coding department. Each face became a button that would take you to a listing of the character's sexual exploits. (For the record, Illustrator 7 and above let you assign URLs to objects and save client-side image maps, but Benjamin was using Version 6 at the time.)

18.7

After exporting a GIF file from Illustrator, it's always a good idea to open it in Photoshop and make sure you like the results. "I usually export a few different versions of the graphic from Illustrator — one with antialiasing turned on, another with it turned off, one with dithering on, et cetera. Then, I combine the pieces I like into the final image inside Photoshop."

ANTICIPATING 256-COLOR MONITORS

As a Photoshop artist, you would have to own a 16-bit or 24-bit monitor. But about a quarter of the people who visit your site will be looking at 8-bit monitors. When your image is viewed on an 8-bit screen, the browser redraws the image using the Mac or Windows system palette. The two palettes share 216 common colors, which make up the so-called Web palette.

"Any color in the graphic that falls inside the Web palette looks fine; any color that isn't in the palette appears dithered. Sometimes dithering is okay. With soft edges and continuous-tone photographs, dithering doesn't usually matter. But dithering looks crummy inside flat-colored areas, like the green shapes and the text in the cast toolbar."

The solution is to fill the flat areas with a Web-safe color. Illustrator 8 and above offers a built-in Web palette. And Photoshop lets you downsample to the Web palette using Image ➤ Mode ➤ Indexed Color. But the best trick is to memorize the RGB recipe for Web-safe colors, as explained in the sidebar "How Ben Anticipates 256-Color Monitors."

18.8

EXPLOITING BROWSER CACHING

Deke's experience with *Melrose Place* was nil, but it seemed quite clear that the ambition of the show's cast was to put every known form of contraception through the most grueling test possible. To wit, each of the 10 characters had his or her own scorecard. We've grouped the headers for these pages into one big figure (18.10). As you can see, each header features a row of the characters' faces, along with elements highlighting the face and name of the character at hand.

If Benjamin had created each header as a separate graphic, the browser would have had to load a new image for each page, thereby slowing the user's enjoyment of the site. Luckily, Benjamin would have none of that. "The one common element in each header is the row of heads inside the little washing machine windows. So, I made that element a separate GIF

graphic. That way, the browser downloads the image once, caches it, and doesn't have to load it again until the next session.

HOW BEN ANTICIPATES 256-COLOR MONITORS

Benjamin explains, "If each of the RGB values for a color is divisible by 51, then it's safe." That's a total of six permutations — 0, 51, 102, 153, 204, and 255 — in each of three channels. As it just so happens, $6 \times 6 \times 6 = 216$.

"When I reduce the bit depth of the image using Photoshop's Indexed Color command, I usually apply the Adaptive palette. Then, I go back and check the flat areas with the eyedropper to make sure they haven't changed (18.9). If a flat color has changed, I return to the RGB mode and use the paint bucket set to a Tolerance of 0 to make it Web-safe again."

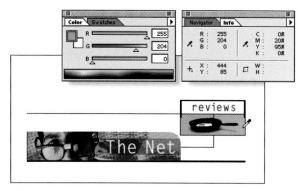

18.9

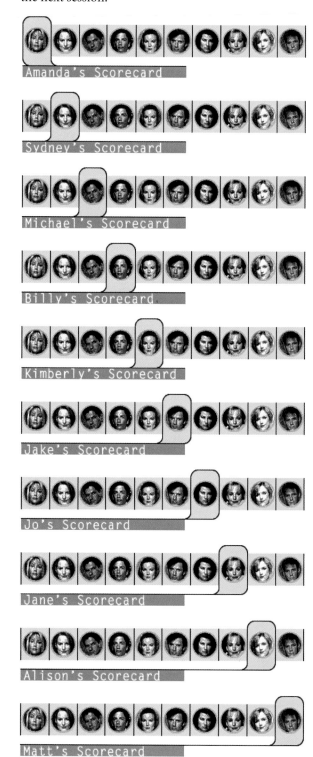

18.10

"The parts that change are the yellow cap above the washing machine heads and the yellow bit with the text below the heads (18.11). The cap is incredibly tiny. It's just three colors — yellow, black, and white — so that's a 2-bit GIF file with lots of flat areas for compression. Naturally, that's a Web-safe yellow. The bottom part is a little bigger, but I managed to get it down to a 4-bit palette.

"These elements have to line up perfectly, so I put together a layered file in Photoshop with the washing machine heads, all the caps, and all the bottoms. Then, I exported each layer to a separate GIF file. Because I cropped each element tight vertically, with no extra pixels hanging off above or below, they appear to merge into a single graphic inside the browser."

ANIMATED BANNER ADS

Banner ads are the current craze for advertising on the Web. They burst and sizzle at the top of your screen in an attempt to entice you to click them. Some folks hate banner ads because they're intrusive, they prolong the overall download time, and they generally make a mockery of the original, civic-minded intentions of the Web. But we don't have any problem with them. Advertising is the fuel for just about every prevailing medium that's come down the pike. Without advertising, some excellent professional sites would have to fold up their tents. Even with advertising, some of these outfits are running on shoestring, loss-leader budgets. What we need is more advertising, not less!

HYPING *TALK SOUP*

Whatever your feelings are on this fascinating topic, you have Benjamin to thank for some of the banner ads you've seen. Included on the CD-ROM at the back of this book is an ad Benjamin created for the television show *Talk Soup*. In case you're not familiar with it, the show compiles sensational highlights from the current glut of fatuous daytime talk shows. It's like a Reader's Digest condensed guide to the daily sleaze. (Though Deke never watched *Melrose Place*, he is guilty of having sat through entire episodes of *Talk Soup* with mouth agape like a motorist passing a train wreck.)

"E! wanted a simple animated banner for a contest they were running. It had to feature a little person rising from the *Talk Soup* bowl. That little person was you, if you won the contest.

"Like usual, I made a comp for the animation inside Illustrator (18.12)." To prepare the illustration, Benjamin set up the individual frames for the face, the soup bowl, and the shaking E! logo inside Photoshop. To keep things tidy, he painted each frame on a separate layer. Then, he dragged and dropped the layers into Illustrator. "I created this particular comp for myself so I could remember the order for the animation. I sent a more simplified version to E! for approval."

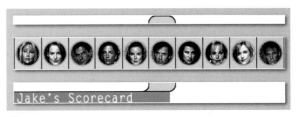

18.11

18.12   *(c)1996 E!Online*

COMPILING THE FRAMES IN GIFBUILDER

After getting the idea accepted — "no one seemed to like how I made John Henson's eyes wiggle, but everything else was okay" — Benjamin set about compiling the frames in Yves Piguet's popular shareware utility, GifBuilder. "GifBuilder does a pretty good job of dithering and reducing file sizes. And in GifBuilder, you can drag and drop whole layers directly from Photoshop. That way, I don't have to worry about adjusting the Indexed Color settings or saving GIF files out of Photoshop."

Benjamin started by dropping in the first frame of the animation, which included host John Henson's face on the far left side of the banner and the soup bowl on the far right (18.13). This frame served as a background for the remaining frames. Rather than drop in completed frames that measured the whole width of the banner, Benjamin dragged over different elements as separate pieces. One set of frames included different views of the bowl, another included alternate text, and the last was a thin set of frames that featured the red E! exclamation point.

Benjamin would have a field day in Photoshop 6.

GifBuilder's basic organization is a lot like Photoshop's Layers palette. The individual frames appear in a list with or without thumbnails (18.14). You can change the order of frames by dragging them up or down in the list. The program lets you specify the duration and coordinate positions of frames. You can even toggle the animation to loop repeatedly after it finishes playing the first time.

FILE SIZE, DIMENSIONS, AND DURATION

Of course, file size is as much of a concern when working with animated GIF files as it is when creating still images. "GifBuilder provides a command called frame optimization that dumps any pixel that's repeated from one frame to the next. If the file is still too big after that, I look at which frames I might be able to delete. The goal is to get the entire animation under 12K or so, which is sometimes a challenge."

File size isn't the only size limitation for banner ads. There's also the issue of pixel dimensions. "Up until very recently, banner ads were a total nightmare. Every single advertising venue had different banner specifications. This ad ran on E! Online and CNET at 476×54 pixels. Yahoo! needed 468×60. So, I'd have to do four or five different versions of the same ad. Nowadays, most sites have standardized at 468×60 pixels.

"But you still have to watch out for weird parameters. At Yahoo!, a banner ad can't be more than 8K, and the animation can't last for more than four seconds." While that makes life difficult for the ad

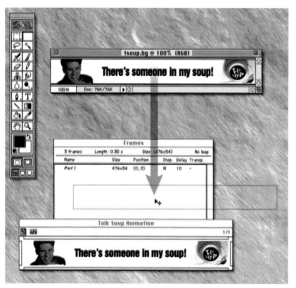

18.13

LOOPING WITH A LOW SOURCE

If you write your own HTML code, you're probably aware of the <LOWSRC> tag, which instructs the browser to download a preliminary version of an image. For example, the TomGirl figure (18.15) illustrates the tag <IMG SRC="zellweg.jpg" LOWSRC="zellmono.gif">. This tag tells the browser to load the smaller monotone image first and then gradually display the larger JPEG file in its place. The mono file serves as a proxy until the real image loads.

Benjamin suggests that you can also use this tag with animated GIF files. "I saw this used really well with an animated bee. The <LOWSRC> tag loaded a file that showed the bee flying toward you. Then, the GIF switched out and it became looping animation with the bee flying in space. There's really no other way to pull that off without resorting to JavaScript or some sort of plug-in."

creators, it's wonderful news for Web content consumers. The ad loads in four seconds, plays for four seconds, and the pain is over. Personally, we're happy to give eight seconds of our time if it means keeping a site free.

18.15

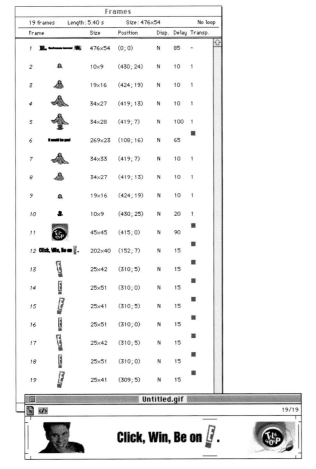

18.14

CHAPTER 19
BUILDING A WEB SITE USING PHOTOSHOP AND IMAGEREADY

Creating a custom Web site is crucial for any business that wants to succeed. Businesses have a plethora of tools to create their own Web sites or Web sites for clients. To create a truly remarkable site, you must incorporate the use of multiple programs. A couple of years ago, Bruce Quackenbush convinced Joe Jones and Art Works Studios to venture off into the area of Web design. Since then, Art Works Studio has been hopping to keep up with the demand. They design fantastic Web sites based on the client's needs. Bruce in particular has been researching and revamping how he does a Web site and has come up with a great work plan. By using ImageReady, a program that optimizes images for the Web and ships with Photoshop, he creates a Web site by purchasing one program.

Bruce feels that the single greatest challenge in creating Web pages is the fact that it requires a blending of a rather diverse range of skills. At a minimum, it requires an artist or graphic designer and a programmer or technician. Between the two, they have to cover interface design, usability studies, marketing and advertising psychology, and the list goes on and on.

Quality Web design requires a synergy of graphic design and layout talents combined with programming talents and technological expertise — a feat rarely accomplished by a single person.

BRUCE QUACKENBUSH

PRODUCING THE ARTWORK

Joe Jones created the original artwork for Art Works Studio's Web site. Joe used a combination of Illustrator, Photoshop, and the three-dimensional program Bryce 4 for the animation. This artwork was created at full resolution (300 ppi) to ensure that it could be used in any printed promotional materials for future use.

COMING UP WITH A BASIC IDEA OR CONCEPT

Bruce explains, "When faced with the daunting task of redesigning the company's Web site, which of course had to be better than any Web site design they had done, Joe (the artist) and I (the programmer) spent quite a few months in discussion, research, testing, and more discussion to come up with a plan."

"To get the effect of a single full-screen graphic without horizontal scroll bars or a 100K-plus file size, we developed a technique of creating a background that doesn't tile, but fades to a solid color. By doing this, we create pages that look well-designed and highly developed no matter what size or resolution the viewer's monitor and browser windows are. On top of that, this technique also minimizes the total file size. This technique was used on both the splash page (19.1) and the main page of the Web site (19.2)."

MAKING THE BACKGROUND IMAGE

Bruce uses a combination of two methods to ensure the background image does *not* tile on a Web page. The first is a brute-force method. Basically, this method involves making the background image large enough to fill a browser window no matter how big it is. Because the extra space will generally be filled with a solid color, the file size won't be too large. The

19.1

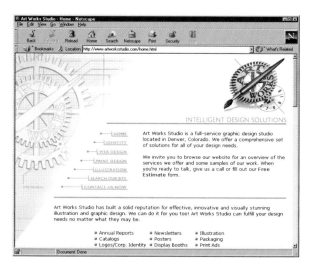

19.2

ARTIST:
Bruce Quackenbush

ORGANIZATION:
Art Works Studio
802 Poplar Street
Denver, CO 80220
303-377-7745
www.artworksstudio.com
bruceq@artworksstudio.com

SYSTEM:
Pentium 250
10GB storage
Windows NT 4.0

RAM:
94MB total

MONITOR:
Dual 19-inch ViewSonic E790s

VERSION USED:
Photoshop 6.0
ImageReady 3.0

OTHER APPLICATIONS:
Adobe Illustrator, Raydream Studio, Netscape Navigator, NoteTab Pro

WORK HISTORY:
<u>1974</u> — Read book on Harold Edgerton and became fascinated with electronics.

second method is to use Cascading Style Sheets (CSS) to tell the browser not to tile the background. That would look something like this:

```
body { background-image:
URL(images/splashback.jpg);
        background-repeat: no-repeat;
```

Bruce makes the background image about 800×800 pixels and then adds the preceding CSS code. His theory is that people who are using Version 3 browsers (that don't support CSS) probably don't have large, high-resolution monitors. Figures 19.3, 19.4, and 19.5 show more examples of a nontiled background using these two methods.

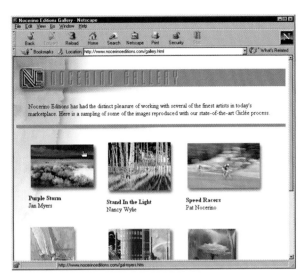

19.4

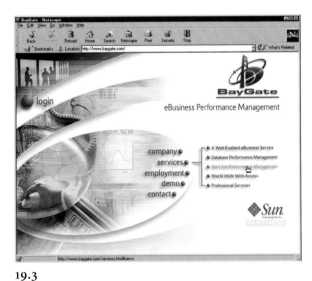

19.3

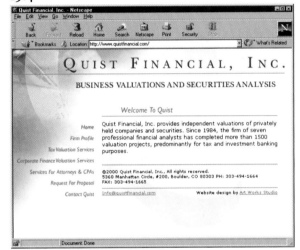

19.5

1976 — Enrolled in electrical engineering course at UVM and learned to program Fortran.

1977 — Flunked out of UVM in spectacular fashion.

1980s — Succession of manual labor jobs.

1992 — Received a degree in electronic technology from Denver Institute of Technology.

1996 — Convinced Joe Jones and Art Works Studio to expand into the Web design market.

FAVORITE SONG:

"In-a-gadda-da-vida" by Iron Butterfly ("jazz, rock, classical — this song has it all").

19.6

WORKING WITH THE FINAL FILE

The final file ended up being approximately 60MB and contains more than 50 layers. You can only imagine how long this file would take to come up on a Web site as it was originally created. The first task Bruce tackled was to carefully render and flatten all the effects. Then he combined all the layers into the minimum number of elements. This isn't strictly necessary because ImageReady 3.0 fully supports all of Photoshop 6.0's effects and features. By flattening and rendering the effects, the file size becomes much smaller and easier to work with. Some issues also occur with the way effects are applied when a file is resized that make this compression desirable. This left Bruce with four basic elements:

- The background layer containing the texture in the top-left corner, fading gradually to pure black (19.6).
- The graphic elements with bevels and drop shadows rendered and flattened (19.7).
- The words "Art Works Studio" with bevels and drop shadows rendered and flattened (19.8).
- The 20 frames of the animation, each on a separate layer (19.9).

19.7

19.8   19.9

RESIZING AND RESOLUTION

The next step is to resize the file to the final size and resolution to be used on the Web page. Using the Info palette and Eyedropper tool, Bruce located the point on the right side of the image where it became pure black and placed his first guide there (19.10).

Because the design criteria called for the actual (nonbackground) graphics to fit in the smallest browser window (640×480) without a horizontal scroll bar, he used the Measure Tool to determine the pixel distance from the left edge to the placed guide as 1,200 pixels. Then he calculated the percentage to reduce the file to give him 640 pixels in width (640 / 1,200) × 100 = 53.3 percent. After applying this percentage (Image ➤ Image Size) in the Image Size dialog box with Constrain Proportions and Resample Image: Bicubic selected, he went back to the Resize dialog box again and unchecked Resample Image and set the resolution to 72 pixels per inch, which gave him the final Web size and resolution.

USING IMAGEREADY

Final processing for this file was done in ImageReady. Bruce says, "Because 'splash' pages that contain only a 'click here to enter' link are, in my opinion, generally pointless, I was determined to add a menu identifying the Web site's main sections without impacting the 'clean' graphic design. This required the use of DHTML to show the hidden menu when the central image was clicked. To create the menu, I flattened and cropped the portion of the main image where the menu would be placed, and then he used the Text tool to create the menu items. I duplicated each of the menu items and applied a contrasting color for the rollover effects (19.11)."

"I turned off the background layers, and sliced the image to produce the simplest possible table. Then I named each slice and assigned 'No Image' (in the Slice palette) to the blank slices. Selecting each slice in turn, I used the Rollover palette to create an Over state, turned on the layer containing the highlighted colored text, and turned off the other layer."

After some experimentation, he determined that eight colors were sufficient to achieve a smooth anti-aliasing effect while minimizing the file size (19.12).

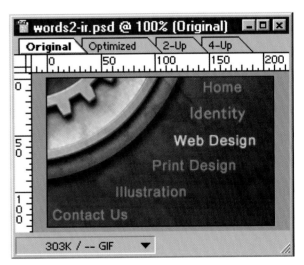

19.11

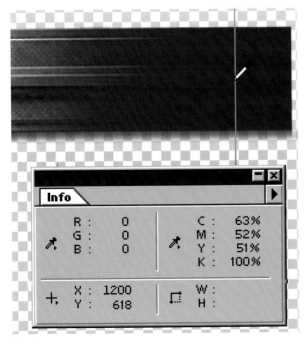

19.10

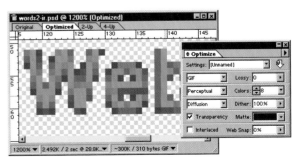

19.12

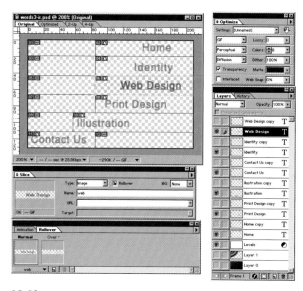

19.13

19.14

19.15

Bruce assigned the Matte color as black and applied the appropriate optimization settings to each slice. He was then left with a master file for the menu in PSD format that he could go back to at any time to change the wording, add/remove menu items, change colors, or make any other modifications and still be able to generate new graphics with just a couple of mouse clicks (19.13).

BACK TO THE MAIN IMAGE

The first and possibly the most important (and difficult) step is to place guides and start slicing. The first issue to consider is the animation in the center circle. To keep the file size to a minimum, this animation has to be as small (in pixels) as possible. Keeping this in mind, Bruce placed his first of four guides there (19.14). Immediately the second issue rears its ugly head. To keep the file size down and simplify the table as much as possible, he decided to leave large parts of the page empty showing the background graphic. He moved the guides around the circle out a bit in each direction so they included all of the linear graphic elements and their shadows (19.15).

FORMAT AND OPTIMIZE

Now the first four guides are placed where they realistically have to be to cut out the animation segment and not overly complicate the table layout. The next step is to slice the rest of it in such a way as to remove as much of the empty background texture space as possible. In this case it was fairly obvious because of the linear graphic elements radiating from a circular shape (19.16). In other cases, you may have to play around with it for several hours to get the best layout. The key is to balance three interrelated variables: the total file size, the total number of files, and the complexity of the HTML table that puts everything back together, to get the minimum average of all three.

The next step is to choose a file format and optimization setting for the majority of the image. This is done now because in the following step Bruce is going to create slices from guides and the settings in the Optimize palette will be applied to all created slices. Because of the wide smooth gradations in the image, JPEG was the obvious choice. In other graphics with large areas of solid color, sharp transitions between colors, and/or a fairly narrow range of colors, the GIF format might provide a smaller file size and maybe even better image quality.

The trick to optimizing JPEGs is to first understand a little about how the JPEG compression algorithm works. First it divides the image area up into small squares. Then it tries to smooth or average the color within each square (19.17). What this means in practical terms is that the image will start degrading first in areas of high contrast and small detail.

ImageReady is an especially useful tool for optimization because you can switch to Optimized view in the main window and adjust the quality slider in the Optimize palette while you watch the changes in the image and the finished file size in the status bar at the bottom. In this case a JPEG with a quality of 22 turned out to be the best setting.

MAKING SLICES

Now it is time to make the slices from the guides. In the olden days (before ImageReady 2.0 was released; Bruce is now using ImageReady 3), this was a painstaking process involving the Crop tool and multiple Save As and Revert commands. ImageReady 2.0 has a menu item called Create Slices from Guides (found under the Slices menu). This command does almost all the work in a single click! This applies the current settings in the Optimize palette to each area as defined by the guides.

ADJUSTING THE SLICES

Bruce explains how he adjusts the slices. "Next I had to go through the image and adjust the individual slices as necessary. First I selected each of the slices that contained nothing but the background image and assigned Type: 'No Image' in the Slice palette (19.18). Next, I adjusted the optimization settings for the individual slices. In this case, the low quality setting that worked well for most of the image caused a bit too much distortion in the most important part of the page, the words 'Art Works Studio.' My first response was to combine two of the three slices comprising that part of

19.16

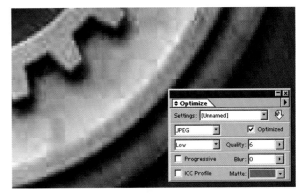

19.17

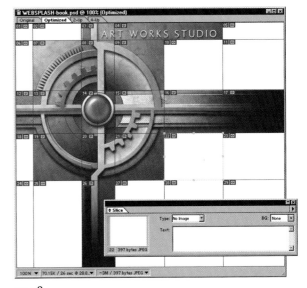

19.18

the image. Using the Slice Select tool, you select the slice in question, and then you can grab and drag any of the four handles. When doing this, be sure to select and delete the slices that you are going to cover up; otherwise, ImageReady creates those files and ends up confusing both you and the HTML file that ImageReady creates. After fixing that problem, I selected both slices that contained the text and adjusted the Optimize palette until I got the quality I desired."

The other slice that required some adjustments was the center circle where the animation is. Being an animation, it had to be a GIF file. Because it is an animation, Bruce wanted to make it as small as possible, so,

using the Slice tool, he cut a new slice out of the bottom area to remove the part of the image that didn't move (19.19).

CREATING THE ANIMATION

Now that the animation slice is as small as it can possibly be, it is time to actually create the animation. ImageReady has a whole bunch of animation tools to help create animations. In this case, however, the animation was created in Bryce 4 and rendered as separate layers for each frame. This made it a fairly simple matter of creating new frames and turning on successive layers. Bruce selected the frame that showed the widest range of color and adjusted the number of colors in the Optimize palette to just short of the point where the image degraded to an unacceptable level (19.20).

Bruce notes with interest that turning on the Transparent option, even though no transparent areas exist, results in a significantly smaller file size —38.8K instead of 55.7K (19.21). Bruce honestly has no idea why that would be, but it goes to show that it is always a good idea to try all of your options at least once.

FINAL THOUGHTS AND TOUCHES

Combining GIFs and JPEGs in the same seamless layout can be problematic because some color shift is unavoidable between the two formats. Bruce feels, "If at all possible, you should set up the slices so that the

19.19

19.20

19.21

transition takes place on a line in the image or in an area of mostly solid color. In the case of the Art Works Studio Web site, the color shift is slightly visible, but isn't really noticeable because it follows an implied line in the graphic." In the next image the cursor is pointing to the color shift between the GIF and JPEG (19.22).

The only task left for Bruce to do now is to issue a Save Optimized command. This generates 15 JPEGs, one GIF, and an HTML file containing the table. Although he writes all of his own code, including JavaScript that shows and hides the main menu, he frequently uses the ImageReady-generated HTML files as a starting point. You can view the finished site at *www.artworksstudio.com.*

19.22

CHAPTER 20
BUTTONS, BUTTONS, BUTTONS

Computers have a way of completely transforming how we work in a small amount of time. Just as an example, perhaps you've seen the made-for-TV version of *The Shining*—you know, the Stephen King novel about the folks who spend the winter in a really scary hotel. The movie was inspired by and filmed at a hotel called the Stanley in Estes Park, Colorado. The story's theme is a bit gruesome—what with all the bleeding walls and killer topiary animals—but it's worth a few chuckles. It was especially comical when the mom and dad start freaking out about the snowmobile being wrecked and their being helplessly trapped, because in real life the Stanley is about a block away from a supermarket that's open all year. And supposedly, the hotel is poised at the edge of a blizzardy mountain pass that's closed over a span of about 200 miles, when clearly no such place even exists in Saskatchewan, much less Colorado.

But the least believable part comes right at the beginning. The lead character, Dad, is writing a play using a typewriter. King wrote the story in the 1970s, when typewriters were still common. But here it is 20 years later, and we're supposed to believe that an ex-college professor in his mid-thirties hasn't managed to pick up a laptop somewhere along the way? How did he ever manage to wean himself off slide rules, rotary-dial phones, and 8-track tapes?

This is all a roundabout way of leading up to the topic of buttons. The point is, if we had shown you a collection of brightly colored buttons (20.1) three or four years ago, we would have fully expected you to utter a "Hmm" or other bored commentary. Buttons are about as applicable to print-media designers as pressure-sensitive styluses are to stenographers. But

The best buttons are little pieces of art, as elegant and informative as characters in a typeface.

MICHAEL NINNESS

Study Agriculture   **Learn a New Language**   **You Can Be Mechanical**   **Learn to Love Symbols**

20.1

nowadays, we would be surprised if you didn't examine these buttons with at least a glimmer of curiosity. The latest computing rage — the World Wide Web — has turned armies of us into interface designers. Like it or not, buttons and onscreen iconography are fast becoming a part of our everyday lives.

In celebration of this phenomenon, we contacted a fellow whose only experience with typewriters was a tenth grade typing class. Young enough to have taken up desktop publishing in high school, Myke Ninness sees buttons as miniature artwork with a purpose. "Their real function is to guide visitors through your site, multimedia presentation, or whatever. The best you can hope is that the buttons are so intuitive that no one pays much attention to them. Or maybe someone thinks, 'Wow, this is a great site,' but they don't spend a lot of time pondering over each and every button. They just click and go.

"But if you take the time to look closely, the best buttons are little pieces of art, as elegant and informative as characters in a typeface. In fact, in many ways, electronic buttons are to the '90s what PostScript fonts were to the '80s — except you have a lot more options when creating them and they're a heck of a lot easier to make."

THE BASIC BEVELED SQUARE

"I'd like to stress up front that none of the button effects I use rely on third-party filters. You don't need Kai's Power Tools or any of those. All the 3D stuff is done with two filters that are built into Photoshop — Emboss and Lighting Effects. And otherwise, it's all layers and channels."

Probably the easiest kind of button to create is a beveled rectangle or square. Ninness starts off by opening a texture file and sizing it to the desired shape. When creating a square button, he usually crops the texture to about 400×400 pixels. For best results, the image should have a low degree of contrast. "Because Lighting Effects exaggerates the amount of contrast in an image, you may want to mute the colors a few notches using Image Adjust ➤ Levels."

To define the beveled edge of the button, Ninness selects the entire image (⌘/Ctrl+A) and chooses

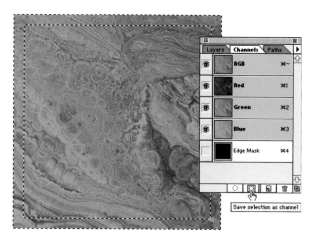

20.2

ARTIST:
Michael Ninness

ORGANIZATION:
Adobe Systems Inc.
801 N. 34th Street
Seattle, WA 98103
206-675-7000
mninness@adobe.com

SYSTEM:
2000 G3 PowerBook
8GB storage

RAM:
512MB total
100MB assigned to Photoshop

MONITOR:
N/A

VERSION USED:
Photoshop 6.0

OTHER APPLICATIONS:
Adobe LiveMotion, Adobe GoLive,
Adobe Illustrator, Bare Bones BBEdit

WORK HISTORY:
1986 — Designed high school yearbook
using Mac 512Ke and PageMaker 1.0.

Select ➤ Modify ➤ Border. "Enter a Width value of 40 pixels, or about one-tenth the width of the file. This expands the selection around the edges of the window. Then switch to the channels palette and click the save selection icon (20.2) to convert the selection to a mask." Ninness names his channel Edge Mask.

"At this point, you can deselect the image (⌘/Ctrl+D) or not. If you leave the selection intact, you'll get a flat button face. If you deselect the image, you get more depth, but it can be a little more difficult to control."

For purposes of this example, Ninness deselects the image and chooses Filter ➤ Render ➤ Lighting Effects. "Keep in mind, Lighting Effects is notorious for generating out-of-memory errors. To work on a 500K button, you'll need about 20MB of RAM assigned to Photoshop." He selects the Edge Mask channel from the Texture Channel pop-up menu at the bottom of the dialog box. Then, he turns off the White is High check box. "From there, it's just a matter of tweaking the spotlight and slider bars until you get the effect you want (20.3). When you press Return, Photoshop generates your beveled button automatically (20.4)."

MAKING BUTTONS WITH CLIPPING GROUPS

"Photoshop's clipping group function is a big help when creating buttons. You can place texture inside buttons and apply highlights and shadows, all with a simple Option+click." To demonstrate, Ninness starts with a simple collection of characters on a transparent layer (20.5). "If you're working with text, be sure to turn the Preserve Transparency check box off." He then creates a vibrant texture on a separate layer in front of the characters (20.6).

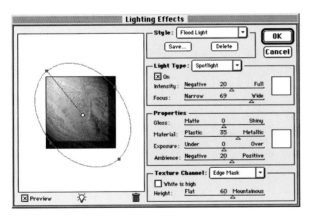

20.3

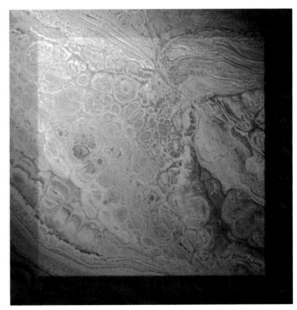

20.4

1990 — Paid way through design school training professionals to use Macs.

1994 — Graduated from University of Washington with BFA in Graphic Design.

1996 — Director of Computer Graphics Training Division at professional photo lab Ivey Seright.

1997 — Group Product Manager for Imaging Solutions at Extensis Corporation.

1999–present — Group Product Manger for LiveMotion at Adobe Systems, Inc.

FAVORITE FISH:
Clown fish ("They freakin' rock!")

"The texture is a stock Noise and Motion Blur technique that's been around for ages. Just take a layer and fill it with whatever color you want — in this case, a reddish orange. Choose the Add Noise filter. Crank the noise as high as you want — higher values result in more streaks. Then, apply the Motion Blur filter at 45 degrees with a distance of 45 pixels. If you want, reapply the filter with the same angle but change the distance two or three times. This brings out the pattern a little bit more. Then, if you don't like the color, you can go into Hue/Saturation and modify the overall Hue. You have endless opportunities to change the overall look of this."

When you get the texture you want (and keep in mind, it doesn't have to be streaks — any texture will do), Option/Alt+click the horizontal line between the two layers in the Layers palette to combine them into a clipping group (20.7). Alternatively, you can press ⌘/Ctrl+G in Photoshop 4. Then, Ninness recommends that you merge the two layers together (⌘/Ctrl+E). Now, in Photoshop 6, you can take full advantage of using the new vector objects feature.

Next, Ninness duplicates the layer and fills the opaque portions with black (Shift+Option/Alt+Delete). This layer will serve as the highlights and shadows for the button. The Emboss filter will give the button depth, while Gaussian Blur will lend some softness to the effect. "By blurring the layer, you give the Emboss filter some soft edges to work with. Trust me, Emboss can do some ugly things to hard edges." Ninness applies a Radius value of about 6.0 for a 400×600 pixel image.

Next, Ninness chooses Filter ➤ Stylize ➤ Emboss. He sets the Angle value to 135 degrees. "I don't know why, but I like my light to come in from the upper-left corner. Then, you match the Height value to the Radius you assigned for Gaussian Blur — in this case, 6. And the Amount is 300 percent (20.8).

"After you apply the Emboss filter, you end up with this crappy gray effect. But we don't care about the

---

MIKE SAYS, "WORK BIG"

Screen buttons are typically low-resolution images, rarely more than 60 pixels wide. But Ninness likes to start out with about ten times as many pixels as he ultimately needs. "It's always a good idea to work on a high-res file and then sample it down. Some filters are very difficult to control at low resolutions, and gradients can band. If you work big, you have a lot more wiggle room."

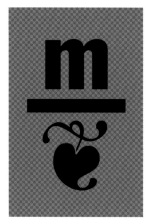

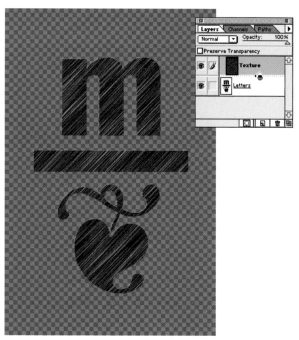

20.5   20.6   20.7

gray; all we want are the highlights and shadows. So change the blend mode in the Layers palette to Hard Light. That nukes all the gray stuff and leaves the highlights and shadows intact (20.9)."

You have one final step. "Because you applied Gaussian Blur, you end up with this residue that drifts outside the original letters. If you don't like the shadow effect — sometimes it can be effective, other times not — then group the shadow with the layer below it, again by Option/Alt+clicking the horizontal line or pressing ⌘/Ctrl+G." This will clean up the edge of the button. Then, add a drop shadow to taste.

"And here's a tip: If the highlights and shadows are too washed out, just duplicate the top layer and adjust the Opacity (20.10). Each copy of the layer remains inside the clipping group. With very little effort, you can have that button popping off the page."

ETCHING TYPE INTO THE BEVELED SQUARE

"This clipping group technique is also a snazzy way to etch text into a button. For example, take the beveled square. A square by itself — that's not a button. But add some text and you've really got something."

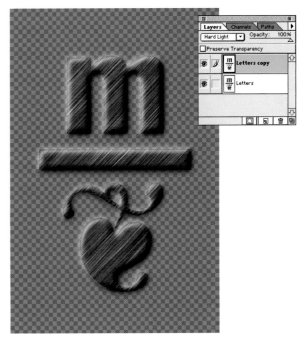

20.9

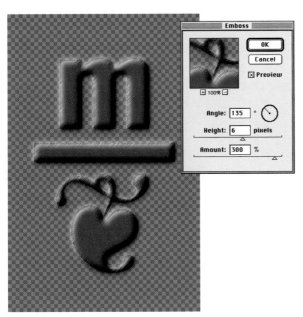

20.8

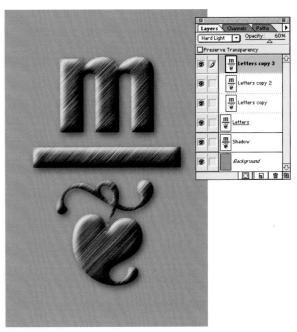

20.10

20.11

20.12

Ninness sets the foreground color to 50 percent gray. Then, he uses Photoshop's type tool to add the words "Click Me" to a new layer. After he centers the text on the button, he turns off the Preserve Transparency check box (which permits blurring later). He also sets the blend mode in the Layers palette to Hard Light to make the gray text invisible.

Next, he duplicates the Click Me layer and fills it with black (by setting the foreground color to black and pressing Shift+Option/Alt+Delete). Ninness then applies the Gaussian Blur filter with a Radius value of 3.0. "The higher the radius, the deeper the etching."

After blurring, he chooses Emboss and sets the Height to 3 (matching the blur radius) and the Amount to 300 percent. "Unlike before, I'm digging the text into the button, so I rotate the Angle value to –45 degrees." The result is a soft-edged effect that looks like the type has melted into the button (20.11). To make the text nice and crisp, group the emboss layer with the text below it by pressing ⌘/Ctrl+G (20.12).

MASS BUTTON PRODUCTION

"From a production standpoint, this technique can be a huge time saver. If you have a series of buttons on your Web site, and they're all going to be the same except for what they say, then you have one source file to go back and edit. Here, I just have to change the two text layers — which takes maybe five minutes — and export the modified button in the GIF89a format. That's because the GIF89a Export module saves just the visible layers.

"It also works in the other direction. If you change your mind about the color of the button, and you still have the original Photoshop file with the various text layers intact, you only have one layer to go back and edit — the Background layer. The text etches into the new background automatically."

CREATING A STAMPED BUTTON

"Clipping groups are a great way to add depth to complex shapes. But they aren't the only way to go. In fact, my favorite button technique doesn't involve clipping groups at all. Using layers and channels, you can stamp an icon so it looks like someone has branded it into a button shape." The buttons at the beginning of the chapter (20.1) are cases in point.

Ninness suggests two techniques for creating stamped buttons: one that involves the Emboss filter, and a more complicated but equally more realistic method that involves Lighting Effects.

THE SIMPLE EMBOSS APPROACH

Whether he decides to enhance his button with Emboss or Lighting Effects, Ninness starts off the same way. First, he creates a new image with the Contents set to Transparent. Then, he creates an icon for the button—shown here as a black cog (20.13)—on the background layer provided with the document. It's very important that the icon be black; even if you want to make it a different color later, use black for now.

Next, Ninness creates a new layer below the first and blocks out the shape of the button in white (20.14). "I just painted a few random strokes using the paintbrush tool with a soft brush. I figure, if the technique works with fuzzy brushstrokes, it'll work with anything." Again, it's very important that you use white for the button. You can always modify the color later.

If you're following along and creating your own button, this is a good point to save your work. In the next section, you'll start from this point when using the Lighting Effects filter. You may even want to duplicate the image so you don't harm the original.

Just so we're all on the same page, Ninness has two layers—one called Cog (black) in front of another called Button (white). With the Button layer active, he presses Option/Alt while choosing Layer ➢ Merge Visible. (On the Mac, you can alternatively press ⌘+Shift+Option+E.) Doing so merges the contents of both layers onto the Button layer.

At this point, you could launch right into the Emboss filter. But again, Ninness suggests you start off with a little Gaussian Blur. "In this case, I'd go with something subtle, such as a Radius of about 2.0."

Then, he chooses the Emboss filter. Because he's working with a layer of white pixels, Ninness sets the Angle value to –45 degrees to create the effect of light coming in from the upper left. "Then, I just experiment with the other settings. A Height of 3 and an Amount of 300 looks pretty good (20.15).

"That's it, really. From here, it's just a matter of assigning your button the proper colors." If you want to color the icon separately of the button, you can fill the icon with color by pressing Shift+Option/Alt+Delete. Try setting the blend mode in the Layers palette to Hard Light. Then, adjust the Opacity

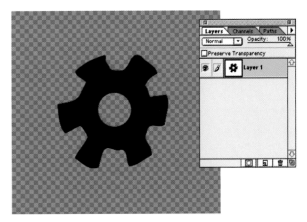

20.13

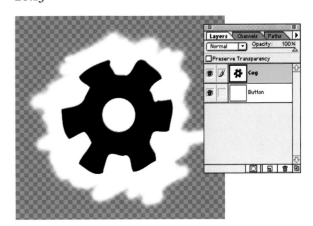

20.14

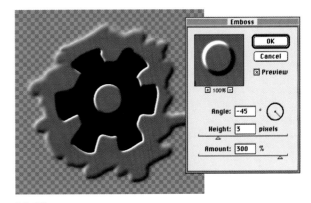

20.15

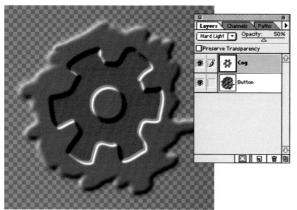

20.16

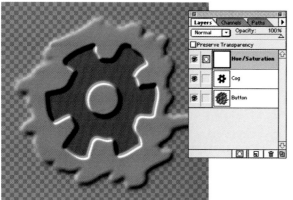

20.17

setting as desired. As a general rule, cool colors tend to require higher Opacity settings than warm ones (20.16).

If you prefer to color the icon and button together, Ninness recommends that you leave the icon black and reduce the Opacity to about 50 percent. You can add an adjustment layer (by ⌘/Ctrl+clicking the new layer icon along the bottom of the Layers palette) and set the layer to Hue/Saturation. Then, inside the Hue/Saturation dialog box, select the Colorize check box and adjust the Hue and Saturation values as desired.

"This is a great way to colorize the button (20.17) because you can always go back and modify your colors later. With your button layers set to neutral grays, your coloring options are virtually unlimited."

THE SLIGHTLY MORE ELABORATE LIGHTING EFFECTS METHOD

To light your button with the Lighting Effects filter, you start with the same two-layer file — black icon in the foreground and white button in the background. You'll apply Lighting Effects to the white button layer, but first, you need to create a mask to give the button some depth. "Lighting Effects creates the best results when you have a texture channel to work with. That's where the mask comes in."

In Photoshop, Ninness ⌘/Ctrl+clicks the Button layer in the Layers palette to select the button outline. Then, he presses both ⌘ and Option, or Ctrl and Alt under Windows, and clicks the Cog layer. This subtracts the cog outline from the selection. Finally, Ninness switches to the Channels palette and clicks the save selection icon to convert the selection to a channel.

To keep things tidy, Ninness names his mask "Lighting FX Mask." Then, he switches to the mask channel (⌘/Ctrl+4), deselects everything (⌘/Ctrl+D), and applies the Gaussian Blur filter, again with a Radius of 2.0.

Ninness switches back to the RGB composite view (⌘/Ctrl+~ [tilde]). With the Button layer active, he chooses Filter ➤ Render ➤ Lighting Effects. Then, he selects his Lighting FX Mask channel from the Texture Channel pop-up menu (20.18), and he leaves the White is High check box turned on. "Switch the angle of the light to wherever you want it. Again, I like it coming from the upper left, but it's up to you.

"If you plan on making a series of buttons using the same basic lighting and texture settings, you might want to take a moment and save your settings. Then, once you get an effect you like, go ahead and apply the filter by pressing Return or Enter." Although Lighting Effects is a more challenging filter to use than Emboss, it also delivers a more credible rendition of depth (20.19). The figure shows the Button layer on its own, with Cog temporarily hidden.

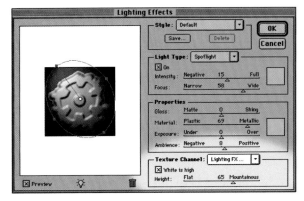

20.18

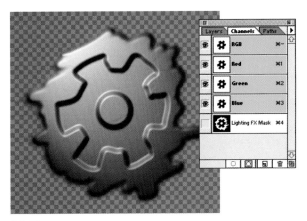

20.19

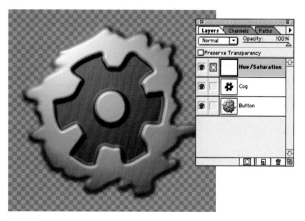

20.20

"To color the button, do the same thing you did with the Emboss effect. Set the Opacity of the icon layer to 50 percent and apply Hue/Saturation on an adjustment layer (20.20).

"You can use the buttons as is, against a white HTML page. Or use the mask channel to clean up the edges of your buttons and then add drop shadows (20.21). This effect takes some effort the first few times you run through it. But with a little practice, you'll be cranking out buttons in no time."

When Good Steer Go Bad

Cowhands of the Orient

I Was a Gear-Head Cowpoke

@Home.OnThe/Range.html

20.21

APPENDIX
ABOUT THE CD-ROM

The CD-ROM in the back of this book contains more than 100 files. That's twice as many files as I included with the last edition of this book; however, that number is relatively small when compared with the CDs included with other computer books. Although the files are few in number, they're big in size and function — sort of the Alamo of CD content.

In stark contrast to the often-reproduced plug-ins and demo utilities that serve as the backbone for a proud industry of CDs at the back of Photoshop titles, all of the 100+ files on this CD are custom content, unique to this book. These files are shockingly relevant to the information conveyed in the text.

To highlight the noble purpose of this CD, I use the eye of an owl as its icon. Famous as the symbol for Great Intellectual Prowess — as popularized in *Winnie the Pooh* books and other dramatic folklore — the owl's eye serves as a signpost for high-minded artistry. It is sheer coincidence that I was in a hurry and came across an owl in the first stock photo collection I looked at.

The files are mostly self-evident. Just double-click a file and watch it go. But because I like to hear myself talk (or should that be, read myself write?), the following sections quickly walk you through the lot.

THE CONTENTS

Insert the CD into your CD-ROM drive. Double-click the owl's eye icon to display the contents of the CD. This action takes you into the CD, where you discover the multimedia side of *Photoshop Studio Secrets*.

The CD content is divided into ten folders. These folders contain a smattering of Photoshop images, HTML pages, and QuickTime movies. Open the

images in Photoshop. Open the HTML pages in your favorite Web browser (Internet Explorer or Netscape Communicator). To open the QuickTime movies, you need QuickTime, which is included in standard issues on all Macintosh computers and some Windows-based PCs.

If you do not have QuickTime or need a more recent version, you can download it for free from *www.quicktime.com*.

The CD includes files that are usable on both Macintosh (A.1) and Windows (A.2). Here's how the ten folders work, in alphabetical order:

Ch05 Reinfeld: This folder contains four silent QuickTime movies, which show moving type effects created by Eric Reinfeld (Chapter 5). These files are the only files on the CD that you can find elsewhere — specifically, on the CD included with Reinfeld's own book, *Real World After Effects*. If nothing else, check out Trippy.mov. No mind-altering chemicals needed.

Ch09 Bergman: Inside this folder, you find 15 examples of Eliot Bergman's dazzling glass, smoke,

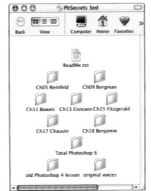

A.1

A.2

and reflections artwork. If you thought that his stuff looked good in print (Chapter 9), wait until you see it in the rich, lustrous RGB.

Ch11 Bowen: Double-click this folder to access two versions of Robert Bowen's stereoscopic view of New York City (Chapter 11). If you have a monster system with scads of RAM, open the Huge3-D.psd file. Otherwise, open Med3-D.psd instead. Then get yourself a pair of 3-D glasses and put them on, with the red lens over your left eye and the blue over your right. (You can hear Bowen personally explain the file by running his movie in the Original Voices folder.)

Ch13 Eismann: Is she a coauthor or an artist? It's impossible to know. But whatever Katrin may be, she's decided to grace this CD with some content from her chapter on digital photography (Chapter 13). All four QuickTime VR movies were created by stitching together pictures from digital cameras. Remember that you need to use the most recent version of QuickTime (*www.quicktime.com*) to view them.

Ch15 Fitzgerald: Inside this folder, you find a total of 24 (7 old plus 17 new) QuickTime VR movies created by Janie Fitzgerald (Chapter 15). Drag inside the movies and watch the world spin around. Press Shift to zoom in and press Ctrl to zoom out. Don't expect to see the stereotypical photographic panoramic views; Fitzgerald proves that art has a place in the virtual world.

Ch17 Chauvin: Double-click the QuickTime movie Dinotopia Full.mov to see Eric Chauvin's vision of Dinotopia live and breathe (Chapter 17). The water comes from Niagara Falls, and the music and sound effects come from Denver-based musician David Schmal. Chauvin includes two silent high-resolution versions so that you can see the water in full detail.

Ch18 Benjamin: Because Ben Benjamin (Chapter 18) creates his images to be viewed on-screen, I figure that you should see them on-screen. Nine of the files are screen shots of his finished Web pages from CNET and E! Online. The tenth file, TalkSoup.gif, is an animated banner ad. You can open it up inside a Web browser, such as Internet Explorer or Netscape Communicator, or a GIF animation program, such as ImageReady. The latter is included with your copy of Photoshop.

Old Photoshop 4 Lesson: Once upon a time, I hosted a cable television show called *Digital Gurus*. The show appeared sporadically in 30 or so million households, but that still left a few billion without. Hence, Jones Entertainment Co. donated this 15-minute segment, minus commercials. Open the Digital Gurus.mov file and click the Play button to see Adobe's Russell Brown demonstrate adjustment layers. Be forewarned, this clip was filmed in — yikes — Photoshop 4! I considered deleting this file (mostly because it reminds me of what a chubster I was back then), but I figured it had nostalgic value. Besides, Russell is funny, and funny is good.

Original Voices: This folder includes snippets from my phone interviews with the 14 original *Studio Secrets* artists that remain in the book. Lasting one to two minutes apiece, these QuickTime conversations (A.3) explore technical topics, personal background, and just plain goofiness. Hear a bit of calming advice from Katrin Eismann. Listen to Jeff Schewe disclose his purchase of a black market Macintosh. Find out why Michael Ninness is known to his friends as "Myke with a *y*." (Keep in mind, these conversations were pieced together from telephone recordings, so the quality is pretty choppy. You may want to crank up the volume.)

Total Photoshop 6: In addition to my various books, I host a 12-tape video series called *Total Training For Adobe Photoshop 6* (or *Total Photoshop* 6 for short). Filmed in the world's only all-digital training studios, *Total Photoshop* 6 (A.4) is an authoritative collection of engaging, self-paced, hands-on tutorials that walk you through every significant feature of the software. But why take my word for it when you can watch them for yourself? Open the Total Photoshop 6 folder and double-click Default.htm. Eight high-resolution lessons await you.

CD TECHNICAL SUPPORT

If you have any problems getting the CD to work with your computer, it's very likely that some of your settings files or drivers are not working properly. For assistance or if you think that you have a damaged CD, call the Hungry Minds technical support hotline at 800-762-2974 (outside the U.S. 317-572-3993) or send e-mail to techsupdum@hungryminds.com.

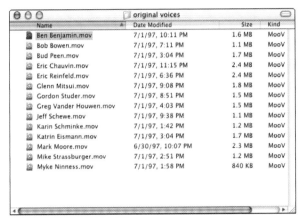

A.3

A.4

INDEX

Numerics

3D effects. *See also* texture mapping
  airbrush, using, 48, 49, 51
  anaglyphs, 160–161
  bevel effects, 11, 16, 292–293
  blur, depth enhancement
    using, 126
  embossing, 23, 60, 61–63, 294,
    296–300
  geometry, 125–126
  gradient fills, via, 5
  highlights, 51–52
  image distortion, via, 13
  modeling, component approach,
    236–237
  modeling, described, 234
  modeling in Alias Sketch!,
    113–115, 121, 122, 125–126
  modeling in ElectricImage, 266
  modeling in Form•Z, 256, 257,
    258, 266
  modeling in Infini-D, 258
  modeling in RayDream
    Designer, 236
  modeling, matte painting, 256
  modeling, path creation for,
    236, 249
  Photoshop versus specialized
    software, 47, 48, 52
  shadows, 51–52
  spheres, 14–15, 52
  wireframe, 154, 234, 245, 256
3D glasses, 160

A

acetate, printing techniques using,
  167, 169–170
acrylic paint, printing over, 171–172
Add Noise filter, 139, 154,
  259–260, 294
Adobe Illustrator. *See* Illustrator
Adobe Streamline, 73, 75
advertising psychology, 145, 146
After Effects software, 28, 256,
  257, 268
airbrush tool, 48, 51–52, 71,
  116, 200
Alias Power Animator, 154
Alias Sketch! 3D modeling program,
  113–115, 121, 122, 125–126
Alien Skin Software, 11
alignment
  layers, 101, 133, 135
  objects in FreeHand, 23
  objects in Illustrator, 23
  paper during overprinting, 170
  scanning, when, 70, 71
  templates, using for, 23
  Web images, 277
alteration requests from clients,
  26, 130, 155
anaglyphs, 160–161
animals, photographing, 192
animation, 28, 277–279, 286, 288
antialiasing wireframe images, 154
Apple QTVR Authoring Studio,
  214, 217, 224
Apply Image command, 59, 62

Apply Image dialog box, 61
archiving, 191
Art Works Studio (design firm),
  233, 281, 289
artist interviews (on the CD),
  303–304
artwork, mixed-media (printing/
  painting), 164, 166–175. *See
  also* printing
artwork, varnishing, 173–174
Atget, Jean, 210
atmospheric effects, 88, 261

B

background
  black, 42, 44, 104
  blurring, 188
  channels, 35–36
  compositing, for, 194–195
  dark, printing over, 31, 34–35
  depth of field, 157, 188
  drapery, 12
  foreground, adjustments with,
    118, 134–135, 137, 139, 188
  gradient, 126, 198
  light source integration in,
    262–264
  paths as background elements,
    73–74
  photography for, 194–195, 198
  texture, 23, 99
  type effects, in, 57, 59
  Web page backgrounds,
    282–283, 286

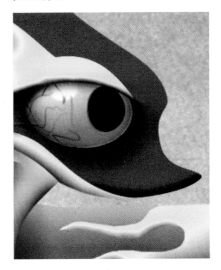

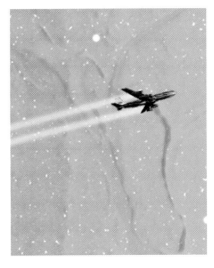

ABOUT THE AUTHORS

Deke McClelland is one of the world's leading experts on digital graphics. He has written more than 50 books on electronic publishing and the Macintosh computer, and his work has been translated into more than 25 languages, with 3 million copies in print. Among these are the award-winning *Photoshop Bible* series and his new *Look & Learn* series, all published by Hungry Minds, Inc., formerly known as IDG Books Worldwide. The first edition of *Photoshop Studio Secrets* won the Computer Press Award for the best advanced how-to book of 1997.

Deke hosts the video training series, *Total Photoshop*, and is a contributing editor at *Macworld* magazine. He started his career as artistic director at the first service bureau in the United States.

In 1989, Deke won the Benjamin Franklin Award for Best Computer Book. Since then, he has received honors from the Society for Technical Communication (once in 1994 and twice in 1999), the American Society of Business Press Editors (1995), the Western Publications Association (1999), and the Computer Press Association (1990, 1992, 1994, 1995, 1997, and twice in 1999). In 1999, Book Bytes named Deke its Author of the Year.

Katrin Eismann is an internationally recognized educator and speaker on the subject of imaging and the impact of emerging technologies on the professional photographer. Katrin is coauthor of *Web Design Studio Secrets* (IDG Books Worldwide, now Hungry Minds, Inc.) and is the conference chairperson for the Thunder Lizard Productions Photoshop Conferences. Her company, photoshopdiva.com, teaches and lectures throughout Europe, North America, and the Asian-Pacific region.

Katrin's creative work is based on investigating concepts and working with the appropriate technologies to create intriguing images. Her images have appeared in the books *Photoshop WOW!*, *Photoshop 4 Studio Secrets*, *Essentials of Digital Photography*, *Make Your Scanner a Great Production Tool*, and *Essentials of Computing* and in the magazines *Macworld*, *PhotoDistrictNews*, *American Photo*, *Photonics*, *Computer Artist*, *Image World*, *International Photography*, *IdN*, and *Mac Art & Design*.

Jennifer Alspach is a world-renowned artist and has spoken at many conferences and trade shows. She has authored many books, including *Teach Yourself Photoshop 5.0/5.5* and *Photoshop and Illustrator Synergy Studio Secrets*, both published by IDG Books Worldwide (now Hungry Minds, Inc.). Other works by Jennifer include *Illustrator 7 Complete*, *Adobe Photoshop 5.5 and Illustrator 8.0 Advanced Classroom in a Book* (two chapters), *PhotoDeluxe Home Edition for Windows Visual Quickstart Guide*, *PhotoDeluxe for Windows and Macintosh Visual Quickstart Guide*, *Illustrator Filter Finesse*, *Microsoft BOB*, and various articles for *Adobe Magazine*.

COLOPHON

This book was produced electronically in Indianapolis, Indiana. Microsoft Word 97 was used for word processing; design and layout were produced using QuarkXPress 4.11 and Abobe Photoshop 5.5 on Power Macintosh computers. The typeface families used are Chicago Laser, Minion, Myriard, Myriad Multiple Master, Prestige Elite, Symbol, Trajan, and Zapf Dingbats.

Senior Acquisitions Editor: **Michael L. Roney**
Project Editor: **Laura Brown**
Technical Editor: **Susan Glinert Stevens**
Copy Editor: **Michael Welch**
Proof Editor: **Patsy Owens**
Project Coordinator: **Louigene Santos**
Graphics and Production Specialists: **Sean Decker, Leandra Johnson, Shelley Lea, Adam Mancilla, Gabriele McCann, Kristin Pickett, Laurie Stevens**
Quality Control Technicians: **John Greenough, Nancy Price, Charles Spencer**
Media Development Manager: **Laura Carpenter VanWinkle**
Media Development Supervisor: **Rich Graves**
Permissions Editor: **Carmen Krikorian**
Media Development Coordinator: **Marisa Pearman**
Proofreading and Indexing: **York Production Services**
Book Designer: **Margery Cantor**
Cover Images: **Anthony Bunyan**
Illustrator: **Kurt Krames**
Special Help: **Diana Conover, Paula Lowell, Tim Borek, Angela Langford, Rev Mengle, Beth Parlon**

END-USER LICENSE AGREEMENT

READ THIS. You should carefully read these terms and conditions before opening the software packet(s) included with this book ("Book"). This is a license agreement ("Agreement") between you and Hungry Minds, Inc. ("HMI"). By opening the accompanying software packet(s), you acknowledge that you have read and accept the following terms and conditions. If you do not agree and do not want to be bound by such terms and conditions, promptly return the Book and the unopened software packet(s) to the place you obtained them for a full refund.

1. **License Grant.** HMI grants to you (either an individual or entity) a nonexclusive license to use one copy of the enclosed software program(s) (collectively, the "Software") solely for your own personal or business purposes on a single computer (whether a standard computer or a workstation component of a multi-user network). The Software is in use on a computer when it is loaded into temporary memory (RAM) or installed into permanent memory (hard disk, CD-ROM, or other storage device). HMI reserves all rights not expressly granted herein.

2. **Ownership.** HMI is the owner of all right, title, and interest, including copyright, in and to the compilation of the Software recorded on the disk(s) or CD-ROM ("Software Media"). Copyright to the individual programs recorded on the Software Media is owned by the author or other authorized copyright owner of each program. Ownership of the Software and all proprietary rights relating thereto remain with HMI and its licensers.

3. **Restrictions On Use and Transfer.**
   (a) You may only (i) make one copy of the Software for backup or archival purposes, or (ii) transfer the Software to a single hard disk, provided that you keep the original for backup or archival purposes. You may not (i) rent or lease the Software, (ii) copy or reproduce the Software through a LAN or other network system or through any computer subscriber system or bulletin-board system, or (iii) modify, adapt, or create derivative works based on the Software.
   (b) You may not reverse engineer, decompile, or disassemble the Software. You may transfer the Software and user documentation on a permanent basis, provided that the transferee agrees to accept the terms and conditions of this Agreement and you retain no copies. If the Software is an update or has been updated, any transfer must include the most recent update and all prior versions.

4. **Restrictions on Use of Individual Programs.** You must follow the individual requirements and restrictions detailed for each individual program in the About the CD-ROM appendix of this Book. These limitations are also contained in the

individual license agreements recorded on the Software Media. These limitations may include a requirement that after using the program for a specified period of time, the user must pay a registration fee or discontinue use. By opening the Software packet(s), you will be agreeing to abide by the licenses and restrictions for these individual programs that are detailed in the About the CD-ROM appendix and on the Software Media. None of the material on this Software Media or listed in this Book may ever be redistributed, in original or modified form, for commercial purposes.

5. **Limited Warranty.**

(a) HMI warrants that the Software and Software Media are free from defects in materials and workmanship under normal use for a period of sixty (60) days from the date of purchase of this Book. If HMI receives notification within the warranty period of defects in materials or workmanship, HMI will replace the defective Software Media.

(b) **HMI AND THE AUTHOR OF THE BOOK DISCLAIM ALL OTHER WARRANTIES, EXPRESS OR IMPLIED, INCLUDING WITHOUT LIMITATION IMPLIED WARRANTIES OF MERCHANTABILITY AND FITNESS FOR A PARTICULAR PURPOSE, WITH RESPECT TO THE SOFTWARE, THE PROGRAMS, THE SOURCE CODE CONTAINED THEREIN, AND/OR THE TECHNIQUES DESCRIBED IN THIS BOOK. HMI DOES NOT WARRANT THAT THE FUNCTIONS CONTAINED IN THE SOFTWARE WILL MEET YOUR REQUIREMENTS OR THAT THE OPERATION OF THE SOFTWARE WILL BE ERROR FREE.**

(c) This limited warranty gives you specific legal rights, and you may have other rights that vary from jurisdiction to jurisdiction.

6. **Remedies.**

(a) HMI's entire liability and your exclusive remedy for defects in materials and workmanship shall be limited to replacement of the Software Media, which may be returned to HMI with a copy of your receipt at the following address: Software Media Fulfillment Department, Attn.: *Photoshop Studio Secrets, 3rd Edition*, Hungry Minds, Inc., 10475 Crosspoint Blvd., Indianapolis, IN 46256, or call 1-800-762-2974. Please allow four to six weeks for delivery. This Limited Warranty is void if failure of the Software Media has resulted from accident, abuse, or misapplication. Any replacement Software Media will be warranted for the remainder of the original warranty period or thirty (30) days, whichever is longer.

(b) In no event shall HMI or the author be liable for any damages whatsoever (including without limitation damages for loss of business profits, business interruption, loss of business information, or any other pecuniary loss) arising from the use of or inability to use the Book or the Software, even if HMI has been advised of the possibility of such damages.

(c) Because some jurisdictions do not allow the exclusion or limitation of liability for consequential or incidental damages, the above limitation or exclusion may not apply to you.

7. **U.S. Government Restricted Rights.** Use, duplication, or disclosure of the Software for or on behalf of the United States of America, its agencies and/or instrumentalities (the "U.S. Government") is subject to restrictions as stated in paragraph (c)(1)(ii) of the Rights in Technical Data and Computer Software clause of DFARS 252.227-7013, or subparagraphs (c) (1) and (2) of the Commercial Computer Software - Restricted Rights clause at FAR 52.227-19, and in similar clauses in the NASA FAR supplement, as applicable.

8. **General.** This Agreement constitutes the entire understanding of the parties and revokes and supersedes all prior agreements, oral or written, between them and may not be modified or amended except in a writing signed by both parties hereto that specifically refers to this Agreement. This Agreement shall take precedence over any other documents that may be in conflict herewith. If any one or more provisions contained in this Agreement are held by any court or tribunal to be invalid, illegal, or otherwise unenforceable, each and every other provision shall remain in full force and effect.

CD-ROM INSTALLATION INSTRUCTIONS

To install or access the content on the accompanying CD-ROM, insert the CD into your CD-ROM drive. Windows users, if you have autorun enabled, you will be taken immediately to a window displaying the contents of the multimedia side of Photoshop Studio Secrets. Mac users, double-click the owl's eye icon to display the contents of the CD.

The CD content is divided into ten folders. These folders contain a smattering of Photoshop images, HTML pages, and QuickTime movies. Open the images in Photoshop. Open the HTML pages in your favorite Web browser (Internet Explorer or Netscape). To open the QuickTime movies, you need QuickTime, which is included in standard issues on all Macintosh computers and some Windows-based PCs. If you do not have QuickTime or need a more recent version, you can download it for free from *www.quicktime.com.*

The CD includes files that are usable on both Macintosh and Windows. For a complete rundown on the files, please see the appendix of this book